S bl ngs

Sex and Violence

Juliet Mitchell

polity

The right of Juliet Mitchell to be identified as Author of this Work has been asserted in accordance with the UK Copyright, Designs and Patents Act 1988.

First published in 2003 by Polity Press in association with Blackwell Publishing Ltd.

Editorial office:
Polity Press
65 Bridge Street
Cambridge CB2 1UR, UK

Marketing and production:
Blackwell Publishing Ltd
108 Cowley Road
Oxford OX4 1JF, UK

Distributed in the USA by
Blackwell Publishing Inc.
350 Main Street
Malden, MA 02148, USA

A catalogue record for this book is available from the British Library.

Library of Congress Cataloging-in-Publication Data
Mitchell, Juliet, 1940–
Siblings : sex and violence / Juliet Mitchell.
    p. cm.
  Includes bibliographical references and index.
  ISBN 0-7456-3220-3 (hb : alk. paper) –
  ISBN 0-7456-3221-1 (pb : alk. paper)
    1. Brothers and sisters. 2. Sex (Psychology) 3. Violence.
  4. Psychoanalysis. I. Title.
  BF723.S43 M58 2003
  155.44′3—dc21

2003007589

Typeset in 10.5 on 12.5 pt Sabon
by Graphicraft Limited, Hong Kong
Printed and bound in Great Britain by TJ International, Padstow, Cornwall
For further information on Polity, visit our website: www.polity.co.uk

Contents

Illustrations

Acknowledgements

I would like to thank Ann Bone, John Cornwell, Susan Cross, Jack Goody, Bogdan Lesnik, Carol Long, Polly Rossdale, John Thompson, Lisa Young and the generosity, intellectual and material, of Jesus College and its Fellows, Cambridge.

Early versions of some of the chapters in this book have been given as lectures or parts of lectures at a number of venues, including the Institut Français, London; the Institutes of Psychoanalysis, Berlin, London and Stockholm; the London School of Economics; the universities of Essex, Florida State, Ghana, Llublyana, London and Stockholm; the European University Institute, department of History and Civilization, Florence; the Institutes of Group Analysis, London and Cambridge; the Institute of Philosophy, Naples; the Institute of Contemporary Arts, London; to the British Association of Psychotherapists, the London Centre for Psychotherapy and at the 2001 John Bowlby Memorial Conference. Part of chapter 4 was published as ' "Seitwärts schauen": Die Psychoanalyse und das Problem der Geschwisterbeziehung' in *Jahrbuch der Psychoanalyse*, vol. 43 (Frommann-Holzboog, 2001).

Preface

All human beings are born free and equal in dignity and rights. They are endowed with reason and conscience and should act towards one another in a spirit of brotherhood.
Article 1, United Nations Universal Declaration of Human Rights (1948)

Recent analysis has pointed to the absence of women in the brotherhood of men, in particular in the ideal of fraternity which characterizes the social contract of contemporary Western societies. Brotherhood has been seen as one of the faces of patriarchy. My own view is that, although it is an aspect of male dominance, it is importantly different – the assimilation of 'brotherhood' to patriarchy is an illustration of the way all is subjugated to vertical understandings at the cost of omitting the lateral. Indeed, I have come to think that this 'verticalization' may be a major means whereby the ideologies (including sexism) of the brotherhood are allowed to operate unseen.

I was first led to the importance of siblings through a study of hysteria published as *Mad Men and Medusas: Reclaiming Hysteria and the Effects of Sibling Relations on the Human Condition* (2000a). Since then, I have found that 'thinking siblings' leads to a seemingly never-ending series of questions – material for yet further analysis. I am naturally aware of the only child. Although this may change, I believe so far in the world's history we all have or expect to have a sister or brother and this is psychically and socially crucial; in a complex way, peers replace siblings. Everyone always, of course, knew about the importance of siblings but linking them to everybody's actual or potential pathology, to the depths of our loves and lives, hates and deaths, opens up a rich vein of enquiry.

The present book is something of a second way-station (*Mad Men and Medusas* was the first) to which my clinical material as a psychoanalyst has brought me, but out of which a large number of tracks lead to various places in all the disciplines that study human society through observation, 'testing', fictional creation or any other means. My use of a range of sources, from anecdote to neuropsychiatry, via politics, gender studies, novels, films, anthropology . . . is not the result of a doctrinal commitment to interdisciplinarity, but simply because I believe we need to use anything available that helps us create a picture and make sense of the object under investigation. Thus, like the long and deep clinical exchanges which are at their base, the reflections and propositions developed here are 'up for grabs' – they can be confirmed, elaborated or repudiated – any response adds something in this field which asks us to look differently. The book is thus hopefully part of a dialogue.

In what was indeed a famous dialogue that became a heated debate in the 1920s, anthropologist Bronislaw Malinowski argued that the permissions and prohibitions in relations between sisters and brothers may be more important than those between parents and children. Ernest Jones, a leading psychoanalyst, powerfully disagreed. Jones asserted the universal centrality of the totems and taboos on child–mother incest and child–father murder (the so-called Oedipus complex) for the construction of all human culture. The argument was not resolved but the general tendency in all the social sciences has been to greatly privilege over all else the vertical relationship of child-to-parent; since the 1920s in particular, that of the infant with its mother. How far may this emphasis be ethnocentric, how far may this be an analysis in the service of an ideological prescription that exists in ignorance of what everybody knows – the importance of siblings? Recently in a small village I know well in southern France, a friend discussing her young daughters with me commented, 'Of course they are much more important to each other in the long run than I am to them – after all, they'll know each other all their lives.'

Our ignoring of siblings is, paradoxically, part of our emphasis on childhood at the expense of adulthood as the formative part of human experience. This tendency, I believe, starts in the Western world's seventeenth century (Ariès 1962); thereafter it gathers momentum until its intensification in the nineteenth then the twentieth century. Yet those who study children are, of course, adults, with the effect that the vertical relationship of parent–child is replicated in the mode of enquiry. This is clearly true of psychoanalysis, which uses the 'transference' of a child's feelings for its parents to the person of the

The Princesses Sibylla, Emilia and Sidonia von Sachsen by Lucas Cranach the Elder (1535), Kunsthistorisches Museum, Vienna

adult therapist as its central mode of investigation. Malinowski's emphasis on brothers and sisters became understood as the importance of the mother's brother – in other words, it was 'verticalized' onto the problem of descent rather than the concerns of laterality.

According to Malinowski, among the Trobrianders eighty years ago child–parent relations were affectionate, with little suggestion of any sexualization either as infantile desire or as parental abuse. Brother and sister relationships were forbidden territory:

> [A]bove all the children are left entirely to themselves in their love affairs. Not only is there no parental interference, but rarely, if ever, does it come about that a man or woman takes a perverse sexual interest in children . . . a person who played sexually with a child would be thought ridiculous and disgusting . . . From an early age . . . brothers and sisters of the same mothers must be separated from each other, in obedience to the strict taboo which enjoins that there shall be no intimate relations between them. (Malinowski 1927: 57)

The strenuous prohibitions on sibling love were internalized already by very small children but would themselves seem to have produced the psychic conditions so well described by psychoanalysis in relation to parents – the prohibition sets up repression which creates the desires as existing only unconsciously. At the same time, the affectionate ties to parents and the tabooed sister–brother relationship are socially endorsed by the formation of what Malinowski labels 'a republic of children'. The children form social groups (from any one of which a sister or a brother are excluded) but within which enquiry, sexual exploration, social organization, control of violent feelings through play – all without adult intervention – take place.

A number of thoughts arise from reading Malinowski's material. It confirms the suggestion in chapter 5 which separates sexuality from reproduction. Further, it raises the question as to why we put so much emphasis on biological parents. Jones vigorously contended that in recognizing a social rather than a biological father, the Trobrianders were living in a state of denial; Malinowski responded that the open sexual play of the children did not lead to reproduction so it was quite natural for Trobrianders not to connect sexuality and procreation unless a certain marital status and its conditions had been put in place – producing a social rather than biological meaning of fatherhood. This leads me to consider the fact that we take for granted the importance of biological fatherhood. Once again, I think we find that looking from the position of social siblinghood gives a different perspective on biological parenthood.

We do not need to get bogged down in a debate about social versus biological fathers – both arise in specific socio-historical conditions. I suggest that what is apparently a 'universal' emphasis on the exclusive importance of 'natural' paternity is in fact a marked feature of Western societies that are organized around 'liberty, equality and *fraternity*' – the so-called 'brotherhood of man'. Freud explicitly considered that the intellectual leap needed to accept the role of the biological father without the material evidence of parenting, as in motherhood, constituted the single greatest achievement of human ideational progress. However, it is not only the Trobrianders for whom this leap has been unnecessary. We need to look at the issue the other way around: when and why did the biological parent become so crucial for us? The history is an uneven one – for instance, the biological mother was not considered crucial for the poor working-class child until the Second World War; likewise the upper-class mother – one of the first disagreements between the present Queen of England and her daughter-in-law Diana centred around the Queen's contention that William, Diana's young baby, should not accompany his mother on a trip to Australia.

One important moment for the so-called leap to conceptualizing the biological father as the abstract idea of the only possible father is the late seventeenth-century debates between them (chapter 9). It is not that the biological parent is the conscious point of the controversy between patriarchalists and contract theorists – rather that it is interesting to read this parent into the controversial concepts of the family. For the patriarchalists, notoriously Sir Robert Filmer, the father was the only parent of the family and therefore of society – one was a microcosm of the other. (Until the eighteenth century the mother was thought to be only a vehicle for the father's seed (Hufton 1995).) For the contract theorists my initial reading suggests that the new division of private and public depended on the notion of the biological parents being at the centre of the 'private'. Instead of 'nature' being the basis of society (the patriarchalists), the 'natural-biological' equals the private sphere within, but separate from, the polity. 'Nature' is one of those 'switch' words that mark the transition of a concept: natural is both the most basic relationship and at the same time what is illegitimate – belonging to a nature that has not been socialized. When Shakespeare has Gloucester compare his 'legitimate Edgar' with his bastard ('natural') son Edmund – 'the whor'son must be acknowledged' – it is as though he is pointing to the new emphasis on the place of biology within the law.

Not only Freud, but Engels, indeed 'everyone' since the rise of 'modern times' has argued that the all-importance of biological paternity explains the need to know the wife is the mother of the child. The supremacy of biological kinship may be a crucial ideological postulate of the social contract – it takes over from 'the state of nature' that previously explained and contained women as outside the polity. Within contract theory biological fatherhood and motherhood is the placing of nature within society – as an untouchable, no-go, rock-bottom unchangeable enclave. Thus not to recognize its importance is in Jones's arguments to rely on a delusory denial. From the viewpoint of the West, Jones is correct – but not from the viewpoint of a society that is concerned instead with the biological contiguity of sisters and brothers and the social meaning of fatherhood.

It is almost as though social parenthood and biological siblinghood on the one hand, and social siblinghood and biological parenthood on the other, run in these coordinated pairs. If parenthood is constructed as biological in the thinking of societies largely based on the social fraternity of contract theory, the biological relationship of siblings is not constructed as a structural moment in the social organization – the creation of the all-important social brotherhood. This absence of a social significance for biological siblinghood may be why we have overlooked the extent and significance of sibling abuse (Cawson et al. 2000 and chapter 3), which would have been not only utterly appalling but highly visible to the Trobrianders.

Yet without deliberately intending it, we may have created structures of lateral peer group organizations that do recognize biological sibling taboos. We establish schools which by and large are age-specific enterprises so that rarely are siblings in the same class and hence the same peer group. Schools thus function somewhat as Malinowski's perception of the 'republic of Trobriand children'. However, there is the same major difference – we preserve once again our vertical structures through teachers standing *in loco parentis*.

So it seems that our concentration on the child since the seventeenth century has been exactly that – an adult focus on the child and the analytic modalities which see the child within the context of the adults on whom it depends or is made to depend. This surely is, in part at least, why siblings, even as children, have been missing from the picture – they can get on with it on their own but are not visible except in the presence of adults. Children in Western societies are thought to commit incest with each other because of insufficient parental care and control. It is as though our elevation of the social, political and economic story of the ideals of brotherhood depended on a diminution of the significance of blood sibling ties. A brother's murder of an adulterous sister in a Muslim family, or a brother's rape of a younger sibling in an impoverished lone mother household are seen as alike. In fact they are alike only in being outside the Western social contract. They are, however, different. The first belongs to a social order based on a blood relationship, whereas the second arises from the absence of a social place and understanding of such blood relationships within a Western system. The rise in childhood violence and abusiveness can thus be seen as not only due to the loss of parental or other vertical authorization of care and control but also to the absence of a social place for biological siblinghood within a polity based on abstract ideals of social brotherhood. This does not of course condone the death of an adulterous sister in the example above: I have simply taken the instance of another social system to illustrate that Western shock at other practices demonstrates not just so-called 'othering' but more pertinently, the intrinsic repudiation of the socialization of blood siblinghood under the banner of Western 'liberty, equality and fraternity'. Relying on the socially bestowed authority of natural parents in the private sphere (and their replacements in the social sphere, as though those replacements were likewise natural) ensures the dominance of social brotherhood as an ideal while natural brotherhood can go on the rampage unnoticed (or deplored only as the absence of vertical authority) because it is given no social place.

Likewise, because of our preoccupation with vertical relationships we believe that it is parents and their substitutes who must restrict children's violence. We also argue that violence is primarily against the authority figure who has the power – the mother, father or teacher. Yet, of course, in schools, in South Sea island children's republics, boys fight each other and girls get their own back. I believe we have minimized or overlooked entirely the threat to our existence as small children that is posed by the new baby who stands in our place or the older sibling who was there before we existed. There follows from this an identification with the very trauma of this sense of non-existence that will be 'resolved' by power struggles: being psychically annihilated creates the conditions of a wish to destroy the one responsible for the apparent annihilation. This plays out as stronger against weaker; larger, smaller; boy, girl; paler, darker. In adult wars we defeat, kill and rape our peers. However, ironically, it is in societies based on the social contract of brotherhood that these activities are not laterally controlled. Our social imaginary can envisage only vertical authority. Our image of a South Sea island republic of children is *Lord of the Flies*: boys' interactive mayhem and murder.

Behind the social contract ideal of brotherhood dependent on the absence of lateral controls lies the tyrant brother. Looking laterally changes the analysis. No one in their right mind could have believed that the construction of a great empire would depend, or indeed be in the slightest degree enhanced by the destruction of a disparate population labelled 'Jews' – why did so many people believe it could? Why does the playground bully get support for his redundant act of picking on a harmless victim? The victim does not represent a tyrant's hidden vulnerability as is usually understood, but rather some traumatic eradication of his very being which can only be restored by manic grandiosity: there is only room for me. Then the tyrant/bully's followers are 'empty of themselves' in a shared eradication of selves with the empty but grandiose tyrant/bully: a trauma is induced. In the manic excitement of the rhetoric of tyranny, individual identities and judgements vanish until all become as one. The 'original' moment, replicated endlessly if not resolved, is when the sibling or imagined sibling replaces one – when there is another in one's place. Bullied victims, madly, are imagined to be standing in the bully/tyrant's place. Others support the crazy vision because somewhere they too can call on this 'universal' trauma of displacement/replacement.

The desperate grandiosity of the tyrant self and visions of empire contain both the sexuality and violence that mask the self-love and the need to preserve it in its endangered moment. However, as children have found, only the proper social organization of siblings/peers can countermand the continued living out of the unresolved trauma of the tyrant/bully's endless moment of experienced annihilation – a sisterhood and brotherhood in which there is room for equality of dignity and rights. Looking at siblings is looking anew at sex and violence. Bringing in siblings changes the picture we are looking at.

— 1 —

Siblings and Psychoanalysis: an Overview

This is a strange time to be insisting on the importance of siblings. Globally, the rate of increase of the world's population is on the decline; in the West it is mostly below the point of replacement.[1] China, with over a fifth of the world's population, is trying to make its 'one child' family policy prevail – with considerable success in urban centres. Will there be any (or anyway, many) siblings in the future?

Yet this book argues that siblings are essential in any social structure and psychically in all social relationships, including those of parents and children. Internalized social relationships are the psyche's major elements. More particularly, the work here considers that siblings have, almost peculiarly, been left out of the picture. Our understanding of psychic and social relationships has foregrounded vertical interaction – lines of ascent and descent between ancestors, parents and children. During the larger part of the twentieth century the model has been between infant and mother; before that it was child and father. Now we learn that such concerns as parental (particularly step-paternal) sexual and violent abuse have hidden from us the extent of sibling outrages (Cawson et al. 2000). Why have we not considered that lateral relations in love and sexuality or in hate and war have needed a theoretical paradigm with which we might analyse, consider and seek to influence them? I am not sure of the answer to this question; I am sure we need such a paradigm shift from the near-exclusive dominance of vertical comprehension to the interaction of the horizontal and the vertical in our social and in our psychological understanding. Why should there be only one set of relationships which provide for the structure of our mind, or why should one be dominant in all times and places? Even if there will be fewer full siblings in the world, there will still be lateral relationships – those relationships which take place on a horizontal axis starting with siblings, going on to peers and affinal kin. In polygynous societies, in social conditions with high rates of maternal mortality, or with divorce and remarriage or serial coupling, half-siblings will persist.

It can and has been argued (Winnicott 1958) that it is essential we work out the problems of future social interaction with siblings in our early childhood. If we fail to overcome our desire for sibling incest or for sibling murder, will versions of these be more insistently played out with later lateral relationships, with peers and so-called equals – in love and in war? Freud argued that in order to marry our wife we need to know in childhood that we cannot marry our mother (the Oedipus complex).[2] I suggest that at the very least we also need to know we cannot marry our sister if we are to be able to marry our sister's (not just our mother's) psychological successor. But do we in fact marry someone who resembles in some way our sister or brother? It has been suggested that the ideal situation for a successful hetero-sexual relationship involves a mixture of prohibited incestuous wishes from childhood for someone who is not too like the original infantile love-object and the contemporary adult desire for someone who is like oneself, but not too alike. We often hear it said that she's married her father (mother) – is it not, perhaps, that we have married a sibling? Similarly, the literature emphasizes the Oedipal desire to kill the father – do we predominantly kill fathers or brothers?

How can we assess the relative importance of our vertical love or hate for our parents and our lateral emotions for our siblings? In wars we fight side by side with our brothers – not our fathers: the resolution of fraternal love and hate would seem to underlie whom we may and may not kill. It was widely noted in the First World War that 'fraternal' loyalty was essential for success – and, as the poet Wilfred Owen described, the killed enemy is also a brother. What happens between siblings – full, half or step, or simply unborn but always expected because everyone fears to be dethroned in childhood – is a core experience of playmates and peers. What Lévi-Strauss calls the 'atom of kinship' (Lévi-Strauss 1963) has siblings as its centre-point; it is this atom which concerns me here. Psychoanalysis, with its emphasis on the Oedipal and the vertical, has had an influence well beyond its own bounds. I wish to add the lateral axis to the psychoanalytic theoretical and clinical perspective. I am also interested in how this maps on to the theories of group behaviour and to social psychology more generally.

Recently I was talking to a group of clinical psychologists and psychotherapists about the place of siblings in their work. I told an anecdote and asked a question: 'The World Service of the BBC has reported that the southern Indian state of Kerala has announced an extensive expansion of child and baby-care services. Why might it have done this?' Comforting to the feminist in me, everyone in the audience answered that it would be to enable more mothers to join the workforce. This had been my own immediate assumption. In fact, it was so that, in a state with an extraordinarily high rate of literacy to maintain, girls could go to school. Apparently literacy rates had been falling because sisters had to stay at home to care for younger siblings. Once more I was struck by the ethnocentricity of our exclusion of siblings from a determinate place in social history and in the psychodynamics both of individuals and of social groups. Confirming this ethnocentricity, it comes as a shock to the Western imagination to learn of the extent of 'child-headed' households in AIDS-struck sub-Saharan Africa.

The proposition here is this: that an observation of the importance of siblings, and all the lateral relations that take their cue from them, must lead to a paradigm shift that challenges the unique importance of understanding through vertical paradigms. Mothers and fathers are, of course, immensely important, but social life does not only follow from a relationship with them as it is made to do in our Western theories. The baby is born into a world of peers as well as of parents. Does our thinking thus exceed the binary?

There is a second hypothesis, more tentative than the first, and this is that the dominance or near-exclusiveness of our vertical paradigm has arisen because human social and individual psychology has been understood from the side of the man. Looking at my own field of research, psychoanalysis, I have found a striking overlap between the concepts that explain femininity in the main body of the theory and concepts that we need if we are to incorporate siblings. Here, I will simply offer indicators. Sibling relations prioritize experiences such as the fear of annihilation, a fear associated with girls, in contrast to the male fear of castration. They involve fear of the loss of love which is usually associated with girls; an excessive narcissism which needs to be confirmed by being the object, not subject, of love. Siblings and femininity have a similar overlooked destiny.

Psychoanalysis, like all grand theories, has followed the pattern of assuming an equation between the norm and the male. The paradoxical result is that the male psyche is taken for granted and invisible. The current feminist challenge to this ideology means that masculinity is emerging as an object of enquiry. An examination of siblings and sibling relationships will bring both genders into the analytical picture. The sibling, I believe, is the figure which underlies such nearly forgotten concepts as the ego-ideal – the older sibling is idealized as someone the subject would like to be, and sometimes this is a reversal of the hatred for a rival. It can be an underlying structure for homosexuality. Siblings help too with the postmodern concern with the problem of Enlightenment thinking in which sameness is equated with the masculine and difference with the feminine. Postmodern feminism has been concerned to demonstrate that a unity such as is suggested by something cohering as 'the same' is only achieved by ejecting what it doesn't want of itself as what is different from it. The masculine unity is achieved at the cost of expelling the feminine as other or different. Brothers cast out sisters or the feminine from their make-up.

For beneath the surface of this argument for the structuring importance of laterality, one can see the shift from modernism to postmodernism and from causal to correlative explanations. In the possible link to siblings of explanations of the sameness/difference axis of masculinity and femininity one sees then the role of feminism (and the increasing 'sameness' in the roles of women and men) as promoting laterality over verticality. Social changes underpin the shift. For instance inheritance depends on the vertical but it is said to be on the decline, with stickers on pensioners' cars in Florida reading 'We are spending your inheritance' indicating a trend. If, despite the feminization of poverty, women can be self-supporting through paid work, then the woman provides her own equivalent of what was once endowment. At this stage these thoughts are no more than speculative lines of enquiry that would seem to merit further investigation. They do, however, suggest a decline of the importance of descent and a rise of the importance of alliance.

Hysteria and siblings

The chapters of the book that follow emanate from a long study of hysteria predominantly from the viewpoint of psychoanalysis.[3] This study was also fuelled by a second-wave feminist interest in the hysteric as a proto-feminist (Clement 1987; Cixous 1981; Hunter 1983; Gallop 1982; and others), a woman whose hysteria was the only form of protest available under patriarchy (Showalter 1987, 1997). Rather than studying the feminists' hysteric, I have long been interested in male hysteria. The presence of male hysteria (along with an analysis of dreaming) enabled Freud to found psychoanalysis as a theory built on the observation of universally present unconscious processes which were largely brought into being by social obstacles to the expression of human sexuality. Most obviously, we have all taken on board that we must not commit incest – the hysteric in all of us wants to do just that, wants to do whatever is not allowed. The hysterical symptom such as hysterical blindness, fatigue, immobility or aspects of some eating disorders, once understood, reveals both the illicit sexual desire and the prohibition against it that the hysteric does not wish to recognize. Cross-culturally and historically, hysteria has been associated almost exclusively with women. Male hysteria (charted by Charcot in the latter half of the nineteenth century and analysed by Freud, who had studied with him) demonstrated that these processes did not belong to a specific population – not to 'degenerates' (as was commonly thought in the nineteenth century) nor to the sick nor to women. Through the awareness of male hysteria at the end of the nineteenth century it could be seen that the symptoms of hysteria were the writing large of ordinary and universal processes. The exaggerations of neuroses show us the psychopathologies of everybody's everyday life.

However, once the universality of unconscious processes was demonstrated, hysteria as a diagnosis shifted. It was no longer considered an illness the extremes of which throw into relief the normative; rather it came to be considered an aspect of a personality – and predominantly a feminine personality. Roughly 70 per cent of those suffering from 'Histrionic Personality Disorder' (according to the Diagnostic and Statistical Manual III) in the United States are women. Hysteria has become an aspect or expression of the feminine personality. We constantly come full circle with the collapse of the hysteric into the woman and femininity into the hysterical.

While hysteria had receded as an illness diagnosis, it was still easy in my psychoanalytic clinical work to observe hysteria as something more than (or as well as) a personality disorder. Hysteria had long ceased to be a common diagnosis (Brenman 1985), but in social and political life continuance and prevalence of the (colloquial) term seemed justified. These two factors led me to look not only historically but also ethnographically. There seemed no doubt that hysteria was, and always had been, a universal potential – all of us can have hysterical symptoms or act hysterically or, if this performance becomes a way of life, or these symptoms persist, *be* hysterics. The question then became, why, if it was possible for men, was it everywhere and at all times associated with women?

The psychoanalytic explanation of what we might term the refeminization of hysteria after its initial recognition in men is in terms of the importance of the phase of the pre-Oedipal mother-attachment of girls. A 'law' emanating from the place of the father (Lacan 1982a, 1982b) abolishes the Oedipal desires of the child for the mother (Oedipus' love for his mother-wife, Jocasta). The law which threatens symbolic castration (the castration complex) prohibits phallic mother-love. The result differentiates the sexes – both are subject to the castration threat if the law is flouted, but the girl will never come to stand in the place of the father in relation to a mother substitute. Instead she must change her stance – she must become as though in the position of the mother and object of her father's love. The girl must relinquish her mother as object of her love and become instead like her. In an 'idealized' normative world, she then tries to win her father's love to replenish the narcissistic wound of being forever without the phallus which is what her mother, who lacks it, therefore desires. Flouting the law, the hysterical girl persists in both believing she has this phallus for her mother (a masculine stance, the phallic posture of the hysteric) and at the same time complaining she is without it (the feminine stance, the empty charm and constant complaint of the hysteric) and must receive it from her father.

This classic interpretation has received many new emphases and, indeed, additions. I was interested in the fact that if the propensity to hysteria was claimed as a 'universal' (or 'transversal' – omnipresent but in various forms), what features did its different manifestations have in common? The hysteric is always both too much there and insufficiently present – moving between grandiosity and psychic collapse. How does this expression fit with the psychoanalytic interpretation? I suggest that the hysteric – male or female – dramatizes an assumed phallic position, and at the same time believes that he or she has had the penis taken away, which in its turn means he or she has nothing. So she appears simultaneously hugely potent and horribly 'empty'. She not only introjects phallic potency as though in her mind it were an actual penis, she also feels empty because in not having 'lost' anything, she has no inner representation of it. Despite appearing phallic, she oscillates between an 'empty' masculine position in relation to her mother and an empty feminine position in relation to her father; 'empty' because she has neither internalized the 'lost' mother nor accepted the 'lost' phallus. Her craving for both is compulsive and incessant. In both aspects of the situation she reveals that she has not understood a symbolic law – she believes (like many readers of psychoanalytic theories) that the phallus, present or absent, is an actual real penis. She thus endlessly seduces as though in this way she will get the real penis. What is also at stake in this is the question of narcissistic love (love for oneself) and so-called 'object love' (love for another). I shall return to this question as I believe it cannot be grasped without introducing sibling relations. In fact all these expressions of hysteria need the sibling to explain them. But another factor – the acknowledgement of male hysteria – also of itself calls into question the exclusively vertical, intergenerational explanation.

Male hysteria has seemed unlikely in a commonsensical way. The Western name for the condition is related to the Greek for womb, and many nineteenth-century doctors objected to male hysteria on exactly these grounds. However, this has no bearing on psychic life: men imagine they have wombs and that they do not have penises. The male hysteric believing in his power to conceive and carry and give birth is experiencing a delusion. There can therefore be a psychotic element in male hysteria which in turn entails it being considered as 'more serious'. But believing he has a womb or does not have a penis also puts the male hysteric in a feminine position – and that is mostly where he has found himself in the diagnosis. Male hysteria has been repudiated along with a repudiation of femininity. A strange equation emerges: male hysteria is feminine so that it is its maleness which is cancelled out; the femininity becomes the illness. In the

1920s, the British psychoanalyst Joan Riviere wrote a case history of a female patient whose femininity (or 'womanliness') was a masquerade (Riviere [1929]); some decades later, Jacques Lacan wrote that femininity itself was a masquerade (Lacan 1982a, 1982b). Masquerading is crucial to hysteria, but it is different if one is dressing up in femininity or if femininity itself is fancy dress.

The hysteric must dress up – feeling empty, he needs clothes to ensure his existence – but if he chooses femininity, while still remaining the subject of desire, this femininity will make use of the whole body as though the body were a phallus – the femininity itself will thus be phallic. If he chooses masculinity as the masquerade its phallic posturing will seem no less inauthentic for being paraded by a male. However, what is established in all these Oedipal accounts of hysteria is the importance of unconscious sexuality arising from the failure to fully repress incestuous Oedipal desires. This will raise a crucial question when we come to consider siblings. There is, nevertheless, a second strand in definitions of hysteria which I believe also indicates that we must implicate siblings. This is the importance of trauma. Since Charcot, trauma had been considered crucial in the aetiology of male hysteria; as understandings of hysteria always refeminize it, the traumatic element has been largely forgotten.

When Jean-Marie Charcot announced the prevalence of male hysteria in his huge public clinic, the Salpetrière, in Paris, he also added a new dimension to its aetiology. He claimed there was nothing effeminate about his male hysterics; they were responding with non-organic physical symptoms (hence hysterical symptoms) to some trauma – an accident at work or on the train, a fight on the street, and so on. In the First World War the similarity of the symptoms of male war victims who had no actual injuries and the symptoms of classical female hysterics confirmed this possibility. However, the relationship between trauma and hysteria has remained unresolved (Herman 1992) and is a subject in its own right. My intention here is different. In brief, I would contend that there is a difference between traumatic neurosis (as war hysteria came to be called) and hysteria, but that it is not a difference between the absence or presence of a trauma. Usually the distinction is made that the trauma of traumatic neurosis is actual and real and that of hysteria rather a fantasy of trauma. I put the situation differently. In both cases there is trauma. In traumatic neurosis the trauma is in the present, in hysteria it is in the past. In hysteria this forgotten past trauma is constantly revived through re-enactment – one does make a drama of a crisis. Minor present-day obstacles to getting what one wants are treated as traumatic – but once upon a time, in the hysteric's early childhood, the result of such obstacles was in fact traumatic.

What is trauma? A residual definition is that it is a breaking through of protective boundaries in such a violent (either physical or mental) way that the experience cannot be processed: the mind or body or both are breached, leaving a wound or gap within. What is it which in time fills this gap that trauma opens up? Imitating the presence or object which has created the hole in the body or psyche is crucial. If, for instance, in fantasy, one murders the father and one then becomes like the dead father, it seems to act to fill the gap. Hysteria is definitionally mimetic, imitating a range of mental and bodily conditions. It thus, like a chameleon, takes on the colour of its surroundings, appearing for instance as eating disorders in the 'thin' culture of an obese rich world or as 'railway spine' when railways are new and frightening. Hysteria in this, once again, exaggerates the normal – the hysterical imitation is so accurate that there is no division between what is not there and what one has become to ensure it still is there.

These imitations however, though multifarious, are not random. They have a meaning derived from the person's experiences and history. What I want to look at in relation to siblings is not the individual but the general situation. In all times and places one of the most noted hysterical imitations is the imitation of death in its various guises (King 1993). Though it is known that in severe cases hysterics commit suicide, the general hysterical trend of pretending to be dead has only been understood as living out a wish. While psychoanalysis has highlighted the breaking through of tabooed sexuality in hysteria, it has done no more than occasionally observe the rendering of trauma into an imitation of death (Freud [1928]). Anxious to separate hysteria and traumatic neurosis, psychoanalysis has not integrated this dimension into its theoretical understanding. In trauma, subsequently imagined or enacted as death, the ego or 'I' or subject position is annihilated. Here too siblings help with an explanation.

One can bring the sexuality and the experience of trauma in hysteria together in the story of Oedipus. Before he marries his mother, Oedipus inadvertently slays his father. Prior to this adult act, Oedipus as a baby was exposed by his parents (but at his father's behest) on a mountainside so as to die and thus avoid fulfilling his fate as a father-killer. In the story, at least, this trauma of intended infanticide would seem to be the condition of the later incestuous sexuality. But if so, this trauma is definitionally pre-Oedipal – the baby Oedipus' predicament symbolizes the helplessness of the neonate if no one is there to care for it. The murder of the father is a reaction to the father's wish to kill the son. However, the father's death removes the obstacle to incest with the mother – an incest which is probably what the father feared in the first place.

In dominant psychoanalytic theory, the presence of a sibling, either one already there or one to come, is important because it indicates that the mother has a sexual relationship with a father. The unacknowledged model of the nuclear family assumes this is one's own father. If instead we think of polygynous kin groups then it is clear that the sibling is imbued not only with the sexuality of his or her position in the family as child of the same parents, but also independently of them in his or her own right. In particular it is the advent of a sibling or the possibility of one which brings the sexuality and trauma, so manifest in hysteria, together at the same time. Remembering that sexuality must be understood not as genitality but as a many-faceted or a 'polymorphous' libidinal love, a love that can love a range of objects with a range of feelings, it is this that the toddler feels for the new baby or that the infant feels for the older sibling. But the adored sibling, who is loved with all the urgency of the child's narcissism, is also loathed as its replacement – the baby it can never again be, or the pre-existing older brother or sister that it will never be. The sibling is *par excellence* someone who threatens the subject's uniqueness. The ecstasy of loving one who is like oneself is experienced at the same time as the trauma of being annihilated by one who stands in one's place. I suggest that if the love/hate of sibling replacement is not overcome, then a later hysteria will regress to using just these manifestations of the child's predicament. Sufferers from Histrionic Personality Disorder are described as inappropriately seductive and provocative, emotionally shallow, self-dramatizing, as using their bodies to get attention, having temper tantrums and being highly suggestible. These qualities, which can be seen in any distressed toddler, seem to me to arise as a response to the trauma of sibling displacement.

—— 10 ——

Group psychology and siblings

In the individual's mental life someone else is invariably involved, as a model, as an object, as a helper, as an opponent. (Freud [1921]: 69)

If a man cannot be a friend of his friends, he cannot be the enemy of his enemies. (Bion [1948]: 88)

Some psychoanalytic accounts of group psychology offer not only observations of the importance of lateral relations but also, I believe, the prospect of a theoretical understanding of their relative autonomy. In the earliest accounts siblings get a look in. Thus in *Group Psychology and the Analysis of the Ego* (1921), Freud comments how all aspects of a demand for social justice emanate from the situation 'in the nursery'. The intense jealousy, rivalry and envy among siblings (and later, schoolchildren) are reversed into demands for equality and fairness. For Freud, with his patriarchal bias, all must be equally loved by the father or his substitute; no one must have more than a fair share, or the statutorily agreed unfair shares of primogeniture or gender difference – to which I shall return.

In the chapters that follow, in dealing with the interpenetration of the horizontal/vertical, I have raised the possibility that before they are equal in their sameness to each other for their father, children must be equal in their difference from each other for their mother. This will be the crucial first vertical relation for siblings. I have provisionally referred to it as 'the law of the mother'. However, there are also independent lateral relations to be explored.

In the last twenty years, branches of developmental psychology have charted intersibling relations (for instance, Boer and Dunn 1992), showing the wealth of autonomous interaction and negotiation between them. This helps to confirm the notion that a metapsychology should conceptualize these sibling relations as relatively independent autonomous structures. Considering these from a group psychoanalytical perspective, I would argue that we need to start by thinking about the construction of the ego and the ego-ideal – what I am and what I would like to be.

The human proclivity to neurosis rests in part on the divisions of the human mind. A crucial division is into ego and ego-ideal – we cannot imagine that other mammals feel, at least with any intensity,

—— 11 ——

a problem about who they are, let alone that this is distinct from whom they wish they were like, their ideal. For humans this ideal can be an internalization of someone to whose status (both real and embroidered) the subject (ego) aspires. Alternatively it can be the ego's worst critic in the guise of a nagging conscience. Classically in the theoretical explanation, this ideal is postulated as being modelled on the real object of the father. It is his approval or censorship that the child takes in (internalizes) so that a representation of the father is set up inside the mind as an aspect of the subject's own personality. This is almost certainly the case. But isn't it also likely that the original model may be another child, a heroic or critical older (or other) sibling? For most of us, when our conscience is putting us down, making us feel inferior, the voice we hear is reminiscent of the tauntings not of adults but of other children. Indeed, it is not uncommon for a child during latency (between five and ten or eleven years) to deinternalize these voices and hear them as though they were once more sounding from the external world of the child's peers. This is a decomposition into different 'theatrical' parts rather than the splitting and disaggregation of schizophrenia. But the resemblance indicates that what we may be considering in this establishment and disestablishment of an ego-ideal is not an Oedipal taking in of the father but an internalization based on sibling-peers. The pathological variants would tend to be more psychotic than neurotic as it is in psychosis that fragmentation of the composite ego occurs. The neurotic distorts reality, the psychotic has no truck with it. We see the decomposed ego in dreams which are thus considered to be everybody's every night psychotic experience.

If we transpose this observation of decomposition and psychosis to group psychology, we may get nearer to understanding the delusional aspects in which, for good or ill, groups tend to indulge. The other side of decomposition is false unity. A group illusion such as a shared religion treats all the individual egos as though they were part of one unified ego. This can become a group delusion in which they are really believed to be one against others. An example would be that the original unified group believes another minority group will wipe out the majority or, through what is seen as excessive breeding, become the majority. If this continuum from normal illusion of unity to pathological delusion is, as I am arguing, based on lateral relations, then one of the reasons why theories of group psychology have not advanced further than they have may be to do with the fact that, firstly, siblings have been omitted, and secondly a comparison with individual *neurosis* is made where in fact it is *psychosis* which would be the more appropriate sphere of enquiry. Neurosis does not involve decomposition or delusory unification of the ego.

To return to the possibility that a child is forming its ego-ideal not so much on the Oedipal father as on the peer: not enough has been made of the very common observation that an infant is delighted to the point of elation by another child. A small baby squirms with glee when watching the antics of an older child. A baby on a bus becomes animated by the sight of another baby: does it know it is like itself – if so, how? This ecstasy of the infant as it watches an older or other child would also bear an important relationship to the pathology of mania in manic depressive states. Mania and depression are also group phenomena – the highs of group experience can be excessive, their aftermath melancholic. Again manic depression has been understood as depending on a vertical, in this case maternal, axis. But if we take it back to normal elation and sadness, the experience of the infant with the other child would seem to be at least as marked as it is with adults, if not more so, as it grows beyond a year. Certainly an infant can be elated by the sight of its mother, or by its ability to shake its own rattle – but the kinesics of another child fascinate it and induce high levels of joy.

Freud pointed out that most of us love children and animals who appear to us to be particularly self-sufficient, such as cats – finding in their completeness a narcissism with which we can identify and through this identification imaginatively restore our own. Why should the infant not do the same? If so, a criticism made by René Girard (1978) of the Freudian postulate of primary narcissism would seem to me a fruitful possibility. Girard uses the writings of Marcel Proust to suggest that we do not come into this world in a state of narcissistic completeness (the Freudian contention) which is gradually diminished as we start to love others on whom we are dependent. Instead, our neonate selves are 'empty' and become filled through mimetic identification with others who seem full of themselves – this would include older children as well as parents. The infant would then develop his own narcissistic ego from these initial identifications with other children – particularly siblings.

Classical psychoanalysis, however, describes the neonate as in a state of 'primary narcissism'. This needs to be specified further if we are to connect it with the impact of siblings and peers. The first narcissism is a notional 'at one-ness' with its environment, uterine and then maternal. There is little or no ego, however, in this narcissism. That will develop by primary identification. To a large extent such identifications will be mimetic, although the baby's own body, its needs and impulses will deflect the mimesis and contribute a powerful individuality, establishing in this way a matrix of exchange, intersubjectivity and reciprocity. The so-called 'secondary narcissism' that results will thus include an ego which will not so much 'develop' (though it will) as swing between presence and absence – a sense of fullness and emptiness. Melanie Klein accounts for this observation through the process of splitting and projection of good and bad reactions to the mother. However, the contribution to this process of siblings/peers such as other babies at her breast seems crucial.

That the individual is from the outset social would seem to me to be axiomatic. I think, however, we can additionally specify the social as the fact that the individual also becomes itself within a group which, even in a nuclear family, will involve other babies, at the very least in post-natal check-ups, in the street, or on the bus. The concept of 'child' will vary both historically and cross-culturally, yet we always seem to take it that its meaning is derived (and as such taken on board by the child) as being that which is different from the adult (in particular the parent). Such an understanding, while true, may be unduly adult-centred. The baby becomes a child not only in relation to learning that it is not its parents (the Oedipus and castration complexes within psychoanalytic theory) but also positively both mimetically and interactively with siblings and peers. Where the primary identifications made with parents are subject to trauma (you think you are like your parents or one of your parents but you are not – at least, not yet), the primary identification with the peer group is positive and subject not to negation but to differentiation: you are like the others but with differences. This means that in later life the peer identification can be total or can incorporate diversity – groups are at times constructed in uniformity, at times they dissolve into their individual parts. It also means that love and hate, rivalry, jealousy and envy are social, and can be specifically lateral acquisitions in a group.

In any baby clinic one sees a baby on its mother's knee disturbed by the fact that another baby on another knee is feeding – getting a pleasure it already recognizes and wants for itself. Such an incident not only indicates the baby's envy of the breast (Klein 2000), but also its jealousy of the other baby. Social justice would involve the breast being available to neither baby or both babies in equal amounts. But it does not take only an adult authority to establish this; it is intrinsic to lateral jealousy and the aspiration to grab toys; it means a baby will try to crawl faster than its neighbour but that it will also start to pass the objects back and forth between them. My daughter crawled brilliantly at six months, not because she was a budding Olympic runner, nor because someone taught her, but because we lived with a nine-month-old child and the two babies learnt together to play up and down a short flight of stairs.

Group psychology, like hysteria, has been understood as deriving from a vertical paradigm. But here again there is a point in the founding text that can be pressed to open up the lateral. In *Group Psychology and the Analysis of the Ego* (1921), Freud refers to the myth he constructed from his clinical work with individuals to explain humankind's group historical, ancestral or phylogenetic past. The reference is to his earlier work, *Totem and Taboo* (1913), in which a gang of brothers slays the primal father who has hitherto kept all the women for himself. The brothers must then institute their own laws and prohibitions on each other, else chaos will come again. But one man exceeds the terms of the brotherhood. The story is fanciful but we can use it (as Freud did not) to point to the problem that arises if we understand everything along only a vertical paradigm. It links up with the question of the ego-ideal discussed earlier and opens up a possible lateral perspective. The man who exceeds the brotherhood is the hero in Freud's fictional hypothesis about the origins of humankind: it is he who tells the tale of the murder of the father – this poet is the 'ego' or subject of the story; he is one of the bold brothers and is made a god. 'The lie of the heroic myth culminates in the deification of the hero. Perhaps the deified hero may have been earlier than the Father/God . . . The series of gods, then, would run chronologically: Mother Goddess – Hero – Father God' (Freud [1921]: 137). In other words, a psychic chronology of important people runs mother, then siblings, then father.

Freud argues that the archetypal poet – let us say of the epic story of the origin of the race – is himself the first hero; it is he who claims that the murder of the primal father was not the work of a group of brothers but the solitary act of the poet himself. This is 'the lie'. History recounts this solitary heroic deed in the epic and then all the other brothers come to identify with the poet-hero. The poet tells his story of derring-do and thereby puts himself as heroic revolutionary killer in the place of the father. Thus if Freud, along with some nineteenth-century anthropologists, postulates the primacy of a matriarch, then it will not be the father that is being killed and identified with – it will be the triumphant oldest brother. Maybe (as is a frequent feature of Western mythologies) the poet-hero father-killer is the mother's favourite, the youngest rather than the oldest son. If this is so, then this last-born could be using the mother's first-born, his own eldest brother, as his aspirational model – while being the adored youngest, he may also want to be the one who satisfied his mother's primary desire for a son.

In Freud's terms this first son stands for what the mother hasn't got, the phallus. If this is so, the identification of the poet-hero is first with the eldest brother rather than with the father. In, for instance, British ethnic minority patients with large sibling cohorts, the youngest son is often 'the professional' (because, with the older siblings working, there are funds for his education), but nevertheless the favoured younger son feels excluded from hearth and home – sent out into the world of another social class and envious of the eldest son who occupies what Western society thinks of as the father's place as head of the family. The youngest wants to be eldest. Beyond this particular example, such a sibling origin to the heroic ego-ideal seems likely. Either way, other brothers identify with one brother as their heroic ego-ideal.

In Freud's work, the notion of an ego-ideal became subsumed in the concept of a superego. This latter is the internalization of the authority of the father-figure. The notion of an ego-ideal should be resurrected as it is not identical with the superego. Of particular relevance here is that, with its supercession, we lost the notion of a 'heroic self' as fantasized by Freud in group psychology and recently explored in relation to specific clinical observation. Extrapolating from several patients, but using one in particular, Riccardo Steiner proposes that the creative artist uses his predecessors (other artists) as internal models (Steiner 1999). What, from my point of view, is interesting about this claim is that these models – though long dead and buried – are imaginatively experienced as the same age as the subject. In other words, these artistic ancestors are 'lateralized'. However, before Steiner's patient could use them as fully creative and not just rivalrous/imitative models, he had to learn to differentiate himself from these former artists – he had to discover that they were generically the same as him (all were artists) but individually diverse. Before he was able to do this, he imagined they were the same as him and the only way he could conceive of going forward artistically was to eradicate each self-same rival who threatened his uniqueness. Because of this murderous rivalry, he wanted to rid the world of all the great masters.

This instantly suggests not my sibling model but Steiner's vertical explanation – 'great masters' are fathers. However, this wish made Steiner's patient recollect a time when he had managed literally to remove all his schoolfriends' artwork from a particular exhibition – so that only his own work was exhibited. Steiner is a Kleinian analyst and so subscribes to the importance for creativity of a resolution of the so-called 'depressive position'. In this the individual feels remorse for its imagined envious destruction of the mother's creativity (synonymous with procreativity) and through artistic endeavour tries to repair the damage that is felt to have been done. What Steiner points to in emphasizing the importance of a heroic self is that it is specifically the mother's other babies that the individual feels he has murdered and now wishes to bring alive through continuing the creative tradition which the predecessors represent. These babies, I argue, are most importantly autonomous siblings.

Steiner notes that the Kleinian maternal-related depressive position is a position of infancy; in adolescence the depressive position is repeated but this time the heroic other, not the mother, is the person with whom one first competes, triumphantly kills and then reparatively resurrects so that one can emulate 'him' in a great tradition. If we consider how the intervening period of latency between infancy and puberty, whether spent at school or in child-labour, has been a period of all-important peer relations, this shift from a focus on the mother of infancy to the peer of puberty would make sense. However, I also believe the foundations for the importance of sibling and peer group relations for heroic ego-ideals and their negative are already laid in infancy.

—— 17 ——

Neurosis, psychosis, narcissistic borderline conditions, psychopathy and siblings

The historical conditions in which psychiatry, various clinical psychologies and psychoanalysis arose favoured a focus on a vertical axis of understanding. In this background both religion and medicine were salient. But an aspect of this historical condition was the decline of religion and its supersession by psychologies which replaced the soul in religion with a stress on memory (Hacking 1995; Shepherd 2000). In accounts of the decline of religion, what is not commented on is that Western religions are patriarchal. If psychologies replaced religion, it was a patriarchal religion they replaced. The medical model which these psychologies used was likewise a patriarchal vertical model. Yet, although the religion and the medical models on which psychology depended were patriarchal, an ideology of motherhood was also coming to prominence. In the late nineteenth century, England boasted a heyday of 'moral motherhood' – the confinement to the home of the wife in the hegemonic middle classes in order that she might care for the husband but even more particularly for the child (Seccombe 1993). The rise of the importance of the mother accompanied what has been described as a shift over the period of the next century from public to private patriarchy (Walby 1986); this meant an increasing isolation of the family from the wider polity.

Psychoanalytic theory moved within this framework, its practice echoing the privatization of the individual psyche as the focus shifted from the patri- and phallocentric schemas of Freud and his early followers to 'mothering psychoanalysis' (Sayers 1991) and back again (Lacan 1982a, 1982b). In all cases, accounts of neurosis are dependent on a vertical framework. The context in which the theory is formed is the private consulting room which echoes the private family. However, lateral relations exceed this private space – occurring in the wider social world of street, school and workplace and bringing these spaces and their rich occupancy into the family.

Classical psychoanalysis claims to be able to work with neurosis because the patient/analysand has retained a relationship to reality even if it is largely in his imagination. He 'transfers' this key relationship of his childhood on to the therapist and relives its pleasures and problems. The psychotic has severed contact with reality. The middle ground between the two positions of neurosis and psychosis has gained ever increasing importance throughout the twentieth century. It is variously labelled as the domain of narcissistic disorders or border-line conditions which have a neurotic and a psychotic dimension. I want now to insert on to this middle ground, psychopathy. This is for a number of reasons. Psychopathy is a psychiatric term which describes an individual who is compulsively asocial and amoral. Psychopathy is all around us, yet by and large it has escaped psycho-analytic elaboration.[4] It is important for group practices and their understanding – I believe it needs 'siblings'.

Although some of its patients and hence its case material involves psychopathy, psychoanalysis by and large is concerned with neuro-sis, psychosis and the umbrella category of 'borderline'. All three conditions involve particular social relations. The neurotic's reten-tion of a relationship to reality is indicated by the fact that he still loves others; the psychotic has no such relation; the patient in-between is not without love but the love is for himself and only fluctuatingly or artificially for others, who are usually perceived as versions or aspects of himself. I suggest that the introduction of a lateral paradigm reframes the classical neurosis. I believe it is not that hysteria and obsessionality are only neuroses; it is rather that there can be psychotic, borderline and neurotic hysterical and obsessional conditions (Libbrecht 1995). An understanding of the psychoses of paranoia and schizophrenia also benefits from the addition of con-sidering siblings. Paranoia is closely bound up with sibling jealousy, schizophrenia with the thought disorder that features a pinhead irresolution of lateral love and hate and the question 'who am I?' But, I would argue, psychopathy is above all the terrain of siblings and their lateral heirs. Psychopathy is the unexplored borderline.

The neurotic's loves are considered to be displacements of the still desired original love objects of his infancy – his parents. The psy-chotic is understood as denying or repudiating these; the borderline and its equivalents as unable to reach them because of too much narcissism. I suggest instead that if we look at borderline patients as moving on a lateral axis between narcissism and object-attachment, we get a more accurate picture. The borderline is unsure who he is and everyone else gets in the way of his existence unless they are assimilated to him. It is not only, then, that the borderline patient or personality has not entered the Oedipal phase. It is that he is dominated by lateral rather than vertical concerns. In part he is rendering his parents his equals, but he is also using his place among his peers to provide this model: all are children, so to speak. Psychopathy inhabits borders:

> Behaviourally regarded, the psychopath's performance is of the frontier type . . . Frontiers and borders are . . . admirably suited to the working off of compulsive anti-social behaviour; they sparkle with the glitter of personal freedom; the checks and reins of the community are absent and there are no limits either in a physical or in a psychological sense. (Lindner 1945: 11–12)

To be king of the castle the psychopath must live in a levelled world. Freud argues (and others have followed him) that the child first hates the sibling's arrival and then realizes he must love him because his father loves him. This, I think, may be one aspect – but not the most important one. The importance of all being children together becomes even clearer as we look at the main psychic mechanisms in their earliest formation. For Freud 'reversal into its opposite' is the most primitive of all psychic mechanisms; it is illustrated when love for parents becomes hate and vice versa. For Kleinians, this love/hate process is strikingly evident in the oscillating relationship to the present (good/loved), absent (bad/hated) breast of the mother. However, reversal into the opposite is a marked feature too of children's interaction. Indeed exceedingly so: the hugs that turn instantly to blows and vice versa. It is often hard to tell if children's arms around each other's necks are strangling or embracing and this leads from children's play into group behaviour – friends become enemies, neighbours become aliens and vice versa with lightning speed.

Splitting, projection and introjection are all processes that characterize both a psychopathological borderline personality and normal peer group interactions. Both the ego and the object are split into good and bad and, unlike with neurotic processes, ambivalence is rarely accepted – one has best friends, feels one is oneself a honey; one hates the coward one fears to be, wants to have and be everything that the most popular child possesses and represents. What is missing as a dominant mental defence is the neurotic process of repression taken in the strictest sense of the term. Children will suppress their unacceptable desires in relation to each other, sometimes at the behest of authority figures, sometimes as a group-generated response to each other. However, the degree to which, when all is fair in love and war, the desires become anti-social rather than culturally prohibited needs clarification.

The relative absence of repression in borderline states means that these conditions are dominated by other defences; in its turn, this factor suggests how lateral processes may be internalized. Sibling incest is taboo but, rather than this being strongly repressed and hence so unconscious a desire that it can only return in a disguised form in psychopathic symptoms or dreams or in the psychopathologies of everyday life, it is instead transformed into a preconscious, sometimes vaguely remembered possibility, prohibited metaphorically by the mother, but easily indulged in when parents are absent. It is always argued that absence of parental care is responsible for sibling incest and violence. I think this may be ethnocentric. Because Western babies are cared for – it is thought – in the isolated intimacy of the nursing couple or brought up with the parents' constant attention, rules and regulations will be external. Where there is less individual attention to the child the social demands of peer behaviour may be more internalized. Visconti's epic film *Rocco and his Brothers* (1960) illustrates this. Migrants to Milan from the South, the band of brothers is caught between two cultures. Rocco dates Nadia, the ex-girlfriend of his brother Simone. Simone attacks him but Rocco claims he cannot fight a brother. Simone responds that he should have thought of that before he took up with Nadia. In the South, Rocco would have known this; the rule would have been internalized – not so in modern Milan.

Whereas Oedipal desires for the mother are so deeply repressed that no one recalls them, many recall the excitement aroused by siblings or peers. This desire bordering the preconscious and conscious is transmuted into play. In war, both peer-group promiscuity and the rape of same-age enemy women testify to a regression to the prevalence of sexuality between children in childhood.

Sisters and brothers: gender difference versus sexual difference

The stage of sibling interaction which is psychically determinant, I argue, is when the process of distinguishing between sameness and difference is at its zenith: this older sister/younger brother is like me (we have one or two parents in common) but she/he is also different – older, younger; girl or boy. Because this stage is narcissistic and phallic the sameness is expressed in terms of the 'same' genital, that is the clitoris and penis are treated as the same for penetrative play and the same bottoms for being play-penetrated. Children, like some higher mammals, thrust and bump together in fun and a mood of enquiry that uses the body. Until they learn better, siblings (and peers) act too as though each has the same powers of destruction, of strength and of power – kill or be killed. Both genders imagine they can give birth parthenogenetically, the baby which is self-same is entirely of one's own making. Later, in adolescence, if there is sibling incest, the fact of heterosexual reproduction seems to come as a complete shock – it is not, I think, an intrinsic aspect of sibling sexual desire as it is of intergenerational sexual fantasies. Sibling sexuality is sex without reproduction. Anal penetration in heterosexual adulthood is probably the best-kept secret contraceptive method in world history.

Of course, in some cultures sibling couplings have not been prohibited, but rather enjoined in order, it seems, to strengthen a dynasty or preserve group interests (Hopkins 1980). In others, where the father is not known for certain, it is widely feared as it could, and does, easily happen by accident. In some mythologies the world is peopled from heterosexual twins. That sibling incest can both be practised (occasionally) and forbidden (usually) suggests a parallel with its psychic representation of being nearer to preconscious-conscious than to the unconscious process.

If this is so, two distinct, but here related, questions arise. First, psychoanalysis works to understand unconscious processes; if sibling taboos are preconscious rather than unconscious, can psychoanalytic clinical understanding and its resultant theories be of use in understanding lateral interaction, whether psychical or social? Second, are sisters generically different from brothers? The near consciousness of sibling sexual desire is matched or even exceeded by the near conscious murderousness between siblings and subsequently between peers. If these too are suppressed rather than repressed, it could be that psychoanalysis has little distinctive to offer. In fact, however, it seems to me that there is a core aspect that would seem to be so prohibited as to have to be repressed – it depends on who is classified as sibling and this will be cross-culturally variant. In the Judeo-Christian tradition, although in certain circumstances they should kill sisters – for instance when these sisters have had pre- or extramarital sex – brothers of the same parents should not kill each other:

> Oh, my offence is rank, it smells to heaven;
> It hath the primal eldest curse upon it,
> A brother's murder.
>   (Shakespeare, *Hamlet*, III. iii. 36–8)

Death seems close at hand even where it is sexuality that is prohibited: one should not have sex with someone who stands in a sibling or quasi-sibling relationship – this was Henry VIII's problem with his marriage to Catherine of Aragon, the widow of his deceased elder brother. In *Hamlet* it is the offence of Claudius's marriage with Gertrude, widow of Hamlet the Elder, the brother whom he has murdered.[5]

In his mythological anthropological references, Freud always considered sex with sisters tabooed along with, or following from, the deepest incest prohibition on sex with mothers. I have used the term 'gender' here for what arises from the lateral complex, as distinct from a notion of 'sexual difference' which comes about through the vertical Oedipus complex. This distinction has to do with the notion of a drive. A drive (which is not an animal instinct) is a thrust towards something that is or can be missing – hence it can be represented (what is present has no need of representation, re-presentation). The ending of the Oedipus complex through the making meaningful of a symbolic threat of castration makes girls and boys, equally but differently, subject to a sexual division predicated on the absence of the phallus in one group of people. The phallus can be imagined to be absent for anyone because it is definitionally missing in women. What I argue is that the symbolization of lateral sameness and difference does not depend on an absence of a sexual organ in this way. Certainly girls and boys note and indeed make much of any genital differences, but there seems to be little of the trauma of possible absence at stake. There is rivalry about micturition – range for boys, quantity for girls; there is the so-called 'narcissism' of minor differences. But the difference of genitalia only becomes major with the genital and reproductive possibilities of adolescence; penis versus the clitoris is only a minor difference.

— 23 —

'the primal eldest curse . . . A brother's murder'
Cain Slaying Abel by Peter Paul Rubens (*c*.1608–9), Witt Library, Courtauld
Institute of Art, London

The classical position that a girl's *sexual difference* from a boy is modelled on her being like her mother, that is without the phallus, would seem justified. But for this to come into force, both girls and boys have also to accept another absence – the fact that as children they cannot give birth to babies. This, however, does not differentiate them along lateral gender but only along generational lines, and by identification intergenerationally with the same-sex parent. Laterally, the fact that the reproductive aspect of their sexuality is parthenogenetic means that no loss or absence is entailed – as each child imaginatively can produce a baby on its own there need be no heterosexuality. Sexed reproduction entails that each sex appears to offer what the other has not got. This is not so with sibling sexuality. If we take 'absence' as a distinguishing characteristic of the representation of the drive, is there then no representation of a sexual drive with its distinct sibling object?

I said earlier that adolescent sibling incest that results in conception seems to come as an extraordinary shock to the participants. Is the reproductive possibility psychotically foreclosed or denied, or does the parthenogenetic fantasy preclude any fantasy of sexed reproduction? In other words, psychically are the sister and brother not *sexually* differentiated? There is something in this observation that tallies with another: the hysteric, and also sometimes a first-time parent, does not 'know' that the procreated child is his or her child. In addition, hysterical men often fail to father; hysterical women may reproduce successively – the pumpkin-eater syndrome – but without a sense of a difference between one child and the next. These apparently diverse observations have, I believe, a common root. Psychically speaking, the baby in all these instances is, for its progenitor, a replication like a cloning. What the progenitors need not know in all these fantasies of cloning is that in giving birth they themselves are subject to death.

Beyond this general truth it has always seemed important that a mother, in recognizing the inevitability of having a child once she has conceived (even if the child is miscarried, aborted or dies), is at the same time in touch with that other great inevitability, death. To know that a child is one's own child is to know that as its parent one will die. It is this knowledge of one's own individual death that underscores the knowledge that one's lineage continues to live through having one's own child. It could even be – though this is highly speculative – that the few social groups that have promoted sibling reproduction are unconsciously avoiding the knowledge of death. It is usually suggested that they are assuring a future for themselves as a threatened social group through sibling endogamy and also establishing a necessary differentiation between siblings, but perhaps they are also psychically denying that they could ever die out because what is imagined as cloning or replication is a form of immortality.

In Sophocles' *Oedipus Rex*, the only reference Oedipus makes to the fact that he is the brother of his own children is when he refers to his own hands which plucked out his eyes after his discovery of his incest with his mother/wife, Jocasta. This may be a self-castration, but the violence is related to siblinghood. Donald Winnicott, the most benign of the 'mothering' psychoanalysts, had two older sisters. His two sisters had a doll called Rosie which they shared. Living in a progressive household, Donald had his own doll, Lily. One day the gentle little boy completely smashed up Rosie's head. I suggest that sibling sexuality is bound up in violence and that the taboo operates at that interface, Oedipus' self-violence.

Because I am arguing that the absolute sexual difference demanded by reproduction is an Oedipal vertical construction, I am instead using 'gender' to mark the girl/boy difference as it comes about along the lateral axis. I will take my definition, or rather my range of meanings of gender, from the historian Joan Scott: 'The use of gender emphasises an entire system of relationships that may include sex, but is not directly determined by sex nor directly determining of sexuality' (Scott 1996a: 156). With this in mind, I shall distinguish between gender and sexual difference; the latter but not the former is directly determined by sex. Where the castration complex marks the sexual difference 'required' by sexual reproduction, gender difference marks lateral distinctions between girls and boys which include but exceed sexuality.

I suggest that, in particular, the task of the sibling in distinguishing between the genders is to learn that each is serially diverse and not simply a replication of the narcissistic self. In latency, peer group homosexuality is marked and the bisexual possibilities of each gender are explored before puberty makes a new demand for sexual difference. Gender difference between female and male is not a feature, then, of a distinct sexual drive which depends for its representation on a key absence (as sexual difference depends on the absent phallus); boys and girls must both 'lose' the possibility of giving birth to replications of themselves – this is the 'absence' that for both must be represented; it does not distinguish them from each other, but only from their mother. This does not mean there is not sibling sexuality and its prohibition, only that this prohibition does not prescribe sexual difference. What then is the nature of a lateral sexual taboo and its consequences? It is, as I said, bound up with violence.

Sibling sexuality and the death drive

In my view the theme of death is as basic to Freudian psychoanalysis as is the theme of sexuality. I even believe that the latter was largely accorded a more prominent role in order to conceal the former. (J.-B. Pontalis 1981)

Creon: Let Antigone pray to the one she worships – death. (Sophocles, *Antigone*)

He loves her to bits. (Observation of mother of two-year-old child with newborn sister)

Antigone, chronologically the last, was the first to be written of Sophocles' three Theban plays, of which *Oedipus Rex* has become the most famous. Most interpretations see Antigone as representing the values of the family against the state; this entails, I believe, underestimating the importance of the concept of death and its centrality for this play and therefore for the trilogy.

Antigone's two brothers, Polynices and Eteocles, have been at war, each claiming the right to succeed to the throne of Thebes, the city where their father, Oedipus, had been king and from which he was banished after the discovery of his incest. Their uncle (that is their mother's and their father's mother's brother), Creon, has been ruling; Creon favours Polynices as his successor. Polynices and Eteocles kill each other. Creon mourns and buries Polynices with full rituals, but leaves the body of Eteocles exposed. Antigone insists both brothers must be given full funeral rites and breaks Creon's prohibition by herself burying and mourning Eteocles. Creon incarcerates her and secretly has her killed. Creon's son Haemon, Antigone's betrothed, discovers her body at the moment when Creon, having relented, is on his way to release and save her. Haemon kills himself. His mother

(Creon's wife), on learning of her son's death, also takes her own life. *Oedipus Rex* is a play about sexuality and reproduction; *Antigone* is about death.

A penalty of Oedipus' incest is that his brother-sons kill each other. It is only Antigone who knows the meaning of death – near the opening of the play, she claims that she knows that one day she will have to die. She also knows death must be respected and mourned.

Because each sibling evokes the danger of the other's annihilation, siblings are going to want to kill each other. This murderousness is forbidden and must be transmuted to aggressive play and healthy rivalry. However, what can bring about such a transition, beyond, that is, the explicit injunction against violence? Why obey this injunction? Why, indeed, is it not heeded in war? The psychoanalytic theory of the castration complex contends that this threat becomes meaningful for the small child only when, because of its mother, it recognizes that there exists a group of people who are, indeed, without the phallus.

According to Freud, there is no representation of death in the unconscious – something that is nothing cannot be represented. For Freudian theory, castration – the missing phallus – stands for death. Introducing siblings challenges this formulation in a number of ways. What would a representation of death look like if we consider that children are told not to kill their siblings? If we use Antigone, it would seem to be that what is needed is to know that death is both inevitable and absolute – as far as this life is concerned. Death does have dominion. The young child does not know this – if you shoot your playmate dead, he stands up two minutes later. Or is this playing a way of beginning to accept the unbearable knowledge of death? I suggest that the child begins to know about death, and therefore that one must not kill one's brother, because the very existence of that brother in the first place has been experienced as a *death* of the subject's self. A child that Donald Winnicott made famous as 'the Piggle' illustrates this:

> Mother: 'She had a little sister (now seven months) when she was twenty-one months old, which I considered far too early for her. And both this and (I would think also) our anxiety about it seemed to bring about a great change in her.
>
> She becomes easily bored and depressed which was not evident before, and is suddenly very conscious of her relationships and *especially of her identity*. The acute distress, and the overt jealousy of her sister,

did not last long, though the distress was very acute. These two now find one another very amusing . . .

I shall not try to give you any more details of this, but just tell you about the fantasies that keep her calling to us till late at night.'
(Winnicott 1978: 6, my italics)

A sense of one's own absence persists in hysterical conditions and is a trauma that can be revived every time a significant other person dies. In the latter instance, particularly if the dead person is a peer, there is often an instant mimetic identification with an aspect of the deceased before their status as 'other' is recognized. Only the process of mourning establishes the dead person as other than the bereaved. Dunn and her co-workers have observed that sibling interaction is a major facilitator of self–other differentiation. But before this takes place, I would argue, it is as though the self must be mourned. The experience is as if the other sibling, by seeming to stand in my place, has killed me. The initial response is to kill first – as do Antigone's two brothers, each killing the other. The crucial absence here, then, is not the absent phallus (the castration complex) but the absent self.[6]

What enables a child to turn the sense of the death of itself into a mourning process for its unique self so that it can be recreated as one among others – a part of a series? First I think this is not a once-and-for-all achievement; it is one that has to be often repeated throughout life. Its accomplishment is witnessed when analytic patients – indeed all patients, all of us – come to discover the huge relief of that dreaded fate that we are 'ordinary'; at heart we are just like anyone else, as anyone else is like us.

A toddler appears partly to believe that the baby about to be born is another version of itself. When it is actually born, this new being is 'the baby'. The Piggle, who was the baby, is now 'no one'. Into the wish to kill the one who annihilates the subject by its existence rushes the love that was also present in the anticipation of another self. One can see the near simultaneity of murder and adoration on the face of the toddler who 'loves the new baby to bits'. This psychic mechanism of the 'reversal into its opposite' can also be seen in the love replacing hate as the 'life drive' flooding in to mitigate the death drive. It enables the displaced, annihilated subject to love the sibling and at the same time gradually to restore the self.

Sibling sex and death then are intricately entwined. The narcissistic love of the-other-as-the-self explodes in murderousness once it is realized that there cannot be another self, but once the murder is resisted the love comes back in a new form. The unique self can be mourned and it is here that the loss on which all drives depend for their representations makes itself felt. Narcissistic self-love has only a mirror image; the new self-esteem which depends on the loss of the grandiose, unique self has a representation – a symbolic version of one's own subjecthood. What is forbidden is to kill the one you must love – your own life is ensured by respecting that taboo: love thyself as thou lovest thy neighbour. Sibling sex is about life and death, not sexual difference, even though the genders play different roles.

'Gender difference' along lateral lines and 'sexual difference' along vertical ones will come together in adolescence when actual fertility enters the picture for the first time. Both girls and boys will re-experience the murderousness towards the sibling. However, this can emerge as an ideal imago of a peer or peers who have survived, who really stand up again when you shoot them dead – these are the foundation of the heroic self: one restores one's narcissism by placing it in the survivor peer. Unlike her sister Ismene who placates and colludes with offences against respecting death, Antigone is a heroic ideal. To be this she has had to renounce marriage and motherhood. For neither girls nor boys does the heroic self involve reproduction – becoming mothers and fathers. 'Thinking back through one's mother' (Virginia Woolf), like growing up to be a father, is the task of vertical assimilation. A secondary taboo on incest with the sibling is established in adolescence by virtue of the fact that each is a potential parent. For this reason, among others, adolescence is the heyday of homosexuality with its avoidance of reproduction and its creation of gangs and intense friendships.

Psychoanalysis, siblings and gender difference

Psychoanalytic theory is a good illustration of its own thesis: only what is absent can be represented; what is present cannot be represented and hence cannot be seen. Didier Anzieu, one of Freud's most interesting biographers, illustrated how Freud could see the patriarchal structures of high modernism as they were disappearing (Anzieu 1986). The subsequent identification of psychoanalysis with a patriarchal position, particularly in ego-psychology, entailed the invisibility of its own phallocentric position. It is likewise with the matriarchal premises of Object Relations theory. The mother's psychic importance was recognized when it was missing from psychoanalytic theory. Once it was established, it was identified with and thus made present so that it could no longer be the object of re-presentation and subsequent analysis: the analyst herself stood in the position from which 'the law of the mother' operated; so this law was invisible.

Classical psychoanalysis starts with the adult. Maternally dominated psychoanalysis both grew out of an interest in child patients and came to influence other developmental psychologies with a focus on childhood, just as they influenced it. Patients/trainees/actual children were 'the siblings' and because the role was thus present it was not available for analysis. When sibling transference – the patient and analyst as lateral peers – is noted, it tends to be squeezed back into vertical Oedipal models. Melanie Klein's early work which featured siblings vividly is an instance of this. Group psychoanalysis, always given impetus by wartime conditions, realized that this lateral dimension was what was missing (Brown 1998; Holmes 1980; Hopper 2000). *Antigone*, the play of siblings, is a drama for wartime (as with Anouilh's version, first produced in 1944).

Perhaps we can now see a distinction between sexuality (lateral) and reproduction (vertical) because, in the hegemonic white social groups of the Western world, reproduction is not the nearly inevitable consequence of sexuality, and above all because it is sharply on the decline. 'Gender' as a concept comes into being in this context to describe differences which do not depend on reproduction. Crossing gender boundaries, 'gender trouble' (Butler 1999), gender transformations, are all possible if sexed reproduction is not at stake. Sibling and peer cohorts are the personnel of postmodernism with its focus on sameness and difference, its concern with 'time present' rather than 'time past'. Siblings do not on the whole reproduce, but they can cherish, show concern and care for. Social groups not constructed along the apparent binary of reproduction rely on managing the violence unleashed by the trauma of threatened replication; representing seriality is crucial. Life and death, sex and murder, the mechanisms of 'reversal into its opposite' and the splittings of love and hate are all expressions of the psychic representation of the sibling-lateral relationship, as in their extreme versions it is these mechanisms and these lateral images that inhabit the pathologies of the borderline.

2

Did Oedipus have a Sister?

When I first thought about psychoanalysis and its missing siblings, I asked of all and sundry the question: did Oedipus have a sister? My friends, colleagues and acquaintances were all unable to answer the question, and they were so annoyed by this that I decided I had better forego what I had intended light-heartedly and start with the answer. Yes, Oedipus *did* have a sister, he had two: Ismene and Antigone, his daughters. (He also had two brothers, his sons.) Yet only once in Sophocles' play *Oedipus Rex* is this sibling dimension of the chaos that has been introduced by Oedipus' crime of maternal incest referred to. It is referred to when Antigone and Ismene enter the room where Oedipus stands, self-blinded:

> Oedipus: Where are you, children?
> Come, *feel your brother's hands.*
> It was their work that darkened these clear eyes –
> Your father's eyes
> As once you knew them
> Though he never saw nor knew
> What he did when he became your father.[1]

As far as we know, Jocasta and Laius had no children other than Oedipus, so Oedipus' children are his only siblings, or rather, half siblings – they share the same mother but not father. Oedipus' crime of sleeping with his mother confuses generations, but in the play, as in its deployment as 'the Oedipus complex', the central paradigm of psychoanalysis, the axis of son to mother overshadows, or all but obliterates the lateral dimension. We completely forget that Oedipus and his children are brothers and sisters. I want to take this as a metaphor for what I see as the suppression of the significance of laterality – of siblings, and their successors, peers and affines – from a psychoanalytic understanding of the construction of psychic life. However, I also want to question it: in Sophocles' original play, is the focus so exclusively on the vertical generations, or does what I am pointing to as the omission of siblings result from there being in the Thebes of the period less of a psychic distinction between mothers and sisters, or for that matter, fathers and sons?

My awareness of these hidden siblings came through puzzling for many years about hysteria. Hysteria was prevalent in my clinical practice but was largely absent in the late twentieth-century diagnostic and theoretical literature. There seems to be something similar, some analogy here; both siblings and hysteria are obviously present at times and not noticed, and widely observed at other times but made nothing of. To the extent that hysteria is defined within psychoanalysis, it is seen as a bodily re-enactment through anxiety, phobia or somatic 'conversion' of an illicit Oedipal incestuous desire that has been inadequately repressed. In other words it is understood only within a vertical paradigm. Although I shall be referring to it from time to time, hysteria is simply my background material; I want to take further some suggestions which I made earlier in *Mad Men and Medusas: Reclaiming Hysteria and the Effects of Sibling Relationships on the Human Condition* (Mitchell 2000a) about the significance of siblings. Here I plan to look two ways: on the one hand to take siblings to psychoanalytic theory to address the implications of their omission; and, on the other, to use psychoanalytic theory to help in understanding the significance of siblings outside its parameters – it is not only psychoanalysis that hitherto has missed the importance of siblings.

Thus I shall focus on the problem of siblings within a psychoanalytic framework, but my questions are informed by a 'layperson's' reading in other social science and humanities disciplines, above all by anthropology and English literature. This means that the baseline is a conviction, whose ultimate resting point is a particular type of clinical practice and the theory that arises from it, that there are unconscious processes, that these are significant and that they are organized and expressed differently from conscious processes. Crucial unconscious processes are set down in infancy and in the transition from infancy to childhood. It is in this early period, which we for good reasons forget, that we internalize the meanings and implications of human sociality. In psychoanalytical theory a sexual desire comes up against a prohibition and as a consequence its representation is repressed. The repression fails to some degree, and the illicit desire returns in a way that makes it initially unrecognizable – it cannot be expressed directly so it is concealed in neurotic symptoms, dreams, the psychopathologies of everyday life, the power of jokes – the various manifestations of something that was made unconscious through repression, but then in part escaped unconsciousness – although its significance remains unknown until its expression is deciphered. This is a theory that emphasizes the importance of infantile sexual desire and hence infancy in the context of cultural taboos and learning processes: how does a human animal become a human being, with mind, language, spirit, social relations and so on? These postulates of psychoanalysis have, of course, been widely taken up by other disciplines and widely diffused in the general culture both in opposition to them and in endorsement of them.

Although prohibitions on sibling murder and incest may be weaker than on their parental–infant equivalents, they are essential and thus form part of the acquisition of sociality and contribute independently to the construction of unconscious processes. They cannot be subsumed under the *vertical* taboos. In other words, sibling relationships are important not only for conscious but for unconscious processes. It is thus essential that they are included in psychoanalytical theory and practice and all that has been influenced by it. Siblings, and what I call all *lateral* relations that follow from these, have an importance both socially and psychically.

The importance of siblings has been noted in developmental psychology and by therapists working in group therapy. Even within psychoanalysis they surface both as observation and as a question from time to time (Colonna and Newman 1983; Holmes 1980; Hopper 2000; Oberndorf 1928; Volkan and Ast 1997). My point is different from these extremely valuable, but sporadic and unintegrated observations. It is that while siblings are classically subsumed into the Oedipus complex, I have come to believe that, although the vertical and the lateral axes are always interactive, each dimension has a relative autonomy. Sibling violence and incest are not the same as that directed at parents. The prohibition on them is weaker and

I shall offer a possible reason for this weaker taboo later – but never-theless the prohibition is there. In most cultures, some key prohibi-tions are internalized and the representatives of the desires repressed so that they become unconscious. If, as I argue, the vertical and the lateral are not the same, but are qualitatively and structurally differ-ent, then these different desires – active or repressed – will manifest themselves differently.

My emphasis on siblings and their equivalents proposes a different dimension to the emphasis on sexuality. Sibling displacement evokes a desire to kill or be killed. Within the vertical Oedipal story, there is also a prohibition on killing represented by Oedipus' unwitting (for which read unconscious) murder of his father, Laius. Again, I would argue that this is not the same as the sibling prohibition. Following the First World War, Freud hypothesized a death drive. However, as I mentioned in chapter 1, he also argued that there could be no representation of death in the unconscious. I consider that there is such a representation and that we have not seen it because we have suppressed the importance of siblings. At the level of theory, that sibling murderousness is psychically crucial gives, I believe, a new emphasis, perhaps a different understanding, to the controversial hypo-thesis of a death drive. I shall explore this in a number of ways. I am interested more in the psychic role of 'death' than in arguing the case for or against the controversial notion of whether or not there is a drive towards annihilation.

Killing your father and having intercourse with your mother are two related but separate events – you want to murder one and have sex with the other. Violence and sexuality between siblings are much closer together in their construction and what matters is that both acts and emotions of sex and of murderousness are *for the same person*. This proximity of sex and violence between siblings affects both aspects of the equation. There is a fundamental desire to mur-der your sibling. It too meets a prohibition: you must not kill your brother Abel; you must instead love your brother (neighbour) *as yourself*. The violence must be turned into love – but the possibility of love is already there in the love one has for oneself, what, in psychoanalytic terminology, is called narcissism. How does narcis-sism become love of another, object-love? It seems to me that the ambivalence towards siblings is an integral part of this transforma-tion. What is the violence that is born at the same time as love?

We are sexually 'polymorphously perverse' before the rigours of the Oedipus and castration complexes; are we not as children also 'polymorphously perverse' in our wish to kill? Repression – the making unconscious of this wish to kill and the prohibition against it – fails and violence against siblings or their substitutes is acted out. War is a de-repression. The prohibition on murder and on self-murder means that this desire (or more accurately, its representation) must also to a degree be repressed and become unconscious. Here, as with infantile–parental sexuality, there is also the alternative route of sublimation – diverting the drive to other culturally acceptable ends such as competitiveness and friendly rivalry. The failure of repression or sublimation of murderousness, on an analogy with the failure of the repression or sublimation of infantile sexuality, can be enacted in what I will call a violence-perversion, which is psychically structured like a sexual perversion. A sexual perversion is a failure of repression. We are all considered sexually 'polymorphously perverse' in infancy. As a species we are at least as violence promiscuous as we are sexual promiscuous.

I suggest loving one's sibling *like oneself* is neither exactly narcissism nor object-love. It is narcissism transmuted by a hatred that has been overcome. Within this more general framework of the particular relationship of sibling murderousness to sibling love and therefore to subsequent love-relations and/or to sexuality, is a further thesis that sibling sexual love differs in an important respect from Oedipal/parental love and that this has an enormous importance for child-bearing. These claims on behalf of siblings explain a number of observations and entail a different dimension to psychoanalytic theory.

It has always been claimed, at least within psychoanalytic theory, that hate comes before love, and there are a number of explanations of this. Here I will use our awareness that 'hysterics love where they hate' (Freud). In other words, hate in hysteria is primary. As there is latent or potential hysteria in all of us, the primacy of sibling hate may help explain 'hysterical' sexual violence. Important manifestations of hatred have been inadequately explained. For instance, the paediatrician and psychoanalyst Donald Winnicott (arguing implicitly with Melanie Klein's notion of innate envy and destructiveness in which the baby in fantasy attacks the mother) emphasized that from his work, very much contrary to Klein, he *knew* that the mother's

'The small child loves, even adores the sibling . . .'
Two sisters, courtesy Claire Coleman

hatred of the baby comes before the baby's hatred of the mother. Winnicott, however, did not wonder where the mother's hatred came from if she herself had not first hated as a baby or young child.[2] But Winnicott also made a casual remark in passing which he never linked up with his conviction about a mother's hatred – this was that sisters and brothers could love each other provided they *first* had access to enough hatred of each other. I think, however, that before committing ourselves to the primacy of either hate or love, we need to specify further what is meant by them.

Ambivalence is a condition of human relations. But even to think about ambivalence involves a dualistic splitting: love and hate. Language, thought itself, necessitates a division. To live on the pinhead of ambivalence is impossible. In clinical work one sees and experiences the flash moments of it. Usually we think it is untenable because we make ambivalence indicate that there is negativity in our apparent lovingness and we do not want to own the negative. But this is not the problem. The problem is that one experiences two completely contrary emotions simultaneously – and the sensation is unlivable. Yet this is every child's experience – and it is an experience that is typified (or incarnated) by siblings. The small child loves, even adores the sibling that is already there and also the prospect of one to come – whether it does or does not arrive. This is an affectual narcissistic state which will be taken up in the later love that, hopefully, will appear. This cuts across the narcissistic love. It is, however, the hatred that makes what we might call the first psychic mark. The narcissistic love for the new baby (or the child that is already there) is comparable to what Michael Balint (1952) called 'primary love'. 'Primary love' is the baby's first feeling for the mother. However, I think we can see that the baby's self-love spreads out to include those whom it literally takes to be itself. The potential eradication of oneself by another must be dealt with intellectually – the situation of someone replacing one forces the mind to work and the affectual state of love is mentalized. Asked by her expectant father, Carl Jung, what she would do if her baby brother were to be born that night, two-year-old Agathli had a ready answer: 'I would kill him' (B. Clark in Farmer 1999: 8). Agathli had thought about the problem.

Sibling sexuality and murderousness are, then, contiguous. However, sibling sexual love differs from Oedipal or parental love in a highly significant way. All children want to make babies; all children have sexual feelings. It is in relation to parents – the Oedipus complex, Oedipus and his mother, Jocasta – that a desire for reproduction, fantasies of giving birth and a sexual drive come together. We can read Oedipus' choice with a somewhat different emphasis from its usual interpretation as the Oedipus complex: the polymorphously perverse sexuality of the child must come under the sign of love for the mother if reproductive fantasies are to shape the randomness of the drive. No desired mother equals no wish to mother or father, to reproduce in general. The emphasis is on the need for a positive wish for incest rather than on its prohibition or the tragedies of its enactment: if we do not want our mother we will not want to be parents. However, in relation to siblings there are sexual feelings but not, I think, reproductive fantasies.

Two diverse characteristics of hysteria illustrate the difference. Hysterical birth, phantom pregnancies, and either 'unacceptable' or socially sanctioned male couvades are all instances of a fantasy of parthenogenetic birth (Mitchell 2000a) – the hysteric, like the child, believes it can make babies on its own. When his father asked him from where he was going to get the babies which he insisted he was about to produce, Little Hans, the first child of psychoanalysis, answered, 'from myself of course'. If this is unconsciously maintained in later life, it is related to a failure of an Oedipal repression. It is not, however, as is always argued, bound to the father's threat of castration which comes into action if one persists in *having* the mother incestuously. Instead this hysterical possibility arises from a refusal of what I referred to earlier as the 'law of the mother', which prohibits a child from *being* a mother while it is a child.

There is also another equally prevalent characteristic of hysteria – childlessness, or childfree-ness, whether actual or psychological. This is the other side of the coin of fantasized parthenogenetic birth. Like the oscillation between florid sexuality and sexual frigidity, both phantom births and childlessness are characteristics of the hysteric – for the same reason. The hysteric is a Don Juan – that Don Juan would become a father is unimaginable; if by chance a child is produced, then the parent of either sex does not know, psychologically speaking, that it is 'his' or 'her' child. One of my patients – one among many – evocatively described looking at his handsome sons across the dining-room table, and while liking them, not being able to grasp what they had to do with him. 'Where has this baby come from?' is famously the toddler's question on the birth of a sibling. It all too easily carries on to later life and is repeated in the parents' bafflement. Fantasies of parthenogenetic birth and psychological childfreeness are two sides of the same coin.

Sibling sexuality ranges from sex with someone whom one experiences as the same, to sex with someone whose difference one wants to obliterate. It can be part and parcel of the imaginary twin or imaginary sister or brother which is so frequent a fantasy of childhood: this will be a kind of babes-in-the-wood comfort in loneliness, as it is with the twins in Arundhati Roy's prize-winning novel, *The God of Small Things* (1997: ch. 2). At the other end, it will be a precursor of the rage witnessed in wartime rape. In this case the sibling continues to threaten one's existence so that murderousness and sexuality are ways of coping – with dire consequences for the victim. Freud's 'Wolf Man' is a psychoanalytic case in point. The intrusion of the sexual fantasies and sexual assaults of the Wolf Man's older sister drove the small boy and future patient of psychoanalysis absolutely witless. But as the contemporary NSPCC report (Cawson et al. 2000) makes clear, the sibling abuse origin of the disturbed child is often missed.

Sibling incest is less strongly tabooed than intergenerational incest. In most cultures sexual intercourse with one's mother, or even one's father, is more or less unthinkable because the desire's core representation is more than repressed, it is demolished. This elimination of the fantasy is not the case with sibling incest. Childhood sexual play is both normal and consensual to a certain point. Many therapists report the prevalence of adolescent sibling sex and note the frequent absence of guilt or even of a sense of wrong-doing. This absence of concern by the patient or client is all too often echoed in the neglect of the therapist, who himself – incorrectly to my mind – does not find it an important indicator of problems. It would seem that because sibling relations have been given no autonomous place either in the theory or in the therapy, if they go wrong this is interpreted as not mattering much in the practice. If they were understood to produce their own unconscious processes, then the possible pathological outcomes could be grasped as well. The occurrence of full sibling incest is usually blamed on parental neglect. The result is that the neglect, rather than the incest, receives the attention. It seems that it is only when sibling conception actually occurs that the patient's horror and fear of monstrous progeny break in and the clinician becomes worried too.

So sibling incest is widely not considered to be deeply serious unless there is a pregnancy. This attitude replicates the fantasy of the child and seems to me to be incorrect. In terms of the future playing out of sibling fantasies in marriage, in partnerships and in parenthood, what took place either in fact or in fantasy in the child's sibling past is crucial. I think the oversight of siblings then has to do with the absence of reproduction in the sibling sexual fantasies – children are having sex not making babies with each other. Sexed reproduction demands two people of different (so-called 'opposite') sexes; sexuality does not. Siblings are not sexual 'opposites' even when they are of different genders. In the mind of the adult: no pregnancy possible, no sex. This is obviously to miss the sex – more importantly even than that, it is to miss the violence, overt or latent.

There is, then, definitely lateral sexual attraction both homosexual and heterosexual. I would argue that the distinction between the two

– lateral homosexuality and heterosexuality – is relatively unimportant. It is anal-phallic and, at a deep level, gender indifferent; the genital that is imaginatively used is either the same (the anus) or homologous (the clitoris and penis). This lateral sexuality differs from vertical incestuous desires in that reproduction does not appear to be part of the fantasy. This distinguishes it from Oedipal fantasies where, as the original story makes clear, having babies with your mother (or father) is a key component of the desire. In Oedipus' case, this is enacted and the problem neatly encapsulated: if you were to have children with your mother, those children you had fathered would be your siblings. We repress this knowledge because it relates to the taboo, so no one remembers that Oedipus has a sister. A child of sibling incest, if socially condoned, is considered only a child – as among the Ptolemies – not a sibling; if not socially condoned, it is imagined as a monster.

Siblings may play 'Mummies and Daddies', but this is vertical imitation like being a fire-fighter or nurse in the world of work. The sexual desires of children for each other are more likely to be those that come under a widely observed masturbatory fantasy of 'a child – usually a sibling – (is) being beaten' (Freud [1919]: 179; see chapter 4).

The non-reproductive nature of sibling sexual fantasy is bound up with the importance of murderousness in relation to love. What is this murderousness which should be mitigated, like the incest, to something milder, such as competitiveness and rivalry, and its lethal sting thus lost? Melanie Klein emphasizes the envy of the baby for all the mother has and is, and hence its wish to destroy her (Klein [1957]). I am suggesting that sibling hatred is first and foremost hatred, not envy. It can become envy and this envious rivalry can then become sublimated into emulation or competitiveness. It does not need – as does the baby's destructiveness towards its mother – to be 'repaired' (Melanie Klein's emphasis on the baby's reparative fantasies), nor does gratitude seem to be its positive other side as it is with the maternal relation. Envy can be overcome and replaced by gratitude – you realize you have been given enough of what you craved and felt deprived of. Hatred has no such resolution – it can, however, reverse into love. Hatred and violence are, I believe, related not to envy but to trauma. Psychically obliterated by a traumatic experience, the first signs of life are fury and hatred.

—— 41 ——

For a traumatic response to wear itself out, some adjustment has to be made – loss of a home in an earthquake or a friend on a battlefield has in time to be overcome. The object has to be psychically lost so that it can be restored as an internal image – this is the process of mourning. But, contrary to this, the hysteric cannot mourn – his symptoms re-enact something that cannot be given up. This is an extreme expression of the quite common inability to accept that the past is the past. If mourning cannot take place, then the 'haunting' which is so commonly a noted feature of cross-cultural studies of hysteria takes place:[3] the object is not lost, then represented and internalized; instead it persists as though it has not been lost, but is everlastingly present.

Briefly, and schematically, the hypothetical history I shall construct as one that underlies the significance of murderous siblings goes like this: because it is born prematurely, the human neonate and infant is always subjected to some trauma or traumata, which is to say, some excess of stimulation – the world is too much with us – which, on a strict analogy with a physical trauma, breaks through the protective proto-psychic layers and is experienced as a blasting out, an annihilation of the proto-subject, a gap in its existence. We can all imagine the experience by recalling some completely unexpected and pretty large shock, the creation of a black hole where we thought we stood.

Within psychoanalytic theory, the implications of human neonatal helplessness are widely accepted, but they are differently understood. I think that this black hole, like the vortex of a whirlpool, attracts things to it – a manifestation of this would be the way in which, if later traumata occur, after the initial shock a person goes repetitiously over and over the same ground – accidents come in threes. This 'repetition compulsion' is a feature of what Freud called 'the death drive', something that drives a person back to a state of stasis, the inorganic. To me, 'the inorganic' as a psychic state is the internalized trauma, the experience of annihilation, the absence of the yet-to-be subject. The trauma becomes 'death', a nodule or nucleus of death within.[4] However, for life to continue, the hole of the trauma seals over, and all the active elements of life and the instinct to survive contribute to its diminishing importance. Sometimes, as in some premature babies, these life drives are insufficient and observation has shown that only the extremely active intervention of the mother or her substitute can educe enough 'life drive' from the baby for the baby to survive.[5] However, the successful fusion of this drive-to-live with the death drive within will manifest as destructiveness and aggression – a turning out of the passive experience of the violence done to the proto-subject. Both destructiveness and aggression are essential for life. Hatred is the first expression of this turning outwards of the experience of death. Even in later life, it is quite usual for hatred of everyone and everything to be the first sign of recovery from a trauma.

This description is simply my rendition (arrived at through thinking about hysteria) of the hypothesis of life and death drives that Freud put forward in 1920 after the end of the Great War. I offer it only as background, for it is the next stage that is the focus of my concern. I suggest that on this neonatal-to-infantile ground plan a second trauma takes place: the realization that one is not unique, that someone stands exactly in the same place as oneself and that though one has found a friend, this loss of uniqueness is, at least temporarily, equivalent to annihilation. It is easier to visualize this when a younger sibling is born, but I think it goes both ways. The second or later child 'knows' about hatred as it has of course been hated itself by the older child, hated to death. The last child's affectual love is pre-psychic or narcissistic and it will be shocked into psychic 'hate' at roughly the same age as the older child feels threatened by the newborn arrival – actual or expected. However, where for all children the earlier experience was of annihilation (what Freud calls 'death') and the demand to live, at this later level we have murderous desires, as a response to the danger of annihilation. I do not think this sibling experience replaces or follows from the trials and tribulations of the vertical Oedipus and castration complexes. Nor can it be reduced to the underlying sense of annihilation of the so-called primal scene, the fantasy of the parental intercourse in which one is absent from one's own conception. The sibling experience interconnects with these experiences and fantasies but sets up its own structure. It has its own desires and its own prohibitions: Jung's little daughter, like all children, is simply not allowed to kill her brother.

I want to call attention to the 'law of the mother' which needs to operate to intervene at the level of sibling murderousness and incest. This is a somewhat provocative reference to Jacques Lacan's notion of the 'law of the father', which is the law of castration – the symbolic penalty for trying to stand in the father's place with the mother.

Where according to Lacan the 'law of the father' is cognate with what he designates 'the Symbolic' and the child's accession to language, my notion of the 'law of the mother', I suggest, introduces seriality – one, two, three, four siblings, playmates, school friends . . . tinker, tailor, soldier, sailor. There is room for you as well as me – something of which the hysteric in all of us has no cognizance. Representation and hence language relates to absence – what is not there must be signified. Seriality, although it takes place within language, is about numeracy not literacy. There is probably some hard-wiring for a small range of numbers – birds can 'count' their eggs. The mother's injunction falls over this 'counting' – siblings are the eggs which are the same and different. Later, within the sibling group, there is then a contract: to extend one's narcissism to form a social group in which one loves because one is the same, and to find another group to hate, because they are different.

I now briefly want to set my hypothesis about the importance of siblings within the context of hysteria – the source material for this argument. In particular I shall situate siblings within the question of male hysteria and the debates about it that took place during and immediately after the First World War. Similar issues arose during the Second World War, but there was less interest in psychoanalytic circles in defining the category of hysteria. The same holds true for equivalent war responses today (Showalter 1997). As I think the category of hysteria is still useful, the First World War serves my argument best.

The non-organic illnesses which struck the combatants on both sides in the war, in almost all their symptoms, resembled well-recorded manifestations of hysteria – overwhelming anxiety, physical anaesthesia, paralysis of bodily parts, mutism and, behaviourally, mimetic identification and manipulativeness, seductiveness and dishonesty – but there would seem to have been more nightmares than is usual in peacetime hysteria. The conditions are well portrayed in Pat Barker's trilogy, *Regeneration* (1996). These illnesses, at first officially called 'shell shock', were eventually defined as traumatic neuroses, and within the widely influential psychoanalytic paradigm, the absence of sexuality, more specifically of unresolved *Oedipal* sexuality, was taken as the marker that these men were not hysterics.[6] Yet in the argument as to whether these are cases of traumatic neurosis (or of 'Gulf War Syndrome', its contemporary equivalent) or whether they are instances of hysteria, the connection between trauma and hysteria is overlooked. Furthermore this overlooked connection is twofold: there is more sexuality in traumatic neurosis and more 'death' in hysteria than is usually perceived. With regard to the first, I think we accept too unquestioningly, and without analysis, the sexual compulsiveness that characteristically follows excessive shock – the wartime rapes, surely hateful sex, or even just the driven, compulsive promiscuity rationalized along the lines of 'for tomorrow we die'.

At the other end, the suicidal proclivities of entrenched hysteria are noted but their motivation is not included as part of the aetiology of the condition. There is a strong likelihood that in serious cases of hysteria the outcome will be suicide. There is a marked drive to death. This drive to death is mapped over an internalization of something shocking or traumatic. There would, then, seem to be more sexuality in traumatic neurosis and more of a nucleus of an internalized 'death' in hysteria than has been accounted for. Yet there are differences between the conditions too.

An observation by W. H. Rivers, the psychiatrist on whose work at Craig Lockhart Hospital in Edinburgh Pat Barker based the study of hysteria in her trilogy, seems to me to go a long way to describing, if not accounting for, the important difference between traumatic neurosis and hysteria. Rivers noted that in time many of the soldiers' symptoms simply burnt themselves out. In my proposal traumatic neurosis is a re-edition in later life of the neonatal and infantile response – first a shock that annihilates the subject and then an identification with this shock which is internalized as a 'death' within. This then fuses with an assertion of, and instinct for, survival and for life which is also sexual; it is a drive to form unities, make contacts, have relations of any sort whatsoever. Subsequently the sexuality may be overloaded with the destructiveness of the death component in a way to which wartime rape bears testimony. The condition of a trauma is that these responses will initially be compulsive and repetitious, but they will wear themselves out in time.

We might make the same claim for those reactions so often described colloquially as 'hysterical'. I believe, however, that full-blown or entrenched hysteria is different in that the secondary stage of sibling annihilation of the subject and murderousness and jealousy rather than the primary stage of an annihilating trauma is used by the psyche. In other words, relationships with people, animals and things are already in existence when the infantile subject is thrown entirely off-balance. In disarray, relationships vanish along with the subject and when the narcissism is urgently put back in place by the hysteric, it looks but only *looks* as though the relationships are restored too. These are at best erratic, but mostly pseudo-loves used to cover the real hatred that is the response to trauma.

Traumatic neurosis repeats the primary pre- or proto-psychic affectual state; the advent of an awareness of siblings (and peers) turns this into a psychic, mentalized condition. The experience of a sibling is of having someone in what initially seems like the same position as oneself. This induces a struggle for survival which will be expressed as a struggle for power; a lust for power, which (*pace* Foucault) is secondary to the need to survive. Before moving on to sibling incest and its prohibition, I will describe a situation as an icon of the effect of sibling murderousness and its prohibition – this is an anecdotal account, not of a patient, but of two children I know. I have no means of testing whether my explanation correctly interprets their behaviour; that is not my intention – I intend it merely as an illustration of a hypothesis.

Emmi is two and three-quarters. Since she was about a year old she has played ceaselessly with 'babies', mainly dolls but also animals, bits of cloth – more or less anything will do. Always a verbal and thoughtful child, she says that what she wants most of all in the world is to find a real baby in the street and bring it home to look after; the focus therefore is on caring for, not conceiving. She has expressed no interest in her mother having another baby. Caring, not giving birth, are what sisters should do. However, recently her aunt gave birth to her cousin and Emmi was extremely interested in this, particularly in the actual birth. She refuses to go to the école maternelle (pre-school) although nearly all the children in this working village attend. Whenever she is taken there, she screams insistently and desperately writhes and struggles to get away. She is successful. Once home and calmed down she explains repetitiously to anyone who is prepared to listen that she 'is really too young. [She] isn't born yet'. It was this formulation that intrigued me. Had she been struck that her cousin was safer inside the womb? The fixating and the repetition of her wish not to be born quite yet suggests that something traumatic rather than just difficult is being experienced.

When Emmi was born out of a very difficult pregnancy and birth, her older sister Marion was appalled. Marion was aged three and a half; she proceeded to play exclusively with dinosaurs while expressing nothing but disgust and hatred for babies. She expressed this disgust very physically. Her denigration, repudiation and revulsion still continues till now, Emmi's own third year, although she occasionally classes her small sister as a child, not a baby, and plays with her. Mostly, though individually lovely girls, they continue to fight and quarrel day in, day out. Their characters and their physical appearance are polar opposites – making it seem as though this were the only way in which they could each find a distinct space to occupy.[7]

Emmi in her fixation on babies seems to be protecting her baby-self from her sister's very real wish for her annihilation.[8] Emmi has a strong life drive but considers she still needs her mother's protection – 'she is not born yet' and she absolutely refuses to be exposed to siblings or peers at playgroup without her mother there – she is truly terrified, not of her mother leaving so much as of being left exposed on her own with other children.

Emmi's sister Marion had quite serious difficulties with speech. When Emmi was born it seems Marion could only express through physical violence her sense of her own psychic annihilation which took place with the advent of this new baby that stopped her being who she was – her parents' baby. Perhaps she felt like a dinosaur – there is a dinosaur park near her home – big and powerful but extinct. Ever since the film *Jurassic Park*, dinosaurs have been popular toys. But, again, Marion's fixation on them has an insistent, slightly desperate quality. In particular she avidly kisses and expresses ecstatic love for an embryo dinosaur that rests in a gelatinous substance within an openable plastic dinosaur egg – the extinct can also be born.[9] What Emmi and Marion demonstrate is the double threat of annihilation posed by siblings. The older child is not just displaced, but for a time is without a place – someone else is what she is. The normal reaction is to kill in order not to be thus obliterated. The new baby registers this threat to its existence from the older sibling and clings to its mother for protection. We may have here in the sibling threat what John Bowlby (chapter 7) labels 'predators' – a universal terror of being attacked. Bowlby is thinking of mammals in the wild; 'where the wild things are' for humans is here within the family.

The experience of siblings introduces a social dimension – it is a social trauma. For the older child the great fear of the one who replaces and displaces breaks through its protective barriers. The younger child must add the fear of being killed by the older sibling to its general helplessness in the face of the world. In most cases these experiences will be healed and the dread and shock will turn into hate and love, rivalry and friendship.[10]

In discussions of 'otherness', whether of gender, race, class or ethnicity, hatred of the other is explained by the obvious fact that the 'other' is different.[11] Sibling experience displays the contrary: the position occupied by the sibling is first experienced as 'the same' – hatred is for one who is the same; it is this hatred for a sameness that displaces which then generates the category of 'other' as a protection. It is the one who can now be imagined to be utterly different who can thenceforth be loathed or loved. The displaced has initially no place to go to – she or he wants to be who they still are, the baby. The new baby must be got rid of; when it does not vanish, then it must be relegated to another place – the place of the 'other'. 'I' must be king of the castle, the new baby the dirty rascal.

Does not the early sibling experience of creating 'otherness' out of sameness underlie the instant 'otherness' of race, class and ethnicity, an otherness that renders invisible the sameness that then has to be rediscovered at a greatly sophisticated level? If so, the sibling situation, being primary, would be the model. Hate for the one who appears as the threatening same-as-the-subject may next transmute to envy or masquerade as envy. After a trauma such as an earthquake the life drive floods the death drive and one rages and hates but gradually one comes to envy the one who has not been traumatized, whose house is still standing, partner or child still living . . . it is simply not fair. As children say, day in, day out.

Although the social category is frequently far more extensive than this, biological sisters and brothers are always the children of the same one or two parents. In concubinage, adulterous unions and sometimes in polygyny in urban situations, biological half-siblings may not know each other, which may make the fantasy possibility of them all the stronger. However, offspring of the same mother tend to stay together and always to be regarded as close siblings. Sibling relationships are always especially important in matrilineages.

It is a common observation that within psychoanalytic theory, the twentieth century saw the shift from the importance of the father to the importance of the mother. Lacan's intervention on behalf of the Symbolic and the 'law of the father' was intended deliberately to go against the grain of this transition. The transition to emphasizing the mother rather than the father is often treated as though it were the product of justice – of righting an imbalance. Although it is realized that the emphasis on the importance of mothers arose from a different clinical awareness often prompted by women analysts and the maternal transference, the full significance of this clinical factor has not received much attention.

It is always difficult to correlate unconscious psychic material with social factors – the social becomes unconscious and then emerges from unconsciousness into accessible preconsciousness only through its utter transformation. However, I will venture where angels fear to tread. Social changes take generations to affect the psychology of the unconscious ego and superego but nevertheless they do have a place there in the end. From the 'moral motherhood' of the mid to late nineteenth-century Europe of the second industrial revolution through what I call the 'psychological mother' of the Second World War and its aftermath, practice, legislation and ideology in technologically 'advanced' countries have brought the mother to a particular kind of prominence. Where once the child belonged to the father, in the twentieth-century Western world care and custody went to the mother, only recently moving in principle though not in practice to either parent. This readjustment came about only when the meaning of paternity had ceased to be coterminous with authority and mothers and fathers had become more alike. In social terms the mother becomes more important for child-rearing rather than just for childbirth. There is a marked decline in reproduction (Szreter 1996). The mother also, in an uneven way, becomes increasingly isolated in this role – the more or less only representative of the category of 'lone parent', despite the rise of serial monogamy.

When it comes to psychoanalytical theories of the mother, how is this mother being presented? For both psychoanalyst and patient, the initial interest in the mother would be likely to be both ideological and conscious, or at most preconscious – as it clearly was for Karen Horney, Helene Deutsch, Melanie Klein, Ernest Jones and others who marked out this path in the 1920s. But the importance of the mother, as the Berlin analyst Karl Abraham (see chapter 4) noted as early as 1913, must also have been there before her recognition in the manifestations of unconscious processes. How do the unconscious fantasies of the patient (and of the analyst) relate on the one hand to the social practices and on the other to the theory for which they must provide the material?

What enters the theory from the 1920s onwards is the pre-Oedipal mother or, in the formulations of Melanie Klein, an exceedingly early Oedipal mother: in all cases an extremely primitive imago whose power is fantasized by the baby as retributive or talionic – an eye for an eye – but not as organizational. There is no later mother portrayed in the observations or the theory – no mother as lawgiver. What has transpired must again be referred both to general ideology – to, for instance, the so-called dread of the all-powerful mother – and to the modalities of the clinical setting. There is, I suggest, no lawgiving mother in psychoanalytic theory because within the clinical setting the analyst herself or himself speaks from the position of the mother as lawgiver. There is thus an enactment of the law of the mother. In social life the mother was becoming more of a lawgiver. The woman analyst was probably in this position in her own life (or in the social ideology) and her practice offered the same possibility. In psychoanalytic practice, when a patient acts something outside the session instead of reflecting on it within the session, it is described as 'acting out'. As is the case with the extreme instance of hysterical enactment, an act takes the place of thought. When the patient engages the therapist in an enactment within the session, it is 'acting in'. In both cases, the act itself substitutes for thought. I suggest that when the therapist *acts* the mother, there is an 'acting in' which has the effect of preventing thought; hence it inhibits the development of a theory. In the theory there are all the mothers that are not enacted – there is no mother as lawgiver because she is the therapist.

I am suggesting that, comparably to the patriarchal masterful posture of the male ego-psychologist therapist (particularly American) which both Lacan and second-wave feminists so deplored, the Object Relations 'mother' analyst is enacting the mother-as-lawgiver and thus is not able to think about the role. If the clinical treatment enacts a maternal law then what will be perceived in the material of the patient's transference will not be this mother but instead the other mother, the necessarily mad (Winnicott), fused and loving

(Balint) or retributive (Klein) pre-Oedipal mother. In psychoanalytic as in early anthropological theory, matriarchy is always conceived as being there before patriarchy; mother-attachment is first. However, what should be emphasized is that this concept of the primitive pre-Oedipal mother derives her definition not from the law-giving Oedipal *mother* (a matriarchy) but from an Oedipal *father* (a patriarchy). Because of this, in the practice and in the theory, no distinction is made between a primitive, imaginatively retributive or loving mother and a lawgiving mother. The distinction is always between the primitive mother and the lawgiving *father*.

In all cases where there has been a shift away from the emphasis on the paternal law in favour of a focus on the mother, this has, despite its intention, been within the terms of this paternal law. This is true even when (or perhaps particularly when) fathers appear not to get a look in. The patriarchy defines the matriarchy as always the more primitive and earlier – never as a different law on the same level. The Lacanian notion of a Symbolic Order which institutes language similarly positions a prior 'Imaginary Order' which belongs to the mother. A philosopher psychotherapist like Luce Irigaray may explore exclusively daughter to mother or female to female relations; Julia Kristeva may indicate the variety, power and richness of the relation to the mother, asserting that before the linguistic there is the semiotic; but the feminine and the maternal come first, and first means earlier, and earlier in this discourse means more primitive. In the introduction to her book *First Things*, Mary Jacobus, a psychoanalytically oriented literary critic, draws the map of this primitive maternal space:

> My subject (insofar as anything so various, multiform and pervasive as the maternal imaginary can be said to be, or have, a 'subject') is the fantasmatic mother who may or may not possess reproductive parts, nurturing functions, and specific historical or material manifestations; but who exists chiefly in the realm of images and imagoes (whether perceived or imagined), mirroring and identifications and figures; who is associated sometimes with feminist nostalgia, sometimes with ideological mystification; who surfaces in connection with melancholia, and matricide, and plays a key part in Kristevan theories of signification; who figures primarily in the writings of Melanie Klein, where terms such as splitting, identification, and projection analyse a repertoire of activities involving fantasised attacks on, and reparations to, the maternal body; who gives the breast its cultural power . . .

—— 51 ——

The 'First Things' . . . are the earlier, unformed yet vitally informing phantasies that shape the infant's emergence as a subject; the first 'thing' is Julia Kristeva's maternal thing, the not-yet object of an emerging, chaotic not-yet subject. (Jacobus 1995: iii–iv)

There is, I would argue, another 'mother' than this fantastical imago; a mother who has been left out of the picture, a mother who is a subject and whose law contributes to the establishment of the subjecthood of her children. It is a law that differentiates generationally as to who it is that can have babies and who it is that cannot. It is also a law that introduces seriality laterally among her children: who can stay up latest, have which piece of the cake and survive the murderous rivalries to win through to sibling and peer love, a law allowing space for one who is the same and different. This mother has been occluded by patriarchal ideology which relegates maternity to the 'first mother' that Jacobus describes above. Within psychoanalytic theory and practice, the analyst-mother's *enactment* of the mother as lawgiver who instructs her baby-patient that it is the analyst alone who can have all the babies/patients, and that the patient must take his turn in the right place with other patients, thus means that the law of the mother cannot be *thought* about.

The law of the mother operates both vertically between herself and her children and laterally to differentiate her children one from each other. Vertically her law decrees that children cannot procreate children. It is exactly this law that is flouted in hysteria. As discussed earlier, the phantom pregnancy, the hysterical birth, the men's couvades, all bear witness to the fact that one imagines one can give birth parthenogenetically, or with someone who is the same as oneself – when the mummies and daddies of children's play are reversible and hence identical and the notions are of anal births in which there is no distinction between girls and boys. In the hysterical fantasy, nothing has been given up, no possibility has been lost and therefore there is nothing to be mourned. Because the prospect of self-generated birth has not been lost and mourned, birth itself and the baby that results cannot be symbolized. If the hysterical male or female does have actual progeny, he or she does not know they are not himself or herself and hence a fertile field for abuse is laid out.

By differentiating between her children, the mother and her law allow for the concept of seriality to be internalized – John has to know he has lost the possibility of being Jane. One is a child in the same position as one's siblings in regard to one's parent or parents, as one's peers in relation to one's teacher or boss, but one is also different: there is room for two, three, four or more. Of this the hysteric in all of us is unaware. Hate for the sibling enables the first move to be made: I hate you, you are not me, is the precondition of seriality. The mother restricts this hate – enjoins its non-enactment. Children's games – musical chairs, oranges and lemons, pig in the middle and all the spontaneous play – are about seriality. The mother has enforced, but the lateral relationship itself instigates its own processes of managing sameness through constructing difference.

The law of the mother thus also operates between siblings or between siblings and peers. Without it would there be murder or incest? As noted, sibling abuse in the West occurs in the context of inadequate parental supervision or concern. This observation of parental neglect in cases of sibling abuse should be specified as the absence of the operation of the mother's law. This is not to make mothers themselves responsible for it, but rather to point to the relegation of this law in the general structure. It is likely that factors such as paternal and marital violence, female social isolation and poverty and/or an intensification of the general denigration of women prevent a mother from occupying the position of lawgiver. However, a question arises. Is this external operation of rules and regulations necessary because our cultural conditions do not allow for their internalization? Where older siblings rather than parents are the main carers of younger children, where children are left alone in their peer groups, are prohibitions accepted and internalized? Can siblings in themselves be each other's lawgiver? What do mothers of twins tell us when they so frequently comment 'he [or she] means more to the other twin than I, the mother, mean'?

The horror of sibling incestuous offspring indicates how, without the intervention of the law of the mother, without some rule generated within the sibling relationship, mothers and sisters become confused. Or maybe in other ethnic and historical contexts they are in any case more confused. In many cultures the age differences of an older half-sister or half-brother and a young parent may be insignificant or nil. Once again analysis has missed the sibling dimension of the confusion. Kleinians in particular write of confusional states – but the objects who are confused are always the parents or the parents and the infant ego; the baby fantasizes a 'combined parent'. The confusion of mother and sister is prevalent in mythology. However, those who comment on the confusion repeat it rather than analyse it. Thus Geiza Roheim, a psychoanalyst-anthropologist, discussing the riddle of the Sphinx in 1934, writes:

> The classical authors do not . . . identify Jocasta [Oedipus' mother and wife] with the Sphinx, but they record a close relationship. The Sphinx appears as the *sister* of Oedipus. Hesiod calls her the daughter of her brother and their common mother Echidna. (Roheim 1934: 17, my italics)

Having observed this sibling relationship, Roheim nevertheless continues: 'This ambiguous creature, enticing and dangerous, who loves but to devour, is therefore the *mother* of the hero' (1934: 17, my italics). Would it have implied she was Antigone, always thought of as Oedipus' daughter?

But by this time this reader at least is as confused as the situation. There are many legends of the Sphinx. The encounter with Oedipus is a conflict; the Sphinx sets a riddle which Oedipus answers. Before receiving this answer, the Sphinx devoured all who failed to guess her riddle. After Oedipus' success in finding the answer, she hurls herself from the rock. It is suggested that underlying the story of the riddle is an earlier version of a physical contest between Oedipus and the Sphinx. The psychoanalyst in Roheim imagines the Sphinx as a mother because she *devours* the contestants: because the baby eats the mother's breast, it is hypothesized that it imagines that the mother in retribution will eat the infant – there are many myths to support this notion of a universal infantile fantasy along the devouring–being devoured axis. But to Hesiod the Sphinx is Oedipus' sister (daughter of her brother and their common mother) and would therefore stand as a more primitive version of Antigone – Antigone not as a daughter but a sister and whom, being a sister, Oedipus must vanquish.

The point about any incest – whether intergenerational or intragenerational, parental or sibling – is that it causes confusion. The sister becomes confused with the mother; it is only the law of the mother or a law of siblings which insists on differentiation. With the vertical differentiation would go a lateral one: sisters and brothers, girls and boys are not generically different as siblings when one classifies them; however, *one* of the points of differentiation between them arises because sisters can become mothers.

Children are not only participants in the world – they are also observers, trying to acquire categories and demarcation. Recently, my four-year-old step-grandson announced to my adult daughter that he was 'a human', but when pressed as to what she was, he replied firmly that 'no, she is not a human', she was 'a grown-up girl'. What we can see here is not the advent of sexism, but the child's need to understand not only generation (the Oedipal question) but types within lateral categories, at least as they are established within the child–parent ideologically dominant axis of the Western world.

Clinicians and theoreticians have followed the young child before it categorically distinguishes lateral from vertical relations. The lateral has then been subsumed within an ideology of an apparently primitive matriarchy, itself a concept of a patriarchal ideology which prefers to pay tribute to the fantasy of all-powerful mothers than to the fact of mothers who are also lawgivers. The importance of daughters and sons and their relationships to each other as siblings is even more extensively occluded.

Anthropologists have long questioned the universality of the Oedipus complex in its monolithic form. For example, Malinowski (1929) argued that in the Trobriand Islands the father and his law is sometimes split, or that the father is replaced by the mother's brother. Having a different practice from psychoanalysts, as participant observers, anthropologists have long recognized the importance of the independent structure of lateral affines; however, they too tend to readjust all to a vertical paradigm. Why shouldn't the mother's brother be just that: an important brother, not another version of an Oedipal father? As descent is in question, the sister is specified as a mother – but this mother is also a sister to her brother and it is this relationship which is overlooked. Indeed Malinowski's observations led him to put great emphasis on sister–brother taboos and their repressed sexual fantasies. His emphasis occasioned a famous debate with British psychoanalyst Ernest Jones, who would let nothing detract from the exclusive role of the Oedipus complex. In matrilineages inheritance takes place through the man's sister. Can we speculate that in Western societies sibling or quasi-sibling relations come to prominence in an increasingly matrifocal situation? Are we noticing them now not just because they have been overlooked,

Oedipus and the Sphinx by Gustave Moreau (1864), Metropolitan Museum of Art, New York

but because social conditions are forcing their presence on our attention?

To overlook siblings may be a highly historically specific and ethnocentric omission. As we saw, currently many developing countries are looking to provide day-care and crèches, not to free mothers to work (as in the West) but so that *girls* can go to school.[12] For the girl and the baby, there may be a considerable fusion (not confusion) of this mother-sister role.

Roheim (1934) typically subjugates all the sororal elements of his ethnographic evidence to the Oedipus complex; we could question this not only by using his own observations, but through a more extensive understanding of the Sphinx. Why is the Sphinx mostly considered to be a monstrous mother? In fact, the Sphinx in Egypt is sometimes male (maybe a representation of a king), sometimes female. There is a subsequent Greek tradition of hermaphroditism. She/he is seducer and destroyer – she seduces in order to kill. Maybe, as Roheim contends, she is sometimes equated with the mother, Jocasta – but maybe too she is the fearful imago of a sister who mothers and is quite negative about her task – loving the baby she nurtures but loathing the sibling who has displaced her. Oedipus' primitive fears would be of an all-powerful older sister Sphinx who wanted to kill him but whom he outwits. Oedipus then has three sisters – the older mother-sibling Sphinx who would seduce and kill, and the younger daughter-sisters, the kindly Ismene and the righteous Antigone. The three faces of the sister who both cares for and destroys: the lateral would-be murderer, the nurse and the lawgiver.

3

Sister–Brother/Brother–Sister Incest

Psycho-analysis has taught us that a boy's earliest choice of objects for his love is incestuous and that those objects are forbidden ones – his mother and his sister.

Sigmund Freud, 'The horror of incest' in *Totem and Taboo*

In general, as regards the existence of sexual relations between children, especially brothers and sisters, I may say on the basis of my observations that they are the rule in early childhood but only prolonged into the latency period and puberty if the child's sense of guilt is excessive ... In any case I think that such relations are much more frequent even during latency and puberty than is usually supposed.

Melanie Klein, 'The sexual activities of children'

Oedipus had to struggle with, and overcome, the sister-mother Sphinx – and 'rest his age' on his sister-daughter Antigone's 'kind nursery'.[1] But what of sibling incest from the girl's point of view,[2] probably the most prevalent form of childhood abuse, at least in England? In a recent rare instance of an arrest of a woman for using child pornography on the internet, the woman in question explained that she had identified with the images of the abused young girls that she had downloaded and remodelled as a means of exploring the significance of her older brother's intercourse with her in childhood. Virginia Woolf, who found her older half-brother's childhood molestation of her traumatic, is a famous reference point. A. S. Byatt's story *Angels and Insects* (1992) (and the film version) is a highly disturbing 'idyll' in which the husband is used as a social smoke-screen to protect the secret passion of his wife and her brother. However, once again, what we find in the psychoanalytic literature is that it is not taken very seriously.[3]

In 1963, the British psychoanalyst Enid Balint published a paper called 'On being empty of oneself'. It was reprinted in 1993 in a book I co-edited, *Before I was I: Psychoanalysis and the Imagination*. 'Before I was I' comes from the poet John Donne: 'And God was displeased with me before I was I'.[4] The paper is a clinical case history of a young woman, 'Sarah'. Balint's thesis can be summed up in what I will call the need for primary recognition: for, necessarily and essentially, the *mother* to see her infant for what it is and to offer feedback for what the infant initiates of its emerging self – before the baby has its identity in place the mother needs to be pleased with who it is she can see her baby is becoming. Without this maternal recognition there will be a sense of emptiness within the infant and a sense of a void without. At the age of six or seven Sarah was seduced by her brother. How does the sibling incest feature in Sarah's symptomatology and in the analytical account of her illness and treatment?

Sarah is seriously mentally ill and has to be psychiatrically hospitalized for a time. She is the third child with two older brothers. It is the brother nearest to her in age who was her seducer; he was presumably the one whom her birth displaced as the 'baby'. When I reread the paper attentively – and discussed it with its author, Enid Balint, in the early 1990s for its inclusion in the collection *Before I was I* – I was struck that the father was not credited with any role in the aetiology of Sarah's illness, in which, lost and empty, she appeared in Balint's words, as 'a stranger in the world'. At the time of Sarah's birth, the father, a violent man, who already had two sons, had wanted Sarah, the only daughter, to be a third boy.

The case came to mind again a few years later when I was puzzling about the fate of hysteria in the diagnostic literature of the twentieth-century Western world.[5] This time it was not her father but Sarah's brothers who jumped out at me. In taking a third look at this case history, my purpose is to make some tentative suggestions about how inserting siblings in the particular case of incest and its prohibition might shift or add a lateral dimension to the monopolistic vertical paradigm of psychoanalytic theory and all that has depended on it or emanated from it. But more than that it is to raise the question of the near exclusive parent–child axis in our social and psychological disciplines in general. This is a question I am examining from an empirical viewpoint in a particular type of clinical work (psychoanalysis), and from a viewpoint that is critical of its ethnocentricity and mindful of its historical specificity. We now know that the child is a historical construct (Ariès 1962) – logically, if this is so, so too must be the parent (Bainham et al. 1999). Sarah's case history and Balint's dismissal of the importance of sibling incest contributed to what I felt was the missed significance of lateral or horizontal relationships, as I subsequently described in *Mad Men and Medusas* (Mitchell 2000a). However, my use of Sarah previously had been to claim her for a diagnosis of hysteria. Now it is the importance of the sibling incest and its relegation to insignificance in the case history and diagnosis that concern me. If the absence of the father's violence and gender-denial of his daughter was striking, the brother's role now seems to me even more so. Indeed, thinking sociologically, isn't it quite likely that with an erratic violent father, a younger son will enact his fear of violence by using violence in his turn towards a smaller sibling – how much of the incest was sex, how much violence? Can we easily separate the two?

The family image was that Sarah had been a problem-free baby, a successful child and glamorous adolescent. She only broke down in her early twenties when she moved to England without her family. However the analytic treatment reveals a different picture of her earlier life:

> During analysis, it became clear that Sarah had in fact always been in difficulties. She described how at a very early age she lay awake terrified in bed, frightened to call out, listening with panic to her heartbeats in case they stopped. From transference reconstruction it also appeared that from still earlier times she would lie rigidly in anticipation of some object descending upon her from above and crashing on to her head. This object was sometimes described as a rolling-pin, sometimes a rock, and sometimes a cloud. (E. Balint [1963]: 42)

It is at this point, which was reconstructed in the analysis, that Balint mentions the possibility that, 'when she was about six or seven years old, the younger of Sarah's two brothers had intercourse with her, and continued to do so until she was about twelve.'

Effectively, that is the extent to which the sibling incest is seen to play a part in Sarah's difficulties. Balint does not refer to it again. This incest took place during the period of Sarah's latency; she was apparently a troubled child prior to it and it stopped before there was much likelihood of pregnancy. But by re-examining some of the material of the case history, we can ask: did it have any bearing on her symptoms and, if so, would that suggest that sibling incest, or rather its prohibition, is important in the construction of unconscious processes and the formation of mental life? According to Freudian theory, neurotic symptoms originate in Oedipal conflicts between the ages of two-and-a-half and five; according to Object Relations theory, psychotic, neurotic and borderline conditions can all arise from different phases within the earlier intra- or interpsychic difficulties of pre-Oedipal infancy. By committing incest when Sarah was six or seven, Sarah and her brother broke a taboo at ages after the resolution (or non-resolution) of the Oedipus complex and long after infancy. However, the actual incest would only be the end result of their earlier relationship, which would have been coincident, for Sarah, with pre-Oedipal and Oedipal periods. We cannot know about how it interacted with these as Balint only informs us that there was 'plenty of Oedipal material'. Balint's understanding however, rests on the pre-Oedipal maternal relationship as it is reconstructed from the transference situation of the treatment – with Balint standing for the mother. We do not know the age gap of Sarah and her brother, but they were close enough to play together. This earliest period will be my ultimate reference point: can a later relationship between siblings have a bearing on the period 'before I was I'? If not, can something that occurs only in latency have an impact on unconscious psychic structures?

Klein, and many other therapists, consider sexual relationships between children to be virtually the norm. Klein's accounts are brief, but rich; she considers sexual 'play' to start very young. However, its significance depends on the degree of guilt and anxiety felt by the child; we should note that in Klein's account this guilt and anxiety is felt towards the parent, not towards the other child. Because there is no structural place for lateral sibling relations within psychoanalytic theory, even such excellent observational phenomenology as Klein's does not link to a clear argument. For this reason, at this stage we will, as Freud said in the context of our ignorance of the psychology of femininity, have to 'turn to the poets' (Freud [1933]: 135). As literature is not my brief, I will use just three instances to indicate the range of effects of sibling incest, from the deeply malign through the disturbed ecstatic to the benign, in order to show the links between these diverse possibilities.

In *War and Peace*, Tolstoy describes the 'hero' Pierre's awareness of the depravity of his wife, Hélène. All St Petersburg's high society sees Hélène as its most intellectually brilliant and beautiful hostess. Pierre is puzzled by the success of his wife's charade, which ends (psychically appropriately) in her suicide. A reference to a childhood sexual relationship with her brother Anatole makes this an insignia of the depravity beneath Hélène's veneer. Anatole is the rake who subsequently seduces the story's heroine, Natasha, in one of the most extraordinary portraits of a seduction in literature. What is important for my purposes here is that to seduce he continually fixes the young girl with his eyes and Natasha looks back to find there is no decorum because *there are no boundaries between them*.

Anatole has concealed his enforced marriage to yet another of his victims; Natasha is already betrothed to Prince Andrei. A liar, a cheat, a Don Juan, Anatole, the seducer, is a boundary breaker. Incest is the crossing of boundaries, or perhaps, if we think about its sibling base, the absence of them. It indicates depravity not simply because it is forbidden but because the other is not 'other'; there is no recognition of the needs, the feelings, the place of the other person; no responsibility, only the osmotic engulfment of seduction. Natasha, whose seduction is not consummated due to the intervention of her cousin Sonja, will eventually marry Pierre, the widower of Hélène. Through her relationship to her seducer, Anatole, and her husband, Pierre, she thus becomes a foil to Hélène. Hélène sleeps with her brother, Anatole, and marries and divorces Pierre in order to try to marry a lover – she can't decide which of two: both Hélène and Natasha have (or nearly have) a strong illicit relationship (incest, proposed bigamy, infidelity) with one man (Anatole) and marry the other (Pierre). A narrow dividing-line separates the Good (Natasha) from the Bad (Hélène) but it is a crucial one and somewhere, residually, it implicates sibling incest – the crossing of that line (see Mitchell 2003).

In Emily Brontë's *Wuthering Heights* (1847), Catherine Earnshaw and Heathcliff are adoptive siblings. Because they are not blood relatives, Brontë is able to portray the almost mystic ecstasies of sibling union in which two become one. Catherine's father has promised to bring gifts to his two children, Hindley and Catherine, on his return from a trip to Liverpool. Instead he picks up an abandoned gypsy

Branwell Brontë's (the model for Heathcliff) portrait of his three sisters, Ann, Emily and Charlotte
The Brontë Sisters by Patrick Branwell Brontë (*c*.1834), by courtesy of the National Portrait Gallery, London

boy who is given the name of a dead child – the children's deceased brother, Heathcliff. Catherine and the fostered Heathcliff become inseparable. The degree of their passion and yearning suggests that Heathcliff, the 'replacement' child (Sabbadini 1988), is a revenant; a longing for the dead is at the heart of their relationship. After their parents' early deaths, Hindley, the eldest sibling, through jealousy, degrades Heathcliff – turning him into a servant. Ostensibly, it is for this reason that Catherine cannot marry him, but they continue to yearn for each other. After a socially acceptable marriage to a landowner neighbour, Catherine dies in childbirth. The union she has craved with Heathcliff has to wait till Heathcliff's death – then, their ghosts are seen to walk the moors together. Catherine's famous description of their relationship could be taken as an account of the ecstasy of sibling unity: 'He's more myself than I am. Whatever our souls are made of, Heathcliff's and mine are the same' (Brontë [1847]: 92).

When the narcissistic child conceives the new baby it imagines it will be more itself than the child itself is; the expected baby will be a kind of supplement to the child's yearned-for grandiosity. We can see this in twins, where, though there can be an intensified struggle for survival between the two, the other can also be used additively: 'I am a we', 'there's two of us and only one of you.' On a twin's death, there is a definite diminution of the survivor's narcissism (Engel 1975). But Brontë's perception of Catherine and Heathcliff's 'twinning' love ('He's more myself than I am') brings forward the various parts played by death in sibling incest: it is as though the bliss of two-in-one can only be realized when both are dead, but a dead brother also precipit- ated the love. The incest is also a pact whereby both can survive if they become one; it is, as it were, a replacement for the struggle to survive in which one must die. Stepping outside the bounds of the novel, one could say that by loving the adopted Heathcliff to the point of her becoming him, Catherine 'undoes' the guilt she uncon- sciously felt as the child that survived and/or replaced her dead brother; and Heathcliff, by his passion for her, similarly mitigates his 'ident- ical' guilt for being the survivor and replacement son who took the dead child's place in the parents' affections. Catherine and Heathcliff psychically *are* the same – both are survivors and, if Catherine was born after the death of her natural brother, both are replacement children; it is this that makes each more of the self than the other –

each is what the other is in their unconscious guilt. We can see through this novel that the guilt which Klein notes as clinically prevalent in the incest of siblings may not be, as she maintained, for imagined violence to a parent, but for thinking that in surviving one must have killed the other child. Does death then feature in all sibling incest? I believe so.

In Arundhati Roy's novel *The God of Small Things* the twins form a unit of friendship self-sufficient unto themselves but within a shared and mutually loving relationship to their strong, lone mother. A third child, their cousin, enters their world. She is drowned. Was there no room for her in the twins' self-sufficiency? The cousin certainly felt so. The girl twin feels unspecified guilt for the accident, unspecified because she had been jealous of her girl cousin. The drowning starts the tragedy which hits the extended Keralan family and the mother has to send her son to live with his father in Calcutta. Saying 'good-bye' at the station, his twin sister suddenly doubles over in agony and lets out a long, desperate scream. In Calcutta, almost mute, psychically empty of himself (or of his sister), the boy survives by carefully shopping and cooking for his father's new family. Roy is too good a novelist to point out her implications, but it is clear that the boy survives by becoming like his twin sister (who is thus more himself than he is) and doing what a girl would have had to do. He doesn't lose his twin, he becomes her. Their mother, first broken and prematurely senile, dies and the twins, their family devastated, rediscover each other forlornly as young adults. Recognition of each other comes slowly and they lie side by side like 'two spoons' just as they had done when children. Except this time there is incest. For me at least, the relief that – in all the devastation and cruelty of their world – they had found each other balanced the shock. Can sibling incest be a refuge in a too traumatic world? Repeated trauma leaves too little of the self – can the sibling replenish it?

Within the model for the boundarylessness of incest must somewhere be the two-as-one of mother and foetus. Trauma urges a return to this pre-egoic comfort of the other as self. But the means of such a regression is not a defiance of the ultimate taboo on incest with the mother (who in Roy's novel anyway is emotionally destroyed) but of incest with a sibling. The small child's expectation of a new baby is of something that will be the same as itself, a replication; an addition to the self – there will be more of me.

To return to Sarah. Balint comments on Sarah's incest with her brother: 'Her mother's failure to recognise the trouble her daughter was in at that time, as well as at an earlier age, was worse for my patient than the experiences themselves' (E. Balint [1963]: 42). As previously mentioned, Western psychiatrists and psychotherapists confirm that sibling incest occurs most frequently in the context of an absence of vertical – usually, that is, parental – care. Although the context will change the implications considerably, the child feels this neglect very acutely. The incest itself can be violent, bullying and brutal from an older child to a younger one, or it can be comforting where there is relative equality; however, the absence of adult protection is present in all cases.[6] This would confirm Balint's observation that Sarah's difficulty was her mother's unconcern, which in its turn would repeat the earlier lack of recognition as to who the infant Sarah potentially was as a person in her self's being. Balint considers then that the sibling incest confirms her contention that Sarah's main problem was this deficiency of primary maternal recognition of who she was. Yet Sarah has fantasies which genitalize this absence of maternal care. Sarah equates her whole self with her womb and it is this womb that she claims has been taken from her. In a repeated dream a dog comes out of the sea on to a beach where she is standing, bites her and steals her womb. She recalls a real incident subtending the dream. Late in her treatment she brings her analyst a pebble from the actual beach she has recognized as the one in her dream. She claims that the pebble represents her womb/self which she now says she has got back largely through the feedback situation with her analyst-as-a-mother who can recognize her.

I believe that the question of the theoretical place of sibling incest hangs on this question of genitalization. In particular it should be noted that though Sarah apparently evinces strong penis-envy, and her active adult homosexuality and heterosexuality are florid, the proto-self or self she could be is not conceived by her as a penis (which is customary for the bisexual phallic Freudian child of either sex), but as a womb. Although the girl-as-phallus has been explored by such writers as Otto Fenichel (1945), it is perhaps easiest to grasp as an idea through Lacan's notion of the mirror stage or 'the imaginary'. In this, the uncoordinated infant of either sex finds its ego (or 'I') as a coherent, unified imago of itself in a mirror reflection to which its mother points, saying 'that's Johnny'. This illusory 'I' comes and goes in the mirror; it either vanishes or is upright and omnipotent – in other words, phallic. But Sarah self-represents as a lost-and-found uterus.

Balint refuses to give a categorization or diagnosis of Sarah's illness – but says it is nearest to being 'borderline'. If so, the Oedipal aspects would be that she was wanting to stay as what her mother wants which is both pre-Oedipally what the mother has not got (the phallus) and Oedipally what the father (but not the growing child) can offer her (the phallus, again). A girl who refuses the implications of psychic femininity, which is to become a love-object for her father, can instead make her whole body-ego take the image of the phallus for her mother (the classic posture of the female hysteric). Those psychoanalysts who subscribe to the notion that girls, like boys, have a psychology that coincides with their biology (phallic for boys and inner space for girls), and with other people's recognition of them as gendered, must logically believe the female ego is represented by a womb.[7] Maybe it is taken for granted, as Balint does in this case history. I believe it needs to be queried. Although womb-envy and the primary femininity of the infant feature in psychoanalytic discourse, there has been as yet no place granted to the womb as a structural representation of the self. I suggest that the failure to give a structural place to the prohibition on sibling incest plays a part in this absence of theories of uterine self-representation: oneself as having a space, a cavity within, that can be filled – or be empty – a hungry womb, the tummy/womb, the anal womb, the space within from which a narcissistic parthenogenetic birth would erupt.

Before we too easily assign a biological base to this psychic uterine self-representation, I would like to stress that I am not sure that this psychic self-representation is sexually differentiated. In fact, more emphatically, I believe there is a stage for both boys and girls when the tummy/womb as an expression of interiority can be used as a representation of an 'inner self' whatever the gender of its owner. Donald Winnicott called this a state of 'being' and saw it as female; he compared it to 'doing' which was 'male'. 'Being' for both genders comes before 'doing'. However, I am talking not of a state but of a body-ego, an 'I', or more accurately a 'me' representation. I would argue that such a representation is necessary for the capacity for memory and for 'holding in mind', which in its turn is essential for an awareness that others are 'other'. In fact, such a representation of interiority is a necessity for there to be a capacity for representation itself. When, however, and in what psycho-social situation does this occur? In what way might we link it to sibling relationships and their taboos?

The history of the fundamental elements of psychoanalytical theory is familiar. First in the 1890s there was a belief in the pathogenic role of actual father–child incest. This was the story that Freud had heard from hysterical patients and that he had confirmed in his own case and in that of members of his family. Ultimately, it was seen that if the presence of neurosis was a universal possibility, it could not be explained by the widespread but non-universal occurrence of paternal incest. (The Recovered Memory Movement reinstates this anti-humanitarian postulate which targets a class of victims as, due to their unfortunate circumstances, having a different psychology – not, as is the case, a different history.) But, equally, if incest applied only to a specific abused population then the neurosis that was linked to it would only apply to this group. Freud's first idea of abuse of an asexual 'innocent' child erupting as hysteria in the sexual adolescent or adult was thus superseded by the notion of infantile sexuality in which the small child desires and fantasizes such incest – the Oedipus complex. Hysteria demonstrated the later breakthrough of inadequately repressed Oedipal desires.

In its turn, the hypothesis of infantile sexuality had a number of consequences. It was a hypothesis of a universal situation. This meant that how it was resolved, and not the advent itself, accounted for neurosis or apparent psychic normality. It also meant that anyone was vulnerable to neurosis by virtue of being human. In that the desires for incest had become unconscious, it was this unconscious that needed to be investigated and its trajectory noted in the symptoms which expressed it.

By moving from the specifics of the hysteric's tale to the universality of the Oedipus complex, the central tenets had shifted place: the father's abuse had become the father's prohibition on the child's universal desire for the mother. The particular experience of actual abuse became a variant experience within a universal rule. What however sets the Oedipus complex in motion in the first place? Answers are usually developmental – the sucking infant becomes the anal toddler, becomes the phallic child. The Oedipus complex comes into being with the phallic stage – when both the girl's and the boy's sexual desires are focused on the clitoris or penis. However, I believe a historical version of the subject, as opposed to the developmental one, could open up another answer to the question. What has happened to the child, in terms of its general history as opposed to biology, for its desires to become focused as incestuous (that is, phallic) ones?

Freud stressed that when the child sees the mother pregnant with another child (or, because of the generalities of culture and its own anxieties and hopes, expects to see the mother pregnant with another child, as for example is its friend's mother) then the exigencies of the situation prompt the urgency of thought. For the child this is a historical not a bodily moment. The feelings stirred up by the historical situation force the mind to work. The philosophical mind is born from a desperate response to the threat of displacement and through this displacement to the possibility of the emergent ego's non-existence – being could become nothingness. The problem that forces the two-year-old to think is specified by Freud as being formulated in the child's question, 'where do babies [that is, where does this interloping baby] come from?' – a question about procreation. But one should add, 'where do I, the baby, go to now?' – a question which the infant or child begins to formulate about death. The desperate plight that underlies this situation necessitates thinking and advances the way the mind separates out from the body, of which it is a part, in order to think the questions: 'where am I now someone else is me?' and 'where was I when someone who is the same as me [a child of my mother] was there and I was not?'

In contradistinction to Freud, analysts such as Wilfred Bion posit the emergence of thought from the nexus of mother and infant: the mother translates the raw material of the baby's feelings into what can be thought about – for instance the baby's sensation of pain is felt and understood by the mother as pain, so the feeling eventually becomes the *idea* of pain. This capacity of the mother is referred to as 'containing'. In *The Cradle of Thought* (2002), Peter Hobson charts the interaction of mother and baby who together produce the mind's cradle. The mother as container or weaver of cradles suggests an association of the maternal mind as womb. Once again, this is different from the notion that concerns me, which is that Sarah's representation of her 'I' or 'me' was as a genital womb. I believe we can understand the genital womb (which is also the womb of hysterical phantom pregnancies) if we read the child's social history on to its developmental pathway.

The developmental perspective continues to play along with the introduction of a historical intervention in which something happens in time. I want to highlight this intervention as a crisis that breaks into development. The threat introduced by a sibling, which means that one is not unique or even irreplaceable, is that the historical trauma halts development. In the classical theory, however, instead of this leading to questions about lateral relationships, a shift of emphasis took place: the discovery of other children who were 'the same' as the subject was deflected into an emphasis on the discovery by the child that the father was the mother's lover. In Freud and his followers' work, this is the only crisis: instead of the Oedipus complex being outgrown developmentally, the father's rights to the mother set up the castration complex as a symbolic 'historical' happening which demolishes the Oedipus complex. In this theory, a castration threat, not a baby's birth, is the traumatic event which intervenes in the child's bio-social development. This threat of castration provides the conditions for symbolizing sexual difference along the lines of who has/has not, or will be in the position of seeming to have/won't be in the position of seeming to have, the phallus. It is as though the original notion of paternal seduction is partially retained in the father's new threat. A historical event – real or fantasized – is always located in the father. Is this a contamination from the unacknowledged ideology of patriarchy? Why not see the sibling as conveyor of the significant moment?

This notion of the castration complex entails the shifting of the potential implications of that first question, 'where does this baby come from?' From a crisis of the subject's uniqueness and existence along a lateral/horizontal level, it becomes a crisis of sexual difference modelled on the prohibition of the father and realized as a trauma because of the absent phallus of the mother; the missing phallus of the mother indicates to the child that it is possible for people to be 'castrated'. The editor of the Standard Edition of Freud's works footnotes a passage in the essay 'On the sexual enlightenment of children' thus: 'In Freud's earlier writings he asserts as a rule that the problem of the origin of babies is the first one to engage a child's interest. . . . In the sentence in the text above, however, he appears to put it second to the problem of the distinction between the sexes; and this is the view to which he reverts' (Freud [1907]: 135). The absence of a penis in women triggers the question: 'what is the difference between the sexes?' (the Oedipal–castration question). The presence of a sibling forces the question: 'where does this baby that is not me come from?' The child's questions then are evenly balanced. However, the Freudian-Lacanian argument has asserted that the difference between the sexes is the dominant question in the theory.

Freud's increasing assertion of the importance of the castration complex as the event which marks sexual difference, and with it the advent of full sociality in the human child, was made in the context of other analysts' assertions of the importance of the pre-Oedipal mother and of biological gender leading in and of itself to psychical sexual difference. Between the two positions, the sibling was forgotten. Where wondering about siblings is a horizontal query, wondering about sexual difference takes in a vertical perspective; it is a matter of making an identification with the appropriate parent *after* the castration complex. However, at the outset, Freud (like the children) is not sure which question has priority. I shall suggest later (chapter 5) that the question 'where do babies come from?' may devolve on to a question of gender rather than sexual difference; the question through which the boy, by being stronger and more valued, hopes to regain his omnipotence so threatened by the sibling that has arrived from 'nowhere' and through which the girl dreads feeling confirmed in her weakness and lack of social value through the same experience. The Egyptian writer and doctor Nawal El Saadawi speaks for many when she recounts how her father helped her to achieve success but her brother always did his best to oppress her (Saadawi 2002). Male dominance is not exclusively, nor even mainly, patriarchal, if we take, as I do, patriarchal to refer to fathers.

We may take the uncertainty as to the child's two great questions as an icon of the greater uncertainty about siblings in psychoanalytic theory – an uncertainty that is resolved by their elimination from a structuring role even while they manifest themselves everywhere in the material. In Freud's theory, the inadequate answer the child finds, despite storks and God, is that the new baby (or the old one that is already there) comes from the mother's tummy (not womb) on a model of orality or anality and digestion. Just as the girl may baulk at the pragmatic answer about the father's phallus, so may the boy resist the empiricism of the mother's role and insist on retaining an inner space as an imagined lodging-place for babies.[8] In other words, both infant girl and boy will want an inner space from which babies can emerge. I suggest that although there may be underlying models of mouths and digestive tracts and anal passages (from the oral and anal phases), nevertheless despite these the exigency of thought about the threatening sibling will necessarily be genitalized, and genitalized not only along the lines that the baby is the equivalent of the mother's phallus. Children put cushions under their jerseys, take off a leg of their doll to feel and see where babies are and how they come out. The phallic 'I' of the Lacanian imaginary phase has an equivalent womb=me – a baby can come out of 'me'. If the phallus is the upright 'I', the womb is the rounded 'me'. The Freudian-Lacanian account has occluded this in its theory. Object Relations theory, by seeing it only as an identification with the mother, not as an intellectual task of understanding where intruder babies come from, has naturalized it. Once naturalized, the notion of conflict which produces psychic life through the exigency of thought and which must therefore be the basis of all psychoanalytic theory – whatever its orientation – is missing.

It is necessary to see the conflict and the resolution or failed re-solution of this conflict which is set up by the presence of siblings as opening the way to an inclusion of lateral relations in the theory. I have suggested that the 'law of the mother' follows the child's wish to give birth and hence for a cavity within. This law operates to prohibit the child's fantasy by as it were saying: it is I, the mother, not you the child, who gives birth. If the prohibition is accepted and the loss of the possibility of giving birth when one is a child acknow-ledged, then an inner space can be symbolized – a place from which thoughts come and in which representations can be held 'in mind'. In phantom pregnancies and in imagined anal births, as in infants' wishes, this womb is literal, it has not been 'lost', and therefore it cannot be re-presented and symbolized. Unsymbolized, what the child wants becomes an imaginary womb producing magical babies – monsters or angels. Unsymbolized, creative thinking (Winnicott) will be aborted.

Balint starts her paper on Sarah with the reflection that we have a phrase 'he is full of himself' and that we need an equivalent 'he is empty of himself'. But fullness and emptiness are two sides of the same coin – the one suggesting the inflated omnipotence of His Majesty the Baby – the other His Majesty's sudden deflation when he is dethroned by another child. Eventually what is needed is not this oscillation which is the nightmare of the later hysteric, but a resolution which transcends both positions. For this we need 'the law of the mother'. I am not suggesting that thoughts and the space to think them originate with the prohibition from the law of the mother; rather that it is in this moment that the process can be symbolized. The baby may well have identified with the containing womb-mother in the way the theories of Wilfred Bion could suggest, but this identification can be with a full or empty womb, and later, a head empty or full of thoughts. This is the possibility to which Balint refers. However, what a prohibition does is to symbolize (or culturalize) this identification: instead of the oscillation too-full/too-empty, we have the alternatives – empty now but can be filled later (as far as procreation goes, female position), empty now/cannot be filled later (male position). In creation, these sexually differentiated positions cannot be gendered (though ideologically they may well be in the assumption of superior male minds). Both boy and girl can be sometimes empty, sometimes full of thoughts – but emptiness precedes the fullness of creativity, just as for the child it did in the laws of procreativity. This 'empty now' is not the obverse of 'full now'; it is a new space, a sublimated space. Instead of being mind-as-womb which is excitingly genitalized, it is a new sublimated space which can be just mind and hence be filled with creative thoughts – and a further differentiation of the mind from its context/origin in the body takes place.

We can see this clinically. If a core fantasy of hysteria in both sexes is pregnancy and a conversion symptom can be a phantom pregnancy, the same overfilling of the mind is also prevalent. The hysteric cannot think, he can only discharge in verbal or actual actions a superfluity of unsorted 'pre-thoughts' – his head is as full (or empty) as his womb. Eating disorders, bulimia and anorexia in particular, so prevalent in peer groups which are the heirs to siblings, demonstrate the empty/full oscillation prior to any symbolization of an inner space. The formation of inner space has been understood in Oedipal terms, but because siblings have been missed and with them the realization that there are other babies in the world, there has been no way to connect this creation of a symbolizable inner space to an all-important 'No', the all-important loss. No, the negative, the prohibition – in this case, the mother's 'No' – is the condition of judgement (Freud [1925]), it is the 'not to be' and the 'not to have' which are the conditions of representation.

The capacity for judgement is marked by a 'no' – 'I do not want that.' The neonate presented with the external world initially makes no distinction between this outer world and what is inside it. (Elaborating this point, Winnicott explores how the mother's breast is the baby's 'self'.) The first differentiation will be along the lines of taking in and keeping in what is good and spitting out what is bad (Klein). For thinking processes to emerge from this, what has been taken in has to become re-presented in the external world. The food that gives a pleasant feeling inside becomes once more the food that was originally outside – but now as a mental conception of what is external and real. A young child (or an old hysteric with eating disorders) cannot predict when it will be hungry because it has as yet no re-presentation of the idea of food. For this to happen, what gave pleasure has to be first lost and then 'refound' in the external world so that the infant can come to know it is available to it as something outside itself. Thinking means that gratification can be postponed – the baby can turn its need for instant satisfaction into a desire for it. (The hysteric and the psychopath still need instant gratification.) However, the small child must also be able to make a judgement as to when it should stop the postponement and take action to get what it needs or wants. The 'no' of judgement indicates that the desire has been repressed while the waiting took place, the 'no' enables it to become conscious so that a decision to ask for one's dinner when the time is right can be made.

Just as the body develops, so too does the capacity to think. We can imagine the first stage as the creation not only of thoughts but also of the space to have them in – at first the food that is either swallowed or spat out only knows the oscillation between the two or between full/empty. Once the food can be re-presented as existing in the outside world, then the notion of a mouth cavity to recontain it also comes into being. One of my patients who had persistent eating disorders said she needed me to tell her where and what her mouth was – we may infer (among other things) that she had regressed to a point of full/empty where there was as yet no notion of a mouth space to hold or wait to hold the food. The unsymbolized mouth and digestive tract are typical of eating disorders as the unsymbolized womb is a mark of phantom pregnancies.

The small child who believes he has a baby inside him initially has it along the line full/empty – so too does the 'pregnant' hysteric who regresses to this point. Without the mother's 'no' being taken on board, this desire to have a baby cannot be known and hence cannot be repressed. When the wish is known to be repressed by an acceptance of the 'no', then the judgement can be made – I will have a baby later when I am grown up and the baby can be a baby to be thought about in the external world. I am suggesting here that the mother's first 'no' which controls feeding, defecation, etc., is taken in by the baby as its first reality-testing judgements, and her 'second' no – what I am calling the law of the mother – takes this a further crucial step by referring to sexual regulations of gender and generation – who can and cannot have babies. If the prohibition is not accepted, the fantasies continue to be enacted as they are in hysteria and so-called 'bovarisme' in which the fantasist, like the 'pregnant' child, continues to believe his fantasies are real, or in perversion where, instead of either sublimation and symbolization or hysterical fantasies, one has only enactment. Perversions seem so active and phallic – and hence for long were associated almost exclusively with men[9] – only because there is no inner space; in hysterical fantasies the inner space is entirely filled with compulsive fantasies so that, as another patient with florid eating disorders put it to me, 'There is simply no room to have any thoughts.' These are some of the consequences of not giving up the child's belief that it can be the mother. They result from a failure to take on board the vertical injunction that there are differences between generations, but they also, I would argue, come into operation in the context of siblings: the new baby or the pre-existent older sibling would not be a threat if it is 'me' the toddler from whom babies emerge. The meaning of the birth of Hans's sister Hanna is not nearly so dire if Little Hans can also procreate (Freud [1909]). There are further consequences.

If the new foetus in the mother's expanding womb forces the small child to think about it, but it still remains in fantasy only a version of what the child can also produce – the child's own forthcoming baby – then it will not be recognized as someone *other* than the child – it will be a replica – a look-alike that again will not be seen as itself, as 'other'. Perverse and hysterical parents see their actual children as such replicas of themselves. If, on the other hand, the 'law of the mother' is accepted, then the longed-for and dreaded sibling will be like the older child – a baby of the same mother – but also it will be different from it, maybe a girl to a boy (as Hanna was to Little

Hans), maybe the same sex but of course younger and with at least a different first name, blue-eyed, black hair, lighter skin colour. The child in this case has the possibility of grasping seriality; he can come to internally realize that a sibling is not a replication, a self-same clone, but instead is both the same and different (chapter 1). The very rapid oscillations of sibling love and hate indicate the negotiation of this recognition of seriality. In turn, sorting out these extreme feelings and representing the missing fertility of childhood sets the ground plan for the non-realization of sibling incest.

Sibling or peer group sexual play ('doctors', 'mummies and daddies') is normal and it stretches along a continuum from caring and loving towards or away from incest. Reading well-known texts with this question in mind, it has seemed to me likely that Freud's famous 'Dora' (Ida Bauer) and her brother Otto engaged together in masturbation, and that the Wolf Man's older sister almost certainly went further and far more intrusively in the sexual seduction of her little brother – the Wolf Man. We can reconstruct Balint's case of Sarah from this perspective. Sarah's mother saw in her third child only the good, easy baby she wanted. Her father wanted a third boy. 'Very early Sarah started to play with her brothers, who were only a few years older than herself, climbing trees and competing successfully with them in every way' (E. Balint [1963]: 41–2); and then around age six, the sexual intercourse with her nearest brother took place. The characteristics of the type of patient Balint is describing would seem to me to accord very well with a history of such a father who wanted his child as a replica of himself (a third boy) and a mother who could not help her child to feel the same yet different from her brothers as they were from each other. Describing patients who are empty of themselves, Balint writes:

> these people do not like to be left alone, and they find it difficult to do anything for themselves by themselves; in spite of this, they often dread human contact and resent being helped by others ...
>
> At the other end of the scale, these people have to withdraw completely from everyday life, but this withdrawal, instead of helping, aggravates their state and may lead to a sort of confusion. If he is hospitalised at this point, the patient's confusion may be halted or even diminished, because he is cared for without any obligation to those caring for him. Thus the patient is not alone, but not actively with anyone. (Balint [1963]: 40)

How, asks Balint, can this state of emptiness of the self co-exist with the need for another person, yet in such a way that the other person does not make the subject feel full of themselves? One can see how these characteristics can lead to an understanding such as Balint's in terms of a mother and baby: the baby cannot survive without the mother, who must be present but the baby must be able to take her for granted and not feel obligated. However, the characteristics just described could also be a response to sibling incest. In its benign version – as in Roy's fictional twins – sibling incest would create a situation like twinning where the other is needed but not as another separate person because they have not been represented as such, nor would their presence bring satisfaction because, not being 'other', they have nothing new to offer. A twin I knew, who was imprisoned for political reasons, could not bear solitary confinement and, in trying to understand his beyond-average despair at this, wrote 'I was not born alone.' One could even argue that at the beginning of life a twin, in Balint's words, 'is not alone, but not actively with anyone'. In later life, though they cannot be alone, the presence of another threatens the possibility of otherness and hence is an irritant. What one half of the twin needs is an institution in which he is accompanied by other people who need not be seen at all as themselves but instead only as the means of satisfying his need to complete himself. The first sense that the other is not the same as the self induces irritation; in clinical work one meets this as a continual, grating, miscommunication. Michael Balint (1968) proposed this was a 'basic fault' in the mother–baby relationship; I believe one feels this irritation when one who is supposed to be same becomes different.

The model I would propose sees the sibling incest as the psychic event which makes use of some previous mother-and-infant condition but gives this earlier pre-psychic state a later genital shape. That the actual incest may happen later in the patient's life than very early childhood means that it only gives shape to a situation that was unresolved and remained *in statu nascendi*. The incest can be relatively egalitarian, as with the twins in *The God of Small Things*, or possibly with 'Dora' and Otto Bauer in Freud's 'Fragment of an analysis of a case of hysteria' (1905) till it ends with Dora being relegated by the doctor to an inferior position to that of her brother – the male child. If it is unequal, as with the Wolf Man and his older sister, and seemingly with Sarah, then the boy or girl victim will

'The incest can be relatively egalitarian'
Siegmund and Sieglinde by Arthur Rackham, from *Arthur Rackham:
Rackham's Color Illustrations for Wagner's 'Ring'* (Dover Publications, 1979)

experience it as a break in protective boundaries, a traumatic invasion of body-mind. In either its benign or its malign version it is problematic, indicative at the very least of not knowing that there is room in the world for someone other than oneself, of breaking or refusing to establish boundaries. It is at the point of Sarah's fears and fantasies of invasion that Balint mentions the sibling incest as discussed earlier:

> [Sarah] would lie rigidly in anticipation of some object descending upon her from above, and crashing on to her head. This object was sometimes described as a rolling-pin, sometimes a rock, and sometimes a cloud. (E. Balint [1963]: 42)

Is Balint's mention of the brother at this point an unconscious association of Balint's: rather than a mother, could Balint the analyst have been standing for the brother in Sarah's transference? Recollecting what she felt as a child of six, could Sarah have imagined her brother's penis as a rolling-pin, his weight on top of her as a rock, the foggy sexual feelings as a descending cloud?

> In the dream a dog came out of the sea and bit her and then disappeared. This reminded her of a previous dream in which a bird swooped down, gashed her on the head, and disappeared. In this earlier dream she said that what had hurt her most was that the bird never came back; it was quite unconcerned, indifferent. She then went back to the dog dream and said that when the dog bit her he took away her uterus, but now she had got it back again and could feel it inside her. (E. Balint [1963]: 46)

The dog emerges from the sea, bites and steals her womb, the bird swoops and gashes her head: the space in the mind for thoughts and in the body for procreation are equated. A week later Sarah dreams that she wakes up to find her ceiling light on fire; in her dream, she rushes to her parents' room but they do not come to help. Instead her tall brother comes and puts out the fire, warning her 'never to touch the bulb again or to turn on the light' (E. Balint [1963]: 47). Then Sarah tells of other dreams which indicate to her therapist that she and her 'objects' are safe if she is empty but if she is full of 'feelings, urges, desire', she will catch fire. But let us reconsider the dreams: though a man might put the fire out, he will then take away what she has inside her, desert her and leave her empty again, finally telling her not to touch the bulb as though it were her dangerous desires that had caused the conflagration. Nor must she turn on the light and let anyone see what is happening. Is this man not her incestuous brother who becomes indifferent to her? Is Sarah not terrified that she may desire him, as in her dream she implies he suggests – she is frightened that her brother blames her for initiating the incest which she may continue to want, as her adult sexual behaviour suggests. Frightened, it is assumed she wanted the incest that destroyed her mind and body; she is safer empty and ill, looked after by people who do not impinge as separate others but instead provide a missing part of herself.

As I paraphrase Sarah's history and dreams, the omission of a determining role for sibling incest seems almost extraordinary. However, it is not: there has been no place for it in the clinical method or in the theory. I suggest that if we take Sarah's case as paradigmatic – there will, of course, be individually different stories – then a new psychoanalytic formulation could run like this: the early parent–infant relationship sets a ground plan, the advent of another child – or, as in Sarah's case, the recognition of an older child – sets up the need to demarcate sameness and difference, to balance love and hate, to find a place in a series. These themes are aspects of the first intellectual question – where does another baby come from? To which I emphatically add – or even place first – *where does that leave me?* If this scenario does not work out more or less satisfactorily, there will be the murder of Abel or the should-be-forbidden sexuality of Sarah and her brother.

Forward-looking formulations, like therapeutic prognoses, are always dubious and what we need is the reconstruction of a history. Given the contemporary, isolated nuclear family with its matricentrism, the failures of Sarah's mother may have provided the scene within which the incest occurs and these failures will then obviously come to feature in the patient's life. A reconstructed history would use the present-day symptoms and dreams with their associations to hypothesize a course of psychic development. Such a history seems to me to warrant starting with the incest in which, in the analytical transference relationship, the analyst may not be the mother but the brother without whom Sarah is empty, who awakens her desires and feelings and subsequently deserts and probably blames her – all important themes in Sarah's spoken material. Her presenting symptom is her sense of non-existence – she is 'a stranger in the world', a sibling problematic.

The case of Sarah illustrates my contention that the advent of the sibling in the psyche is a trauma that organizes the pre-psychic helplessness of the neonate. If the sibling trauma cannot be overcome but instead is reinforced by the advent of sibling incest, then the victim continues to live with the threat of death or annihilation to an unestablished self. We can suppose Sarah's brother handed on to her his sibling problem (possibly irresolvable because of his fear of his father's violence – of his older brother we know nothing). Sarah, like Emmi in chapter 2, was terrified to death *of* death – she lay awake night after night dreading it. The incest would contain the violence needed for survival and, even if not actually violent, this incest revolves around this death of the self. Hélène of *War and Peace* commits suicide, Catherine (*Wuthering Heights*) dies in childbirth, the girl twin, Rahel (*The God of Small Things*), records her personal death in her eyes only – it gets small recognition in the face of the traumatic world around. Sibling incest contains death.

The advent or expectation of a sibling (Emmi or Little Hans with all their 'pretend' ones) gives psychic meaning to the earliest fear of annihilation that threatens if the mother does not look after one or recognize that one is someone (primal dread); this is the place of the sibling in relationship to both the pre-Oedipal and Oedipal mother. We can imagine that Sarah's brother was very threatened by her birth – so he could from the first moment of her existence have incarnated what she feared. By the time she is six or seven they are playmates – she is like him, climbing trees and being a tomboy; sexuality (the life drive) joins the persisting terror, and incest results. As Sarah's case stands, reading the transference as only a maternal transference (as is the regular practice) and not seeing the fraternal threat is to repeat Sarah's problem. Just like her parents, we the analysts have paid no attention to brother–sister, sister–brother incest in its own right; it is a serious matter.

Melanie Klein observed that infantile sibling (or peer) sexual play was common and often persisted into latency and adolescence. It is quite likely that Sarah and her brother started their incest with such play when Sarah was around two years old (this seems a recognizable pattern). Because she considers that such lateral sexuality is about guilt and anxiety *in relation to the parent*, Klein believes that such behaviour can range from the damaging to the helpful – it can intensify or mitigate the guilt/anxiety. In other words, to Klein (as to others) the guilt and anxiety is not about the sibling relationship itself:

> although early experiences like these can do a lot of harm in some cases, in others they may influence the child's development favourably. For besides satisfying the child's libido and his desire for sexual knowledge, relations of this kind serve the important function of reducing his excessive sense of guilt . . . the fact that his proscribed phantasies against his parents are shared by a partner gives him a sense of having an ally and thus greatly lightens the burden of his anxiety. (Klein [1932]: 119)

This can seem quite a shocking commentary, but how different is it from the incest in Roy's portrait of the twins if we substitute 'the world' and their dead cousin for the parents? It is the perspective that causes the problem: because there is no perception of the autonomy of the sibling relationship, the place of the death of the subject, the violence, the sexualization of the guilt *within* that relationship are chronically missed. Klein's insistence on the guilt and anxiety about parents is a variation on Balint's stress on maternal recognition – neither grants siblings a separate space.

— 4 —

Looking Sideways:
'A Child is being Beaten'

Ilse, aged twelve, and Gert, aged thirteen and a half, used to indulge from
time to time in coitus-like acts which happened quite suddenly ... The
analysis of both children showed that they had had sexual relations with
each other in earliest childhood ... an overpowering sense of guilt generated an obsessive impulse in both of them which ... made them repeat
their acts.

Melanie Klein, 'The sexual activities of children'

As mentioned in the previous chapter, in Klein's theory the guilt the
child feels for its destructive wishes towards a parent can be assuaged
in intersibling sexual activity. The guilt towards the parents is unconscious and hence causes the compulsive nature of the acts. However,
in the case history of the instance quoted above, Gert (but not Ilse)
felt *consciously* guilty about the sex with his sister, although he 'for-
got' it had taken place after each occasion. If the unconscious guilt
towards the parents which produces the compulsive symptoms can
be made conscious and lessened then both the ability to play and to
have masturbation fantasies will be released; both childhood play
and sexual fantasies are essential for creative living. Gert, throughout
the long period of compulsive acts of intercourse with his sister, had
no conscious masturbation fantasies at all. Fantasy is a mode of
thinking. We could say that the incestuous act replaced thinking.
Through the therapy, in time the psychological guilt was mitigated,
the compulsive acts stopped being necessary and Gert could have a
masturbation fantasy; it was about a naked girl whose body, but not
her head, was visible. Gradually the head begins to appear and in
time it becomes recognizable as the head of his sister. 'By that time,
however,' comments Klein, 'his compulsion was already done and his
sexual relations with his sister had completely stopped. *This shows*

the connection there was between the excessive repression of his desires and phantasies in regard to his sister and his obsessive impulse to have sexual relations with her' (Klein [1932]: 118, my italics). Here Klein is referring to an extreme individual case; however, it also surely suggests that whatever the degree of violence fantasized towards a parent, there is also autonomous sexual desire for a sibling.

A so-called 'core' masturbation fantasy is often hard to access, but it is crucial: it is a scenario which indicates how the subject sees himself placed in the world; it is not static – Gert's changed with the freedom introduced by his therapy – it can alter simply because of life's variations. We are not given enough of Gert's fantasy or its shifts to make anything of it beyond simply to note that a missing head, while certainly aiding non-recognition, is also a typical castration symbol and more obviously a violence for a violence – 'that Herod's head I'll have' responds the threatened Cleopatra in Shakespeare's *Antony and Cleopatra*. It was Ilse, not Gert, who was initially the active initiator of the incest. The sister and brother throughout the period of their incestuous childhood got on very badly – did Gert fear Ilse? We do not know – but if one reads the occluded sibling relationship into the case history, it seems likely.

Masturbatory fantasies are highly individual but often with recognizable generic features. A *locus classicus* of a common fantasy is known by its dominant content: ' "A child is being beaten" '[1] (Freud [1919]). It is about siblings. The jury is still out as to whether or not changing social practices have eradicated this fantasy. It could, on the contrary, quite possibly be a fantasy so prevalent as to have escaped notice, as Freud thought when he observed and analysed it in 1919 and when Anna Freud supplemented her father's theory in 1923 (A. Freud 1923). My own clinical experience and the exigencies of the logic of theories of unconscious processes make me tend towards thinking that some version of the fantasy or its enactment may be indulged by everyone at some stage of their lives. The support for this contention now rests on what I believe to be the universal psychic (as well of course as social) importance of sibling relations.

I shall make some introductory remarks on Freud's and Anna Freud's analyses of the fantasy and then present a clinical example from my own practice at the end of the twentieth century, returning in the conclusion to make some general remarks that link the Freuds' case histories and my clinical work. This, I hope, will be a contribution to elaborating a psychoanalytic paradigm that takes account of sisters and brothers and lateral relationships in general.

The fantasy is a story which may or may not accompany physical masturbation; it usually culminates in orgasm. It shows the cusp of narcissistic and lateral object-relations being used in the service of the erotic self. Freud saw his essay as helping to further an understanding of perversion. In itself this fact is interesting as 'a child is being beaten' is a common fantasy of women, and women are frequently conceived as neurotic whereas it is men who are perverse. Female neurosis and male perversion are supposed to be two sides of the same coin, yet this essay investigates female perversion. If we bring in siblings, which I argue this masturbation fantasy demands, we can see that neither neuroses nor perversions are intrinsically gendered.

In his paper ' "A child is being beaten" ', Freud makes use of six cases, four women and two men. He mentions that he has many more instances, but these six have been investigated thoroughly. The first two of the six patients referred to are clearly obsessional; the third has some obsessional traits; the fifth suffers from extreme indecisiveness but would not have been given a psychiatric diagnosis; the sixth is mentioned then ignored by Freud, although, from what he says, he must have had this patient very much in mind – probably this patient is his youngest daughter, Anna Freud, whom, to present-day scandal, he had in treatment not long before the essay's conception. It is the diagnosis of the fourth patient to which I wish to draw attention. Of this diagnosis Freud writes: 'The fourth case, it must be admitted, was of a straightforward hysteria, with pains and inhibitions' ([1919]: 183).

Our range then is from 'extremely severe and incapacitating obsessionality', through hysteria, to an indecisiveness which is near 'normal' and probably to that 'ideal fiction', normality itself – Anna Freud! As Freud puts it in his opening paragraph:

It is surprising how often people who seek analytic treatment for hysteria or an obsessional neurosis confess to having indulged in the phantasy: 'A child is being beaten'. Very probably there are still more frequent instances of it among the far greater number of people who have not been obliged to come to analysis by manifest illness. ([1919]: 179)

I suggest that in fact what we have here, in all the cases from severe obsessionality to normality or near normality, is an underlying hysteria. This hysteria subtends, for instance, male obsessionality and is present as a psychopathology of everyday life which, if circumstances are right, can turn into a florid hysteria. Freud explained the hysteria underlying obsessionality in the case of the Wolf Man. The Wolf Man's phobia is an anxiety hysteria but it is his bowel symptom that carries the weight of the conversion hysteria that lies beneath his obsessionality: 'At last I recognised the importance of the intestinal trouble for my purposes; it represented the small trait of hysteria which is regularly to be found at the root of an obsessional neurosis' (Freud [1918]: 75). My point in making this observation is simply that as we are all potential hysterics, the underlying hysteria makes it likely that anyone may have the core masturbation fantasy.

At the other end of the scale from Freud's pathological categories are normal story-tellers, exemplified by Anna Freud's first published psychoanalytic paper in which she describes the case of an adolescent day-dreamer (almost certainly herself) (Young-Bruehl 1988). In this case history, the artistic superstructure of the 'patient's' day-dreams has never come into conflict with reality; it should thus technically be non-neurotic. I consider that what we also have in these instances is what I shall term 'the hysterical potential'. The very 'nice stories' that Anna Freud describes in her explanation can either turn into art (the sublimation) or be used as a defence against something else illicit breaking through to consciousness. However, contrary to Anna Freud's understanding, I suggest that the compulsiveness of the story-telling indicates the presence of a neurotic symptom – just as Gert and Ilse could not stop their intercourse, perhaps, both Anna O (Freud [1895]) and Anna Freud could not stop their story-telling. To me, rather than a sublimation into authentic creativity (which Klein here would have agreed was happening with Anna Freud), I consider there is a splitting process in which there is a bifurcation: the beating fantasies are completely repressed and become unconscious, while at the same time the illicit desires which underlie them are not so much *sublimated into art* as *converted* into 'nice stories', fantasies which apparently, but only apparently, contain care and affection.

This story-telling has been named 'bovarisme' after Flaubert's heroine Emma Bovary. If it stays at this level, this story-telling in which the narrator enacts the events in his imagination is a verbal equivalent of a bodily conversion symptom in which the physical malady enacts the mental desires. In a seeming paradox, it can only be sublimated if it is given up. By this I mean not that the stories are abandoned, but that their wish-fulfilling elements are recognized and relinquished so that the stories, instead of being enactments of satisfaction – the author becomes a hero or a princess – become expressions of desires which will *not* be realized: the created character but *not* the author may be heroic or rich and beautiful. Compulsive rhyming, what was once called 'verbal diarrhoea' and now is known as 'bullshit', some romance fiction, pornography and 'nice' stories all use words as sexually satisfying in themselves. They also have the author as the only 'hero' – His Majesty the Baby in many guises. The author does not know there are other people in the world. When the patient turns the day-dreams of her illness into the written stories of her cure, as did Anna O, the first patient of psychoanalysis, through her giving up of something she may be on the road to sublimation – arriving will entail mourning the loss of the unique self.

Does writing always necessarily implicate *loss* as a condition of its coming to being? Loss is a precondition of re-presentation. However, there would seem to be a type of writing which avoids this. In what we might call 'writing as presentation', the words do not stand for what is re-presented but are the thing itself. This is the type of story-telling, written or oral, to which I think Anna Freud must be referring. It is not to my mind sublimation, because sublimation involves loss. The concrete thinking of schizophrenia uses spoken words in this way. I suggest the 'literal' writing of hysteria uses written words as though one side of the metaphorical equation were the presentation of the thing itself. In Anne Sexton's poem on language 'words are like coins . . . or better, like swarming bees' (Sexton [1962]) – we perceive the tumbling out, the pleasure of an evacuation of words (like a fruit machine), which is exactly the quality of the eloquent 'bullshit', words for words' sake; we do not see words as part of a structured language but rather as the images – money and bees. There is, on the one hand, this wish-fulfilling or day-dream writing, and on the other, 'symbolized' writing – and, of course, the mixture of the two.

Flaubert surely helps us here: Flaubert famously said of his character Emma Bovary, 'Emma Bovary, c'est moi!' A classified hysteric, Flaubert also studied clinical cases of hysteria. I believe he put the hysterical aspects of himself into his heroine, but in so doing 'lost' them, lost that is the pleasurable gain from them such as being always the centre of attention through dramatizing the self's crises. Once they were lost he was able to represent them in a novel which was a sublimation not a realization of his wishes for grandiosity.

Any masturbation fantasy is a story which, above all, is in itself a satisfaction of wishes – hence Freud is seeing it as a perversion. It is a perversion, because usually an actual act – that of physical masturbation – accompanies the story, itself a hysterical fantasy. However, there is gender confusion in its account. It is often asserted that after early childhood girls masturbate less than boys. What I consider to be the case is that as a result of social mores, girls may less often manually stimulate the genitals (Laufer 1989) – they commonly masturbate through dreaming and fantasy which are 'action' stories. If we use the girl rather than the boy as a model, we will see that a major characteristic of 'bovarisme', the dreamy stories, is that they are full of action – either tales of the hero's derring-do or the heroine's conquests. Opposite to this, in what I am calling 'sublimated' or 'symbolic' writing, it is interesting to note some very different characteristics. There are writer's blocks, overwhelming anxiety, enormous pleasure and, most interestingly, the fact that in writing one discovers ideas and knowledge that one did not know one had – about which one had 'no idea', 'no knowledge'. I suggest this is because the act of losing the 'wish fulfilling' aspect entails repression, and with the repression of the wish the curiosity that seemed to be disallowed disappears too. The sublimated wishing allows the return of this unconscious curiosity and, with it, its unknown discoveries.

Read as a hysterical fantasy, whatever the dominant psychic condition of the fantasist, ' "A child is being beaten" ' further illustrates my earlier contention (Mitchell 2000a) that hysteria is said to have 'disappeared' only because our theories and our clinical practice ignore the lateral relationships of siblings and their substitutes, peers and affines. Without these lateral relationships we cannot understand or even see hysteria. Once more, to read in siblings as more than a descriptive category demands an addition and a shift of the theory and practice, and brings the human potential of hysteria firmly into view.

If then, as I contend, this widespread beating fantasy is an indication of the universal propensity to hysteria and the psychic importance of siblings, what is its content? According to Freud, for girls in their fantasy there is a first stage scene of a child, usually a brother, being beaten. Then there is a scene where the girl herself is being beaten; this scene is a necessary hypothesis – it is in fact so deeply unconscious that it is irretrievable and remains a construction made within the analysis from the associations of the patient. The third stage, which culminates in orgasm, is the fantasy that the girl, vague and unspecified, is watching a number of children, who are also vague and unspecified, being beaten by the father or, more likely, a teacher, whom Freud considers to be a father substitute. The vagueness I believe marks both the approaching physical orgasmic culmination and the repression of the ideas about incestuous and narcissistic love-objects.

Boys with the fantasy express a variation on this theme: the boy beating-fantasist replaces the father figure with a mother figure. But more interesting from my point of view is the second stage. For the girl, it is the girl herself who is being beaten, but this stage has become so deeply unconscious that it cannot be reached except as a hypothesis necessitated by the rest of the material. Boys, on the contrary, are quite aware that it is themselves whom they imagine being beaten. I shall return to this gender discrepancy later.

Freud and subsequent analysts explain the beating fantasy as a child's rivalry with siblings for the exclusive love of the parent of the opposite sex. The shame and guilt experienced by the fantasist is explained on the grounds that the fantasy allows a realization of Oedipal desires – the subject sees to it that it is the other sibling who is punished so that she/he alone is loved. I believe that this interpretation once again occludes the siblings in favour of the exclusive importance of Oedipal desires for parents. Making everything dependent on the parental axis can have worrying implications. For instance, I do not believe that when people use the internet for violent and sexual experiences which often seem to be versions of masturbation fantasies, their main aim is to fight for the attention of a father or mother figure.

One of my patients, Mrs X, had so florid an imagination it was often as though she was asking for us to look together at pornographic pictures. Initially, however, Mrs X had come for analysis with considerable resistance and reluctance. She had recognized the urgency of getting help – but she was clearly entrenched in her way of life. She was in the first trimester of a pregnancy after having, for a good number of years, either failed to conceive or, if she had conceived, failed to carry a baby to term. When she mentioned her beating fantasy, I first thought that her telling me this was an act of compliance with the analytic modality; she knew the psychoanalytic literature and this – a well-known topic – seemed a suitable analytic 'confession'. As a result of my inadequate recognition of the fantasy's importance it was only after her analysis was over that certain links formed in my mind and I came to believe I had overlooked the significance of the fantasy and the sibling relation contained in it. My use of Mrs X to illustrate my thesis is thus a post hoc reading of the clinical material.

In Mrs X's version of the fantasy, the third or surface level of the pleasurable masturbatory fantasy consisted of Mrs X watching a non-specific, androgynous child who was being beaten by a non-specific man; it thus coincided perfectly with Freud's record that at this stage the imagined people were vague. Although she was tiny and quite unusually attractive, Mrs X's own physical appearance was markedly androgynous, Peter Pan-like. In the associations she made to the male figure of the beating fantasy, he was a lover or possible second husband that she would marry after the imagined death of her present one. As with Freud's cases there was no awareness at all of the middle stage when it would have been Mrs X herself who was the beaten child; but we did reach back to a first level where the child was explicitly her younger brother.

In fact, Mrs X did not recollect this beating fantasy which so dominated her later teenage and adult years as a childhood fantasy at all. What came to consciousness during her treatment with me were clearly accurate, related memories which had vanished until the moment when she started to have associations to this persistent, compulsive beating fantasy. Instead of, or maybe as well as, an irretrievable fantasy, what she remembered were actual scenes and enactments in her childhood. These seemed so important that it was almost unbelievable to both of us how she had completely forgotten them – but apparently she had done just that, thereby illustrating the crucial amnesias of hysteria.

Almost immediately after her brother's birth, when she was already six years old, Mrs X had contracted polio and been hospitalized. She had recovered from the illness without noticeable impairment. These were some of the forgotten incidents: She recollected her fascinated distress at the nurses' frequent slapping of the babies in the children's ward where she had been placed. She recalled that just before her brother's birth and her illness – probably deeply preoccupied with her mother's pregnancy – she had quite deliberately and thoroughly explored her own vagina and continued to insert her hand and play vaginally. She then remembered having seduced her brother when he was about two and she eight or nine years old. She had got him to play with her in their parents' bed and vividly recalled her genital excitement as she had made him rub his penis against her genitals. At about the same time she used to recount to him her excited desires to smack him as though he were her own naughty child. Her aggression towards him had been quite extreme and had caused their mother noticeable anxiety, she thought. In one analytic session, while she was describing her violence towards her brother, she mentioned an incident when she had cut his lip by throwing a tennis racquet as she chased him 'up a back passage'. Up till the time of the analysis and following her hospitalization, the merest thought of children being hit by adults obsessed, thrilled and appalled her.

When Mrs X was eleven, her parents divorced and both remarried. Mrs X and her brother stayed with their mother and they acquired a small stepbrother. Mrs X never accepted her stepfather as any relation whatsoever. But Mrs X's relation to her own, now somewhat absent, natural father became highly flirtatious and she experienced her father himself as both tantalizingly sexual to a quite explicit degree and very rejecting. Her brother effectively lost contact with his biological father. Here, as is the standard understanding, the parents featured prominently: Mrs X clearly felt she had won out in the competition for their father: the sexualizing of her relationship here was clearly one of the means she had made use of that her brother had eschewed. For Mrs X this was a hysterical version of the Oedipus complex.

In early adolescence Mrs X once more contracted a serious illness, which, although she was again hospitalized, remained undiagnosed because all its manifestations were remarkably like polio. However, as she had already had it, doctors decided it could not be polio, which cannot be contracted twice. Mrs X recalled that when she recovered from her second major illness, one of her tasks was to take her small stepbrother to nursery en route to her own secondary school. She remembered terrorizing him with horrifically frightening stories all the way to school. He grew up to be a nervous and depressed young man – a situation for which Mrs X now recalled she had always felt somewhat to blame. It was, however, only in her analysis that it occurred to her that she might have been a major factor in the disturbed life of her natural brother – he had become unusually passive, suffered night terrors and had a number of disabling phobias well into adulthood. When he had married, she had felt that that was the end of their relationship. Consciously, until this moment she thought she had only adored him and he, her.

Mrs X's account of her childhood reminded me of the Wolf Man's sister. The Wolf Man had beating fantasies: did his sister too before her suicide, or were her violent sexual wishes taken up in actions? My association to the Wolf Man's sister, to whom I refer a number of times in these chapters, actually occurred insistently and prominently for the first time in the analysis of Mrs X. It alerted me to a fear I had harboured that there was something suicidal about Mrs X, though not in any obvious way or ways that she was aware of; it was more like an emanation of the death drive, a compulsion in this energetic young woman towards a deadly stasis, an ultimate passivity, which is also a feature of hysteria. Had Mrs X's suicidal propensities been displaced on to her dead babies – or rather, as I believe, were not both the unconscious suicide and the childlessness aspects of her sibling dilemma?

We discovered that Mrs X's inability to conceive, or alternatively to hold a conception, dated from an abortion of an apparently much-wanted child in the first year of her marriage. She had been so completely convinced that the child was horrendously deformed that doctors were unable to reassure her and had finally agreed to a termination. She had never found out whether or not there had been anything wrong with the foetus – she had satisfied her need to get rid of this fantasized monster. It became clear that Mrs X had aborted, failed to conceive and miscarried because she could not shake off her fear that, in her mind, any baby of hers would be her brother. Even when they were adults, Mrs X would catch herself anxious lest her brother were himself a murderous sex offender, somebody, as she put it, with a 'warped mind'.

What had happened was that her own sexual murderousness towards him as a child haunted her in these flashes of projected rage in which she put her murdering self into him. Her fantasized violence 'deformed' him. The rages need not be felt as persecutory, as she was not the object of them. Rather, it was a matter of confusion and projection, which was later repeated with a series of lovers. Her rivalry, anger and her earlier enacted violence towards her brother convinced her that her own baby would be deformed and that she would be destructive towards it; she saw the fact that she could not give birth – and the abortion – as protective rather than destructive acts. She was saving the baby from herself. There would be no baby to harm. It was also that Mrs X had grasped the fact that children could not have babies only on a realistic not a symbolic level. She appeared, and, to herself (and others), felt, like a child because she did not know in an internally meaningful way what distinguishes adults and children – most importantly, the ability to reproduce.

When eventually she gave birth to a live boy, Mrs X's joy with her baby was so great that it made it hard for her to recognize any negativity or even the possibility of ambivalence. He was – at least initially – a wonderful narcissistic extension of herself. However, this was positive not negative narcissism and, like many first babies, her son initially benefited from the adoration. It would be later, when he not only became more separate, but when the negative dimension of all idealizations played in, that problems would start. Such narcissism as this has always been understood in psychoanalytic theory in relation to a 'vertical' castration complex – according to this, the mother finally receives in her baby a representative of the phallus she always wanted. I would argue that there is something 'lateral' at stake as well. To Mrs X, her son was her baby brother towards whom she had managed to reverse her hatred into love. Thus her love was not only because he was what she had always wanted (and, like a phallus, needed to have in order to complete herself), he was also a replication of her, a self-same playmate. Reversing hatred into love is not a very safe practice as it can always quickly reverse back.

With the birth of her son, the masturbatory beating fantasies stopped – she could recollect them but they had no sexual charge and hence were useless. Which came first, the abandonment of the fantasies to enable the live birth, or the birth to end the fantasies? From the ancient Greeks to the early twentieth century, childbirth has been recommended as a cure for hysteria. A worrying question we might want to insert here relates to what happens to the fantasies. If they are not sublimated, can they be enacted? Could this underlie the prevalence of the corporal punishment of children and, in a worst-case scenario, random physical abuse?

I want now to read Mrs X into the theory. In the first phase of the beating fantasy for Mrs X, as for Freud's patients, 'The child being beaten is never the one producing the fantasy, but is invariably another child, most often a brother or a sister if there is any' (Freud [1919]: 184–5). This child can be of either gender – it doesn't matter. As Freud likewise noted, it is hard to know if the first stage even constitutes an autonomous fantasy but is not rather a reaction to some particular events and some particular desires. This was exactly the case with Mrs X's early hospital experience – the slapping of children there excited and appalled her at a time when she was probably needing a lot of self-comfort as she was in an isolation ward and could not be visited. Masturbation as a means of solace could well have become near addictive at this point in her history. Even in small details that experience of watching other children being slapped matched Freud's observations. For instance, as with his patients, actual beating of children was intolerable to her and there was no corporal punishment in her home environment. The onset of the fantasy could be traced back to events in her sixth or seventh year. These are the years which Binet, even before the rise of psychoanalysis, recorded as the common age of the fantasy's inception.

There are some differences, however, between my understanding of Mrs X and Freud's theorization. Freud comments that the fantasies were an isolated enclave and not an integrated part of a larger neurosis. At first glance, this appeared true of Mrs X's fantasy. However, I think in fact that, to the contrary, it formed a part of her hysteria – the part that arose from the kill-or-be-killed of sibling survival.[2] Freud will have missed this integration into a neurosis because there is no distinctive place in his theory for sibling relations, a marked omission in 1919 when he was analysing Anna, the 'least and last' of his six children – his Anna Antigone, as he called her!

In the second, deeply unconscious but crucial stage of the fantasy which Freud reconstructs, the beaten child is the fantasist herself. Here Mrs X produced something not noted by Freud. With apparent difficulty she told me of many marital infidelities in which she had had encounters with a series of men who actually beat her as an essential prelude to intercourse. I suggest that this enactment obviated the need for fantasy and it thus was a substitute for 'unconsciousness'. I suggest too that it is for this reason that, in men, all stages of the fantasy can be conscious. The perversion – the actual beating – is the other side of the hysteria. We still too rarely note perversion in women and hysteria in men. Mrs X was enacting perverse behaviour instead of, or as well as, maintaining a hysterical fantasy. Freud writes:

> This second phase [in girls] is the most important and the most momentous of all. But we may say of it in a certain sense that it has never had a real existence. It is never remembered, it has never succeeded in becoming conscious. It is a construction of analysis, but it is no less a necessity on that account. ([1919]: 185)

However:

> This second phase – the child's phantasy of being itself beaten by its father – remains unconscious as a rule, probably in consequence of the intensity of the repression. I cannot explain why nevertheless in one of my six cases, that of a male, it was consciously remembered. ([1919]: 189)

So that:

> this phantasy, in which the boy's own self was retained as the person who was being beaten, differed from the second phase in girls in that it was able to become conscious. ([1919]: 196)

In Mrs X the second stage was an action, at least in adult life when she was beaten: it was enacted by her as a perversion – consciousness or unconsciousness would thus be irrelevant. I wonder now if, in Mrs X's case, there was some previous enactment with peers in latency and adolescence.

Conscious of this second phase of the fantasy, men reveal that in it they are always being beaten by a woman; in addition 'they invariably transfer themselves into the part of a woman' (Freud [1919]: 197). Freud does not say that the man imagines himself to be a woman – only that he plays the part of one. We have to take this to mean he is passive. I suggest that the beaten person in the fantasy is vague and androgynous. Mrs X enacts this; a male patient is conscious of it. Because of the unawareness of female perversion, the enactment has not been seen as related to the fantasy. Mrs X's playing

—— 95 ——

out of the fantasy in real life is probably related to the common assumption that women 'ask' to be raped – one of the world's more appalling misogynistic statements. The fact that women or men have certain fantasies is utterly irrelevant to how they should be treated as human beings.

Where the boy's second phase becomes conscious because unconsciously or preconsciously he has become feminine, the girl's third phase does so because in this she imagines that she is a boy (or several boys) being beaten; because she is not a boy she cannot fully enact this (as Mrs X enacts the second stage when she gets herself beaten by lovers), she can only dream about it. Enactment in which there is gender verisimilitude replaces unconscious processes and hence there is nothing to make conscious. Enactment in which a knowledge of sexual difference is either repudiated or repressed leaves that material as either unconscious but inaccessible in the first instance, or as unconscious fantasy in the second: in the conscious second stage the boy who is beaten imagines himself as feminine; in the conscious third stage, the girl who is beaten imagines she is a boy. The girl's third stage corresponds to the boy's second.

Two of Freud's four female cases had an elaborate structure of day-dreams concealing, at first, the beating fantasies. Mme Bovary (and hence probably Flaubert: 'Emma Bovary, c'est moi'), the Brontë children, Anna O, Anna Freud, Klein's Erna, are all famous exponents of this widespread hysterical tendency to elaborate this sort of day-dreaming. Because of the high degree of enactment in her case Mrs X did not transpose her fantasies into elaborate stories in this way. To resume: what we have from Mrs X and Freud's female patients is a conscious exciting fantasy in which a father substitute is beating a series of boys. This fantasy never arises before the age of five. These boys stand for the fantasist. Behind this is a fantasy in which the fantasist herself is being beaten by the father. This stage is a reconstruction of an irretrievable fantasy. Behind this is the first level in which a (probably actual) sibling is being beaten by a father figure while the fantasist is a spectator. This stage almost certainly derives from some real event. Here the gender of either subject or object seems insignificant. This first stage can attain consciousness but it is presented as insignificant. However, if it is real, that is, if it refers to an actual occurrence, then it has not been psychically processed and the dammed-up libido is potentially pathogenic.

I shall now turn briefly to the boy with beating fantasies. Although I have encountered this in my own clinical practice, I never paid it the attention I now believe it merits and hence I will mainly illustrate the argument with Freud's Wolf Man. However, I shall briefly mention one patient of mine, Mr Y, as although the fantasy was not fully analysed, his case raises crucial questions. According to Freud, in the boy the first *conscious* phase that allows the successful masturbation is 'I am being beaten by my *mother*'. However, it takes the form of a scenario in which the subject is represented by a series of unknown boys. It continues to the second stage which can be *conscious*, in which the fantasist himself, not a series of boys, is being beaten by the mother. The deeply *unconscious* phase that can be reconstructed is: 'I am being beaten by my *father*'. Freud did not discover in his patients a stage in boys equivalent to the girls' first-stage sadism towards a sibling, though he suggested this was by accident of selection rather than a fundamental finding.

It is the irretrievable second stage of the girl and the unconscious fantasy of the boy – the masochistic fantasy of being beaten in both cases by the *father* – that is the scenario underlying Freud's theoretical conclusions. I shall 'read in' the girls' excitement at the beating of the sibling or sib-equivalent and the apparent absence of this stage in boys, by looking at the case histories of Mr Y and then the Wolf Man.

Mr Y provides important markers to questions raised in Freud's original essay. Freud noted that it is difficult but imperative to penetrate beneath the male fantasist's insistence that his mother is beating him to the more crucial feature of the father as beater. Mr Y confronted me with a problem similar to that which confronted Freud with his pre-psychoanalytic hysterical women patients: Mr Y's fantasy had all the signs of reality. I believe it is crucial to remember that in many social groups, historical periods or cross-cultural situations, a father beating a son is a usual feature of discipline. It was as this that Mr Y presented his fantasy – as a true and highly plausible account of his upbringing. The extent of his wider use of pseudologia was such that it was often nearly impossible to tell the liar from the lie.[3] All the details of his reported punishment made perfect sense as a presentation of a factual occurrence. However, it was the *repetition* of these details that finally alerted me to the fact that, as with Freud's patients, Mr Y came from a family in which corporal punishment was not practised.

There may have been one actual occasion. There was certainly the memory of one which had the vividness of a screen memory – a memory that encapsulates what matters, fact or fiction. The obsession was with the beating of Mr Y himself, but the focus was that his father was doing this to him in order to please his mother. At this level, the fantasy, then, was Oedipal. But there was a second focus and this was that he was being beaten because of a quarrel with his stepsister. So the father was flirting with the wife by preferring her daughter and beating his own son for quarrelling. Beneath this was the fact that Mr Y had been strongly attracted to his stepsister, a girl of his own age with whom he had been both very rivalrous and erotically affectionate. Desires within real situations that cannot be psychically processed are repressed. So here was an elaborate, highly plausible but repetitious fantasy or actual scene, which moreover Mr Y could not relinquish as he would have been able to do if it had been a reality: in other words, as well as being pseudologic Mr Y, like Freud's 'Dora', suffered from 'supervalency of thought'. This reality could not be abandoned as something that had happened in the past because it was invested with a sexual gain. The presence of a beating fantasy which uses past events suggests that these past events have a present significance – they are still exciting.

Mr Y was persistently preoccupied with the glories of his own, and denigration of others' faecal products. He was also compulsively intrigued, both fascinated and repelled, by a species of frog that produced and raised embryos under the surface of its skin. The desire for this to happen to himself – that he could parthenogenetically produce babies – in its turn referred to a phobic reaction to anything that could 'get under his skin'. Commensurately there was no space in his transference relationship to me as he needed both to stand in my place and get under my skin. The model was clearly that of a mother, but a parthenogenetic mother, either with himself as parthenogenetically produced baby, or himself making imaginary anal babies from his own body – or both.

But siblings, or the threat of siblings, clearly figured too. Both parents had previous families. Mr Y was their only child together. A sibling had been stillborn when he was six years old and possibly there had been intervening miscarriages. In his lateral relationships with friends and with his wife he did not seem to recognize them as other people; they were heirs to missing siblings. As such, and unborn,

'The small child imagines a new baby as himself reproduced'
Archdukes Maximilian II, Ferdinand II and Johann by Jakob Seisenegger
(1539), Kunsthistorisches Museum, Vienna

they replicated himself. The small child imagines a new baby as himself reproduced. The obvious masochism of the beating fantasy could be seen also as a sadistic attack on these doubles. One could take this observation further but, as I failed to pursue it with Mr Y, it can only be into the realm of speculation. The speculative point that can be made is that 'the ground of reality' for a boy and a girl will be different for reasons of social practice – a girl is more likely to see a boy being beaten, a boy to experience being beaten. But the fantasy can rest, as with Mr Y, on the *absence* of that reality. In his case it was a double absence: the dead siblings, and virtually no actual family corporal punishment – the screen memory of his one beating by his father may or may not have been fact. There was, however, plenty of beating at the schools he attended, which therefore, like Mrs X's hospital stay, offered the actual accidental occurrence.

Freud treated a young Russian aristocrat in 1914 but did not write up the case history as 'an infantile neurosis' until 1918, shortly before his paper ' "A child is being beaten" '. Because of a dream of wolves, this patient became known as the Wolf Man. Freud does not state that the Wolf Man is one of his cases of masturbatory beating fantasies. Indeed, he may not have been, as some crucial details such as the Wolf Man's conscious awareness of a father's role do not fit the schema of the later essay. The Wolf Man had sadistic beating fantasies in which he was beating large horses, and masochistic ones in which first a group of boys and then an heir apparent were being beaten in his presence; the person beating was sometimes a mother-figure (his Nanya). This fits absolutely, but sometimes he imagined his father or father substitutes as the punishing person. The focus of the analysis is not on these masturbatory fantasies but on an early childhood dream of six or seven white wolves sitting on a tree outside the patient's window. The adult Wolf Man remembers how as a boy he woke in great anxiety from his recurring dream and thereafter suffered from terrible fears and anxieties. The dream, meticulously charted, is an instance of what is known as deferred action – a scene only becomes relevant at a later date. Two and a half years before the dream, it seems that as an infant of eighteen months he had witnessed his parents' intercourse. This controversial reconstruction is at the root of the dream.

What I want to consider is not, as is usual, whether or not an observation of an eighteen-month-old can either be verified or be significant – but something else: why defer this? What I want to ask here is: why dream it at a specific point in his early childhood? His older sister had terrified him into states of violent screaming by showing him pictures from fairy tales – in particular of wolves. Just a few months before the dream, his sister had seduced him. He had reacted to the seduction with aggressive masturbatory acts to his Nanya, who had scolded him severely. In other words, the active and the passive beating fantasies preceded the traumatic dream and continued beyond it. What is their significance?

The interpretation of the dream of wolves as a later rendering of a previously uncomprehended event – the earlier witnessing of parental intercourse – is clearly important. However, I want to set the dream in a sibling context. Within the history of psychoanalysis the Wolf Man's witnessing of his parents' coitus has acted as a *cause célèbre*. Freud was aware of how controversial his interpretation would be and asked colleagues to collect cases where there seemed to be the evidence of similar earlier witnessing of the so-called 'primal scene' with later serious psychological effects. Karl Abraham provided one. Melanie Klein, Abraham's patient, made observing the primal scene a commonplace of the experience of her child patients, such as Erna. For Klein, and others, it is the scene which provokes the violence towards the parents which is then expressed as the guilt towards parents at the heart of the sibling incest.

Before Freud's request for confirmation, Abraham had however already published an account of a little girl who had undoubtedly witnessed parental intercourse. The child was in a twilight state, with many hysterical symptoms and suffering from anxiety and terrifying nightmares. The father confirmed that his daughter may have seen something and had certainly heard bedroom quarrels to which these nightmares of murderous adult sexuality alluded. My concern is not to question this but to point to another factor:

> Conversation with the father brought further material to light. It appeared that the child was accustomed to associate with a neighbour's daughter who was said to practice mutual masturbation with other girls. It is probable, therefore, that, excited by sexual acts and conversations with this friend, she had reacted much more violently to the incident in her parents' room than she might otherwise have done. (Abraham [1913]: 167)

In other words, the child's sexuality is awakened in the lateral peer group.

Abraham is only called in for a consultation; we know nothing of any beating fantasies, although we learn the girl has visions of terrifying animals, like many a small child, and like a phobic adult, a hysterical patient and the Wolf Man. Freud, like Abraham, traces the Wolf Man's nightmare of wolves to his witnessing of parental intercourse. Again, I am not concerned to question this, but rather to emphasize that what is described as his 'almost insane behaviour' relates to his seduction by his sister and her terrifying him with pictures of wolves and other animals.[4] Abraham's is a one-off consultation with a child, Freud's a detailed analysis of a young adult's reconstruction of his infantile neurosis – but they match in interesting ways. There was external confirmation that the Wolf Man's sister was a highly intelligent and actively sexual child who tormented her brother. In his turn he was very jealous of her and of her high

—— 101 ——

standing, particularly with his father. Was she not the 'heir apparent' of the beating fantasies? In puberty, after a very hostile and sexual childhood, the two became the best of friends and the Wolf Man tried in his turn, in fact in vain, to seduce his sister. Freud comments:

> In doing so he was taking a step which had a determinant influence on his heterosexual choice of object, for all the girls with whom he subsequently fell in love – often with the clearest indications of compulsion – were . . . servants, whose education and intelligence were necessarily far inferior to his own. If all these objects of his love were substitutes for the figure of the sister whom he had to forgo, then it could not be denied that an intention of debasing the sister and of putting an end to her intellectual superiority, which he had formerly found so oppressive, had obtained the decisive control over his object-choice. (Freud [1918]: 22)

Immediately after this comment which follows a substantial digression on the neuroses, psychoses, personality and history of the sister, Freud inserts a brief discussion of the theories of Alfred Adler. Adler was the only analyst to consider siblings seriously and extensively. He was particularly interested in birth order, which subsequently became a very popular area of investigation (Sulloway 1996). With Adler in mind, Freud comments that, had he stopped short at the point of noting the significance of the Wolf Man's sister and not persisted in uncovering the Wolf Man's deferred trauma of witnessing the primal scene of his parents' copulation as determinative, then his analysis would have confirmed Adler's theory which made the will to power and the drive to self-assertion the basis both of character and neurosis. I think Freud was correct to reject this proposition. However, Adler's argument nags at him in a way that is scarcely matched even by Jung's apostasy and alternative psychology. In constantly repudiating Adler, Freud I think missed something different. Power lust and self-assertion need not be considered on their own – they may be an aspect of sexuality and of a death drive. Siblings evoke sex and violence; power lust and supremacy are only their manifestations, not, as Adler thought, their *raison-d'être*.

I consider Freud would not have needed to be worried by Adler's theories if he had granted siblings an autonomous place within his framework of the life and the death drives. Why should it not have been both the vertical intergenerational problem of resolving the

Oedipus complex (and behind this the primal scene) and the horizontal or lateral question of resolving the sibling complex – the sibling in relation to whom one is alike in position and different in identity? Mrs X and the Wolf Man's sister as older children would seem to have felt their very being threatened by a young brother who takes their place. Displaced, they torment, torture and seduce their siblings and those who follow after. Mrs X enacted this with her lovers and relived it in her beating fantasy. At the level of masturbatory satisfaction she imagined a lover or husband (not a father or teacher) beating a child while she voyeuristically looked on. According to Freud, it was the Wolf Man's sister, not his relation to his mother, which led him to his subsequent heterosexual object choices. These correlated with active sadistic beating fantasies; his passive beating fantasies related to his sexual desire for his father to penetrate (rape/seduce?) him – but surely they took their origin from his powerful sister's sexual attacks? Mrs X's sequence involved *both* positions – she attacked her brother and then enacted her father's aggressive love.

How, however, are we to theorize the sibling content of the prevalent fantasy of 'a child is being beaten'? When a number of analysts contributed to a discussion of war neuroses following the First World War, Abraham proposed that the collective factor of war – the group – freed men to be violent in ways that 'civilized morality' would inhibit in an individual. He compared the situation to the eating of the totem meal. Freud wondered how he had missed this observation: soldiers, like children and peers, gang up. The Wolf Man and his sister became the best of friends in their teenage years when they joined in opposition to their parents. Melanie Klein believes this is a positive aspect of sibling sexuality. For good, there is love, friendship and support; and for ill, violence first against each other, then 'ganging up' against another lateral group. Affines, sexual partners, are surely to be included in laterality rather than verticality – the Wolf Man chose his partners on the heterosexual lateral model of his sister. Mrs X fantasizes the beater as a husband or lover – indeed there was much to suggest that she chose her husband because he fitted the figure of the beater in her fantasies. In fact, may it not be because so many marriages repeat the love/hate of children's peer relations that they are violent and yet the partners can be 'in love'?

Siblings, like hysterics, love where they hate. In 1922, again worrying about Adler, Freud nevertheless suggested that an instance of social life was based on the sublimation of earlier fraternal homosexual rivalry (Freud [1922]). If social life is the sublimation of homosexual-fraternal jealousy etc., then its de-sublimation is war. However, can we really say that fraternal homosexual social life is sublimated to produce social life? Or rather, what is homosexuality in this context? Surely it is not a same-sex object choice, but rather the ability to overcome the sense of annihilation that threatens when-ever it appears that someone is the same as oneself? Homosexuality is both an object choice and an identification, and it may be more of one than the other – just like Don Juan's heterosexuality (chapter 8); it is *sameness*. Sameness is what the word 'homosexuality' indicates. Psychoanalysis does not deploy the term 'lesbian', preferring 'female homosexuality' as though in unacknowledged awareness that it is *sameness* that is at issue. Hysterics, like the 'homosexuals' at the conclusion of Freud's paper on jealousy, paranoia and homosexual-ity of 1922, are in fact bisexual both in apparent object choice and in identification, because at the level we are addressing, sisters and brothers are the same. Siblings stand in the *same position* within their kinship network. Hysterics protest that someone standing in the same place as themselves eradicates them unless they can eradicate this other first. The success of the second – killing the other – as in war can provoke terrible anxiety; the wish to annihilate or the fear of being annihilated can be defended against and made unconscious so that it returns only as an aspect of a conversion symptom.

If we reread the beating fantasy through sibling relationships, it goes like this. The first stage involves an eradication of the other. The middle stage is the eradication of the ego as a prelude to auto-erotic orgasm. The boy's masculine ego vanishes into his feminine position. For girls the annihilated ego is psychically absent and thus irretriev-able.[5] The third stage sees to the diffusion of the first stage of one 'other' into a number of others. However, these 'others' also have no particular characteristics of their own; they all stand for the auto-erotic subject. In the interests of total orgasmic pleasure, the third stage incorporates the sadism of the first and the masochism of the second.

The complicated process of the fantasy can perhaps be more easily grasped if we use an illustration. First, however, it is necessary to mention that the hypothesized core physical sensation is the pulse-*beat* of the excited clitoris or penis. From this sensation, or to produce this sensation, the person masturbating elaborates beating fantasies, using, I believe, beating scenes (real or imagined) with rivalled siblings or peers seen as children. A common nickname for the penis or clitoris in many languages is 'the little one'. The most important point, however, is that as the fantasist grows up, the child being beaten remains a child. It would seem that there is no mileage to be gained in imagining an adult being beaten even if sado-masochistic beatings are part of the actual sexual life, as with Mrs X. That the beaten child, usually a sibling, does not grow up indicates that this fantasy probably originates in the fantasist's childhood; the fantasy is a static enclave.

To illustrate this, we can consider the use of child pornography. Such pornography seems to me dangerous precisely because it uses actuality for what should be kept as fantasy. The pornographer has made an image of real sexual and violent torture and abuse of children in order to feed a masturbation fantasy that could well be widespread. If we all have somewhere a version of the fantasy 'a child is being beaten' emanating from the sex-and-violence excitement of our childhood sibling and peer histories interlocking with our physiological stimulation, then it is this very prevalent fantasy that is being appealed to in child pornography. Because the pornographer uses actuality, there is a danger that the viewer could also slip between fantasy and reality. If the fantasist has experienced real violence and/or incest in his or her childhood, then the slippage has a greater chance of taking place and hence we see in social life the compulsion to repeat (the abused abuses) which is evident psychically in the driven compulsion of the masturbation fantasy. Furthermore, there is the danger that in everyone, because of the fantasy, the abused and abuser change places – because everyone is potentially both.

The complexity – or, better, the 'complicatedness' – of 'the child is being beaten' fantasy is, I believe, testimony to the fact that the fantasist does not occupy one position only: as in a dream, she or he inhabits all the characters, is beater and beaten, one child or many, observer and observed. When Sarah (chapter 3) associates to a dream that she is frightened her brother will blame her for their intercourse, it is not only because she probably desired it herself even if she was its victim, but also because, being siblings, she experiences her brother's desire as also her own. Is this not a model for sexual intercourse in general – that the other's excitement is exciting because one is also that other? That other is a lateral relation rather than a mother or father.

The ecstatic state of 'being in love', when two become one in post-coital unity, or the ecstasy of killing, the wish to kill or to get under the skin of the other, all seem nearer to echoes of sibling lateral states than to infant–parent ones. However, this in no way indicates the need to make the drive to power a determinant, as Adler would have it. Sexuality and its repression remains crucial for the formation of unconscious processes. But death as murderousness towards self or other is also prohibited and hence the wish to kill or be killed also features in unconscious processes. Sibling incest receives a lesser prohibition than intergenerational incest, but leaving aside the few cultural exceptions, it too is prohibited. If the desires ignore the taboo on sibling incest then, clinically one can witness that all the loves, ecstasies, hatreds, jealousies, rivalries of patient-to-analyst-as-sibling break forth. They are released too I suspect in the countertransference of the therapist. Mrs X 'got under my skin', 'stood in my shoes', thought she knew my mind. But this unleashed a comparable response in me. Only when I realized that she needed to know (and somewhere I did too, in a way that was different from a parental countertransference) that being in the same place, having the same things, did not mean one had to be the same person – that there was space for difference in sameness – did a crucial level of the analysis move forward. At this point Mrs X discovered, as she herself put it, that the sense that there was space between people who were alike meant there was space in her mind. This is a 'topological' space between positions, thoughts, words; it is not an empty space.

Mrs X was then able to see that her earlier inability to produce a live baby was related to her anxiety about the strength of her sibling death wishes towards her younger brother. As previously mentioned, when she did give birth, she was so overjoyed that the danger was excessive idealization. Parental idealization of offspring is usually an extension of the parents' own restored infantile narcissism – the baby is 'His Majesty' that the father and mother once were themselves. However, although Mrs X (and, of course, other patients) did gain narcissistically in this way, something else was going on too. Certainly, the idealization was a split from the destructiveness in denigrating her mother's babies and therefore an attack on the mother, but more particularly it was the denial of her attack on these babies *as siblings*. But there was more than this in the fantasy: the siblings not the mother were killed.

In poetry, films and novels where sibling love and sexuality flourish, we rarely have offspring – if a baby results, it is imagined as monstrous or doomed to die. Mrs X's fear that her baby would be monstrous was of a degree beyond the absolutely common fantasy of all expectant mothers. But may the common fantasy not have a strong sibling origin? The 'point', so to speak, of an incest taboo is to prevent sex with someone who falls into the category of sameness. When a child plays doctor with sibling or peer, he may produce a fantasy baby with the other child but it is with the child not as different or other, but as the same. Sibling reproduction is thus a variant on, or a replication of, the auto-erotic parthenogenetic fantasy. The prohibition on one entails a prohibition on the other. Symbolically the prohibition emanates from the position of the mother – you cannot now make babies like me: for the boy this indicates never giving birth (just as for the girl of the castration complex it is that she will never be a father); for the girl it is for the time being. Laterally the prohibition may not be relevant, for sibling sexuality may not be reproductive in its desires (see chapter 5). The prohibition here relates to not treating the other as the same, to not continuing with narcissism and grandiosity in the field of the social.

Mrs X's live son was to a degree still a parthenogenetic baby and idealized as her own unique accomplishment. But because he lived, he also served as a place from which she could in time separate and thus relinquish her murderousness towards her brother. The cessation of the masturbatory beating fantasy may have been a prelude to giving up imagining killing her brother. A girl, which Mrs X had next, presented greater problems of self-replication. She was confused about her daughter's gender not only because she had grown used to having a son, but because she had both thought she was her brother's mother and because she had seen herself mirrored in her *brother* as a child, herself as her brother. So she frequently saw her daughter as her brother. Melanie Klein suggests mothers see their siblings in their older children; I suggest that such a vision with all the accompanying ambivalence is there from the moment of conception – indeed before, in the possibility or otherwise of conception, as in Mrs X's case.

Karl Abraham wrote an essay in 1922 on the female castration complex, the penultimate paragraph of which became famous. It contained the momentous observation: 'The mother's anal eroticism is

the earliest and most dangerous enemy of the psychosexual development of children, the more so because the mother has more influence
on them in the earliest years of life than the father' (Abraham 1922:
28). For a woman still to delight in anal pleasures indicates she has
not resolved her Oedipus complex, and she thus may use her baby in
her fantasies as a sexual object. Such a psychic scenario could well be
dangerous for a child – but there is a slippage latent in the argument:
a person's unconscious fantasies are not predictive of their actual
behaviour. The slippage involves the concept of 'character'. Abraham
concludes that if we can free such mothers from the burdens of their
castration complex, we will help to release the coming generations
from their neuroses.[6] The same year, in a brief communication in the
International Journal of Psychoanalysis, the president of the British
Psychoanalytical Society, Ernest Jones, offered three points in confirmation of Abraham's thesis (Jones 1922). The first, which is the only
one I will mention here, recounts the case of a girl with an older
brother of whom she was jealous and envious. The boy had a con-
genitally deformed foot. The father was preoccupied with getting his
son remedial help; as a result, the daughter was neglected. She played
with dolls till age three, when a baby was born in her best friend's
house. Thereafter the girl gave up dolls and any interest in babies,
which she still refused to have even when happily married. In the case
of the hapless little girl we have a scenario with a brother, a father
and a best friend – no mother is mentioned.

In ' "A child is being beaten" ', Freud, in rejecting once more Alfred
Adler's notion of the primacy of a 'masculine protest' and an 'inferiority complex', had rested his case on the importance of the symptom as evidence of unconscious processes at work. From the viewpoint
of ordinary thinking, a protest against being a girl and a sense of
inferiority are easily explicable. A symptom such as hysterical blindness is not – for the second but not the first we need the notion of
something unconscious at work. Freud pointed out that the formation of neuroses (with symptoms) and the construction of character
must not be confused. Yet one year after the publication of Abraham's
1922 essay, Franz Alexander published a paper on 'The castration
complex in the formation of character' (1923). The castration complex
can only be unconscious. Alexander's contribution in the *International Journal of Psychoanalysis* follows immediately after Freud on
'Some neurotic mechanisms in jealousy, paranoia and homosexuality'

(1922). Freud concludes this brief article with a new finding about homosexuality: intense rivalry and jealousy *usually with an older brother* have been reversed so that the once hated object has become a homosexual love-object. He further asserts that social feelings arise as a way-station on the road of this reversal – they are the sublimation of *fraternal* homosexual feelings. Social decency and concern are on that path between same-sex sibling rivalry and sibling love. I would add that social concern has to break down in war. Is what takes place in war and similar situations a de-sublimation and reversion to rivalry and hatred of siblings?

The castration complex is the aggregate of unconscious ideas (and the feelings that accompany them) around the fear that if one persists in incestuous Oedipal desires, one risks the punishment of castration. Although the girl is no less subject to the castration complex than the boy, her anxieties are different because the definition of her femininity is that she is 'already castrated'. Instead she envies the penis – the one masculine condition of fearing castration is as normative as the other feminine one of believing herself phallically lacking; subjection to the castration complex is the condition of humanity. This is not the same as the notion put forward by Abraham, Jones and Alexander of a female castration complex which is all too like the popular notion of the woman as a castrator. A female castration complex, correctly speaking, would imply that the woman is still a psychically bisexual girl who fears the loss of her penis just as a boy does. Technically this would imply possible delusion – not at all an aspect of a character.[7]

The papers to which I am referring were written in the immediate aftermath of the 'Great War', whose traumatized soldiers on both sides contributed so much to the rethinking and reformulation of psychoanalytic theory. It is often claimed that the hysterical woman patient gave rise to psychoanalysis itself. I would add, more controversially, that the male war hysteric and his traumatized brother gave rise to its major revisions. The questions that interest me here are an integral feature of this revision even though they are not the most dominant nor those most often discussed. The major changes in the theory are most obviously the construction of the so-called second metapsychology, that of the id (*es*), superego (*überich*) and ego (*ich*), and the revision of ideas about the place of anxiety. The buried theme to which I am drawing attention, however, is the implications of an unnoticed shift from the neurotic *symptom* (which can be traced back to a particular distorted expression of Oedipal desires and *penis envy*) to the woman whose *character* is defined by the *female castration complex* – in other words, from the neurotically hysterical girl to the characterologically castrating mother. This is a crucial topic in its own right; here, it forms only the context for Abraham's observation on the anal eroticism of the mother and the devastating effects of this on her child's psychosexuality. Abraham's clinical insight into anal eroticism is forced into the theory of the castration complex. But anal eroticism is *also* a dominant feature of the parthenogenetic fantasy and its moment in sibling incestuous play and rivalry. Castrating women were seen as *characters* by Alexander. I wish to reverse this move which promoted a shift of analysis from the unconscious effects of repressions due to prohibitions into a dangerously moralistic characterology. As Freud says in ' "A child is being beaten" ', neurosis and character are not the same. Such a shift to 'character' cemented the notion of a castrating woman.

Instead of reducing analytical insights to ideological injunctions, introducing siblings or quasi-siblings as autonomous structures allows us to return to unconscious processes. From these unconscious processes social questions open up without any need for either character analysis or for the Adlerian postulates of power play and inferiority complexes. Maternal fantasies and enactments with their babies as loved/hated angels or monsters, paternal sexual violence, worldwide wife-beating and the feminization of hysteria, war and peace: these are rooted not only in the interplay of generations but in the dilemmas which jump out at us if we look sideways.

5

The Difference between Gender and Sexual Difference

In Monika Treut's film *My Father is Coming* (1990) the hero, as he drives along, repeatedly muses about his face in the car mirror. He shows a young woman a photograph: 'Is that your sister?' she asks; 'Closer than that,' he replies. Brothers and sisters represent the minimal distance between people that must be preserved if incest is to be avoided. The photograph is not of the hero's sister, it is of himself before he had a 'sex change' operation. I want to suggest that the term 'gender' (at least in the Anglo-Saxon world) has come to prominence even within psychoanalytic discourse because what is being described is not the maximal difference between mothers and fathers but the minimal difference of sibling sexual relations, which themselves are only a shade away from a narcissistic economy in which the other is the self, 'closer than that'. Treut's transgendered hero can stand as an icon of how psychically and physically close siblings can be.

As psychoanalytic theory stands, the concept of 'gender' cannot properly be made to fit into it. There is no position for the subject to occupy that does not involve sexuality; yet 'gender' refers to a wider field of relations in which sexuality may not be a determinant. Furthermore, within psychoanalytic understanding the omnipresence of sexuality in human psychic life includes the notion that the person comes to a recognition of sexual difference (the 'ideal fiction' of normality) or refuses to (psychosis) or fails to (neurosis) or decides not to (character) – the awareness that femininity and masculinity are defined by their difference from each other; one can cross the line (transsexualism), but line there is. Whereas 'gender' can refer to

'Gender can refer to relations along one side of a binary division . . . girl siblings'
The Daughters of Sir Matthew Decker, Bart by Jan de Meyer (1718),
photograph © Fitzwilliam Museum, University of Cambridge

relations along one side of a binary division: boy siblings, girl siblings
– men and boys, women and girls.

I want to make an argument about the concept of gender that
starts with two diverse propositions, the first of which disagrees

with some extrapsychoanalytic (that is, political, sociological and psychological) notion of gender, the second of which disagrees with the current translation of 'sexual difference' as the more fashionable 'gender difference' (for example, Breen 1993) as though within psychoanalysis they were the same. First, I consider that if we are looking at gender relations there is always some at least residual sexuality in play; second, that the degree to which this sexuality does not inform the concept of gender (for example, Scott 1996a) is the reason why it cannot be a seamless translation for 'sexual difference'. What we need therefore above all is a further understanding of the nature of the sexuality within 'gender' and to see where this differs from that within the concept of 'sexual difference'. All aspects of these issues involve the missing siblings.

I shall start with the problem within psychoanalysis and then see its broader implications. In the earliest drive theories the sexual drive is in conflict with an individual's 'self-preservative' drive: the sexual urge expresses internal compulsions and comes up against taboos which, if flouted, will endanger the individual's survival. Subsequently these forces were conceived as not in conflict, but as part of a totality, both together forming the 'life drive' with tendencies to integration and change opposed by a hypothesized 'death drive' which compelled the individual towards disintegration and stasis. The clinical material that formed the basis for this theoretical shift is not my concern here. What I want to point to is a hidden re-emphasis in the understanding of sexuality as it shifted to become the dominant partner in the 'life drive' and, at the same time, to the implications of a relative weakening of the self-preservative drive as it took up its new position. My reasons for looking at this issue are not merely academic – I believe it has contributed to a slippage of psychoanalytic theory into common-sense ideology which, though it has produced some gains, is better seen for what it is.

In brief, the subsumption of sexuality into a life drive has emphasized that it is a drive towards procreation, a reproductive drive. The earlier sexual drive was conceived as a profoundly disruptive force, and though this aspect is supposed to be retained, in fact it was largely split off: sexuality that is areproductive, as in inversion (homosexuality) or perversion, is disruptive. Reproductive sexuality is conceived as hard to attain, but it does not constitute a source of disruption or 'discontent' within civilization; on the contrary. There are no surprises here!

The clinical observation of narcissism initiated the theoretical shift to the combination of sexuality and self-preservation in the 'life drive'. There can be no survival without self-love. However, in the formulation of the life drive, narcissism joined inversion and perversion as developmentally necessary but ultimately disruptive of the desirable reproductive, life-force sexuality – thus we have 'narcissistic disorders'. The problem is not that these shifts of understanding may not be descriptively accurate – it is that we no longer have a theory that goes against the grain of ideology, and once this happens, its progress tends to be additive rather than creative, its prescriptions remedial rather than radical, at least in this area.

Omitting or subsuming siblings assisted the relegation of sexuality as a disruptive force to its attainment as a life drive in the service of reproduction. It also inhibited the development of a critical place for 'self-preservation' as a persistent drive. It did this to a large degree by elevating the role of fantasy over the drive, and then by emphasizing those fantasies that determine psychic life as entirely parental ones. We have seen Freud argue that if he had stopped short in his analysis of the Wolf Man with the boy's seduction by his sister, he would have lost the determinative role of sexuality and given the determinative role to Adlerian notions of a drive-to-power. The key place of sexuality is retained because Freud and his patient were able to reach back earlier to a critical traumatic observation by the eighteen-month-old of his parents' intercourse – the 'primal scene' – the forerunner of the Oedipus complex. Sexuality is coerced into parental and thus heterosexual reproductive channels: the baby Wolf Man was an exponent of universal terrified interpretations of parental sex as the father's violence to the mother and the mother's appropriation of the vanishing paternal penis. The search for the baby's fantasies of the primal scene was on; Melanie Klein was to make it the basis of her theories.

I consider that Melanie Klein's work is a fascinating instance of the repression of siblings from observation and theory.[1] There is a significant shift in her work with regard to siblings which I shall try to indicate by charting a movement backwards from the late to the early work. Klein's first writings are inspired by the theoretical innovations occasioned by the First World War – in particular by a new emphasis on the role of anxiety. The themes were elaborated from the material of child analysis. The new theories she gradually proposed arose from her increasing work with adult psychotics. However, at the time of her death she was correcting the first publication of her analysis of a child she had carried out in the Second World War.

During the Second World War, Klein analysed a ten-year-old evacuee, 'Richard', daily for four months. She kept detailed notes of every session and in the late 1950s reviewed, commented on and 'reinterpreted' her work for publication as what became the last book she worked on: *Narrative of a Child Analysis* (Klein [1961]). In the *Narrative* I believe we can see the suppression of the sibling in the interest of the all-important mother. Richard, who was evacuated with both his parents, mentions in the second session his soldier brother Paul. When Paul comes home on leave, it is clear to Richard that Paul is the mother's favourite son. Richard tells Klein how he resents his mother sending Paul chocolates – though he approves of her act too. Klein's interpretation of Richard's ambivalence does not mention Paul. Instead she explains to him how he thinks that 'If he experienced jealousy and anger, and also wanted to make trouble *between his parents*, he would be the aggressor' (my italics). After a while, Richard agrees, but again 'spoke of his relation with Paul . . .' (Klein [1961]: 25). This time his talk is of past recollections, but they lead him to mention a recent fight with his cousin Peter; to which Klein responds 'that when Peter was rough in a fight, Richard felt him to be a mixture of the nice father and of the bad . . . father'. Richard reminds Klein of the resentment he feels about his mother's welcome to Paul when he comes home on leave. He associates to a dog who loves him, Richard, more than anyone else. Klein now acknowledges Paul but emphasizes the association – Richard can overcome his jealousy of Paul if he himself becomes a Mummy and has a child (dog) to love.

Richard has secrets; this dog, Bobby, becomes another secret – it turns out that he plays with it sexually in bed. Klein first interprets Bobby as Daddy's genital (Klein [1961]: 88), but then as brother Paul whom Richard reveals he wants to kill. As the analysis progresses, Richard makes less reference to Paul and, when he does, we find Klein more frequently interpreting 'Daddy and Paul' together – it is as though in this way patient and therapist unconsciously reached a compromise! Reading together Klein's ignoring of Paul and her understanding that Bobby is Richard's baby, we can see the part played by the omission of siblings in the relegation of the disruptive sexual drive to reproductive fantasies.

Rather than elaborate here the part played by the brother, I will note just one detail which highlights that his omission represents the wider omission of lateral relations and vice versa. It is common to regard a patient's first communication as particularly important. In Richard's case, his instant first explanation of the worries that had brought him to treatment is that 'He was afraid of boys he met in the street and of going out by himself, and this fear had been getting worse and worse. It had made him hate school. He also thought much about the war' (Klein [1961]: 19). Although his fear of and aggression to peers – siblings, heirs or replacements – feature often, they are given no autonomous special place. We can link this via the brother to the conduct of the therapy – the absence of the analyst herself from any lateral position. Although on one occasion Richard draws a fish, calls it 'Paul' and then immediately corrects himself – 'No, it is Mrs Klein' – Klein never makes an interpretation in which she is Paul in the transference relationship. Yet it is Mrs Klein who, by going to London in the Blitz, is, like Paul, exposed to the dangers of war. Richard's parents stay out of the danger zone.

I am reminded of a first case of psychosis analysed by Herbert Rosenfeld (see Mitchell 2000a): his schizophrenic patient Millie's psychotic breakdown occurred on the death in the war of her brother, Jack. Jack, like Paul, has no significant place in the case history. Death and dead internalized objects are indicators of psychosis (as Klein notes in the *Narrative*), yet there is no analysis of a fear of Paul's death, though it is Paul who is away in the army, not the father. Brother Paul is entirely subjugated to the understanding of the primal scene and the parents of the Oedipus complex. When Richard plays sexually with his dog, Bobby, is he really imagining making babies, imagining Bobby as a baby? Is the sexual drive always reproductive? For Klein, yes. But was it always so?

Apart from *Narrative of a Child Analysis*, which constitutes a single volume, the rest of Klein's work from 1945 until her death in 1963 is brought together in volume 3 of *The Writings of Melanie Klein* (1975) in 323 pages of text; the index lists four references to brothers and sisters (there is no listing for 'siblings'). Two of these four are extremely interesting from my point of view. In the essay 'Envy and gratitude', a major theoretical contribution about primary envy of the mother and its resolution in gratitude, there is one patient who experiences envy towards both her mother and her elder sister. The patient is described as 'fairly normal' (Klein [1957]: 209). Her older sister is not. A dream reveals the patient's intense envy and rivalry with the sister, and this leads to her being more compassionate towards the sister's deficiencies and recalling how much as a child she had also loved her. The dream is of the patient preventing a woman falling out of a train; the patient states the woman is herself but she associates to her sister's hair. Klein's concluding understanding is as follows:

> The patient's feeling that she had to keep a firm hold on that figure implied that she should also have helped her sister more, prevented her, as it were, from falling; and this feeling was now re-experienced in connection with her as an internalised object . . . The fact that her sister also represented the mad part of herself turned out to be partly a projection of her own schizoid and paranoid feelings on to her sister . . . (Klein [1957]: 210)

The 'fairly normal' patient is shocked by the discovery of her own 'madness', and Klein comments that a residue of schizoid and paranoid feelings split off from the rest of the personality can be found to be common in many 'normal' people. Split off and projected, they have to go somewhere – siblings, I suggest, are a good location. The brief case history allows us to posit that siblings are also at the origin of the schizoid and paranoid feelings themselves.

The other instance from the four references to siblings in the writings of the second half of Klein's working life is simpler: it is the observation of a small baby:

> From the age of *about four months onwards*, the relation with her brother, several years her senior, played a prominent and noticeable part in her life; it differed, as could easily be seen, in various ways from her relation with the mother. She admired everything her brother said and did, and persistently wooed him. She used all her little tricks to ingratiate herself, to win his attention and displayed a conspicuously feminine attitude towards him. (Klein [1952]: 110, my italics)

This turns into love for the father, whose earlier relative absence Klein notes as if to imply that had he been there more, he, not the brother, would have been favoured. I suggest to the contrary, that the feelings for the father, like those for the mother, would have differed from those for the brother. I have seen the same adoration for a half-brother who, in this case, I noticed was the relative absentee while the father, who was constant, was also, but differently, loved. We should remember too, the little girl is *four months old*. In my own training in infant observation I have noted the same preoccupation in a boy baby for an older brother. Gender may be behaviourally expressed but this is not, I believe, the point. I shall return to this.

However, interesting as it is, that is all we have on siblings from the second half of Klein's life-work. The *Narrative* includes the one brother – he is clearly important to the patient but a reader could be forgiven for not seeing his significance. The other more theoretical works find no place for siblings outside the parental constellation, except for the sane girl's dream of her mad sister. This is not at all the case with Klein's early work.

The early work is full of siblings. Siblings apparently feature even in the transference understandings. I shall discuss the case of Erna – an only child obsessed with brothers and sisters – but first I want to put my finger on the salient moment of Klein's struggle to fit them into the requisite Oedipality. In 1926 Klein wrote of two brothers. From an early age (probably before two years), Günther and Franz had played sexually – not that 'played' is quite the right word for the violent fantasies that accompanied fellatio and anal penetration with fingers:

> The spoon symbolised his brother's penis being forcibly thrust into his own mouth. *He had identified himself with his brother* and thus turned this hatred of him against his own self. *He passed on his rage* against himself for being small and weak *to other children* less strong than him, and, *incidentally, to me in the transference situation.* (Klein [1932]: 115, my italics)

However, all the lateral implications of this powerful observation are forced into the vertical relationship; we are told: 'his brother was a substitute for his parents', his 'brother's penis ... represented his father's penis', 'the younger brother ... stood for Günther's father and mother joined in sexual intercourse', and so on. Maybe they did – but Klein has quite lost that they were destructive onslaughts on brothers as well, indeed surely first and foremost.

We can see the contortion needed to read everything as parental in the case of Erna, a seriously ill obsessional child of six. In a footnote Klein comments:

> As Erna had no brothers and sisters in real life, her unconscious fear and jealousy of them which played such an important part in her mental life, were only revealed and lived through in the analysis. This is once more an example of the importance of the transference in child analysis. ([1932]: 42n1)

But in the main text we read 'these phantasies of Erna's would quickly be followed by feelings of hatred against her imaginary brothers and sisters – for they were, ultimately, only substitutes for her father and mother' ([1932]: 42–3).

Klein's reading of siblings as parents is standard practice – what makes it special is the extent and vividness of her sibling portraits. It is almost as though in order to advance not only her revolutionary understanding of child analysis, but also, more particularly, her extension of the Oedipus complex into the first months of life, she must keep these sibling thoughts at bay. My hunch is that child patients first forced siblings on Klein's attention and she understood them brilliantly while conforming to a Freudian Oedipal theory. These relations directed her towards a revolutionary understanding of the earliest months – but she maintained the Oedipal framework, amalgamating it with the primal scene. She then started to work ever more frequently with the psychotic parts of adult patients. I believe she saw and so extraordinarily described the processes of what she called the schizoid-paranoid phase of the four-month-old baby because her earlier work had observed siblings manifest in the psychotic adult – she forced what she had seen into her revolutionary, but still vertical, model.

After the First World War, when Freud asked colleagues for examples of early witnessing of parental intercourse and demoted the Wolf Man's seduction by his sister, we saw the firm re-establishment of the exclusive vertical dimension. By the Second World War this dimension was deeply entrenched, and maybe this is the context for understanding the apocryphal story that Melanie Klein told her analysand Wilfred Bion to abandon his concern with group analysis as it was leading him away from psychoanalysis. Group work in both world wars forced the lateral dimension on the therapists' attention. The emphasis on Oedipus and then on the pre-Oedipal mother was a triumph of reproduction at the expense of a wider understanding of sexuality and its many varied relationships.

I want now to relate the dominance of the Oedipal and pre-Oedipal and the subjugation of siblings to parents to the terms 'sexual difference' and 'gender'. I shall argue that 'sexual difference', the correct term for psychoanalytic understanding of masculinity and femininity, implicates reproduction. 'Gender', which is now used indiscriminately, has been deployed unwittingly to express a sexuality which is not primarily or predominantly procreative. If we are aware of this, the distinction can prove useful. Sibling relations may be – indeed in some very rare circumstances such as Ptolemaic Egypt, must be – reproductive but I contend we should confine the word 'gender' to non-procreative sexuality, to sexuality that is bound up with survival and hence violence. The prevalence of gender as a concept, in my argument, has come about because since the 1960s, dominant sexual modes in the West have been non-reproductive. Though it may seem to be stretching the point, I would include in this observation the new reproductive technologies, which seem to me to be in some ways about gender relations rather than sexual difference.

It is not, of course, that the reproductive and sexual drive economies are distinct in real life – there is only one drive, which finds different objects. I believe, however, it will help us to understand a number of phenomena if we separate analytically the fantasies into which the sexual drive moves. As Freud wrote in another context, in the clinical situation the colours are blurred; after we have made them distinct like a primitive painting for the purposes of analytical understanding – we murder to dissect – we must allow them to merge together again. For Freud 'reproduction' is impregnated with sexuality because it is the result of channelling the explosiveness of sexuality into Oedipal desires and then repressing them. But reproduction within psychoanalytic theory (and more generally) constantly slips back into an ideology of an asexual dynamic. This asexuality probably arises because (again, in the modern Western world) reproduction is linked to women. Mothers (even wives and women generally) are not seen psychologically as *subjects* of desire. In the ideology women either have too much sexuality or none at all. The Victorian idyll of woman as asexual mother can be taken as the icon of reproduction.

Confining 'sexual difference' to the construction of reproductive relations and 'gender' to the wider category of sexuality must not be taken then in an absolute sense. Yet, despite this caution, I believe the distinction is useful in a number of ways, not least because it helps explain the question André Green (1995) addressed to psychoanalysis: 'What has happened to sexuality?', and to return us to sexuality's insistent, if neglected, history. I shall contend that the clinical and theoretical subjugation of sexuality to reproduction is a hidden version of the repudiation of sexuality itself. Such a subjugation, which Freud argued was central to each and every deviation from psychoanalysis from Jung onwards, is, of course, what is supposed to happen (at least hitherto) in human history: the polymorphously perverse infant must be transformed into the post-Oedipal child. (This history overlooks deviants such as Wilhelm Reich. In other words, we either argue that opposition to psychoanalysis is opposition to sexuality, or we ignore the opposition of the psychoanalytic sexual radicals.)

What is more, our theory and practice may be moving away from its focus on reproduction and sexual difference towards a concern with gender, but at a time when the notion of gender has itself become etiolated as far as sexuality is concerned. I have mentioned how the historian Joan Scott writes of 'gender' as a category of historical analysis; she underlines that the use of gender emphasizes a whole system of relationships that may include sex, but is not either directly determined by sex or directly determining of sexuality (Scott 1996a). For a psychoanalyst to first substitute gender for sexual difference and then contemplate a notion of gender without sex or sexuality at the centre must be problematic – yet that I believe is what has happened. In proposing we reconsider both 'gender' and 'sexual difference', one of my aims is to prevent us slipping away into psychotherapies which find no key role for sexuality in the construction of the psyche, or ones which believe that sexuality is only out there in the actual world of abuse. Siblings show us just how crucial a force sexuality is in psycho-social dynamics.

Robert Stoller, the Californian psychoanalyst, notoriously introduced the distinction between 'sex' as the biological factor and 'gender' as the social contribution to a person's being (Stoller 1968). Feminist sociologists such as Ann Oakley (1972) in Britain and anthropologists such as Gayle Rubin ([1975]) in the USA adopted the distinction. As the distinction entered sociology, the sexuality vanished. However, over recent decades 'gender' has shifted meaning and come also to stand for the relationship between women and men (feminine and masculine; female and male) in any given context and on a par with race: it can thus have both a biological and a sociological dimension; this restores a possible place for sexuality. While I see this as a useful move, I think we need to try to specify 'gender' further, and we need too to interrogate it in the interests of sexuality – to not let sexuality slip out of the picture again. To do this, it is simpler to start with the concept it has largely replaced, but which I argue should be retained while being distinguished from it; this concept is 'sexual difference'.

When Jacques Lacan 'returned' to Freud it was, in this connection, to emphasize the castration complex – the psychic play of a traumatic prohibition around which sexual difference came to be symbolized. Female and male were both equally subject to the possible loss of the phallus but differently so. This distinct subjection depends on the future differences between mothers and fathers. In all instances it is sexed reproduction that necessitates psychical sexual difference – whether, as for some theorists, such difference is introduced by God (Ernest Jones) or the biological body, or, as for others, it is enjoined by the conditions of human sociality. All children fantasize making and giving birth to babies. How our psyches construct the coming to knowledge of the post-Oedipal child that it takes two *different* beings – or rather, two beings whose differences are *conceptualized* – to do this is the condition of sexual difference.

Reproduction, in dominant discourses, is counted on the side of the woman, and the fantasies we hear from patients or observe in children endorse a preoccupation with the mother. If the child is Oedipus, then it will be his mother who is the focus of attention. The repeated claims that Freudian psychoanalysis is phallocentric and patriarchal forget that the preoccupation with motherhood with which it was hoped to counteract patriarchy is instead the other side of the same coin. The recent attempt to make the mother not the object of the baby's needs and the child's enquiries but instead a subject in her own right, and to see the task of the psyche as one of subject/subject interaction, corrects the subject/object of Oedipality and pre-Oedipality but only at the expense of taking sexual difference for granted rather than as constructed with difficulty. Where sexual difference is concerned, does not one sex always take the other as its object? Is not that the point? Subject/subject interaction, I contend, takes place in the zone of siblinghood, where 'gender difference' also belongs.

Subject/subject interaction has long been the focus of feminist analyses, as in Simone de Beauvoir's phenomenological rendition of Hegel. This subject/subject interaction is now attracting some psychotherapeutic and psychoanalytic attention. However, sexual reproduction demands first the attraction and then the overcoming both in orgasm and procreativity of the otherness of the other so that the otherness of the other turns into 'we are as one' – but as a temporary transformation of the binary. That the feminine is constituted as in itself an object as a result of the identifications that follow from the absence of the phallus as a condition of the castration complex makes that fact a crucial problem for feminism. There seems to me no intrinsic reason why each sex could not take the other as object in a more egalitarian manner. But that is not my concern here. My point is simply that sexed reproduction demands some conceptualization of sexual difference, which in turn entails both a subject/object dynamic and heterosexuality. There are other ways of having a child, but not as yet of procreating and giving birth to one.

As soon as Freud had discovered and formulated the Oedipus complex, psychoanalytic theory entered the realm of 'object relations'. And as the perspective was from the pre-Oedipal or Oedipal child, the focus would inevitably become the mother as object. From the very conditions of phallocentricity arose the focus on female sexuality which it had been hoped would be its obverse. Clinically we talk about our mothers; the effort to write about fathers is an attempt to right the balance – to bring the reproductive man in as *object* of our attentions. For this reason it has been male hysteria – what happens to the boy's wish to give birth – rather than the female hysteric as a proto-feminist that has interested me, as noted previously.

The ego is a body ego – female/male bodies are different – morphologically, hormonally, endocrinally, functionally, although, of course, they are very much the same if we compare them with giraffes. Sexual difference is not always what leaps to mind when we first look at most animals. However, for humans with regard to sexual difference, the bodily difference representationally is perceived as a reproductive difference. Eggs, sperm, menstruation, menopause, vagina, clitoris, penis, womb, body hair, voice timbre, pelvic shape, height, weight and size – whether or not they directly affect different reproductive roles – are given their meaning in relation to this: they contribute to the fantasies of sexual difference, to the representations of women and men in their difference from each other. So too do clothes, haircuts, verbal idioms and a wide range of other insignia cross-culturally and socially various. Our egos are thus always sexed egos and they are sexed around reproduction. The hysteric who has not taken on board sexual difference, or the knowledge that it takes two different sexes to reproduce, to that degree is also relatively ego-less, his 'I' a wandering will-o'-the-wisp, 'empty of himself' or grandiose. This hysterical 'mirror stage' precedes the symbolization of sexual difference.

Sexual difference, reproductive difference, although it may find a resting place in biology, is no more 'natural' than the ego of the mirror stage; it is constructed as a representation; it is constructed in the mirror of the other's desire: why, asks Freud, when male and female are in all important respects alike, do we do so much to differentiate them? The answer, surely, is in order to mark psychically the sexual difference of sexed reproduction.

I would argue, however, that there is no reproductive drive – only reproductive fantasies. If reproduction is measured along the line of the woman, sexuality (in the West) is the province of the man. What did Freud mean by saying that there is only one libido and it is a male one, if not that this was so for women as well as men? Psychoanalytic (Freudian) theory is certainly phallocentric, in that Western ideologies equate the male with sexuality and the female with asexual motherhood. That the libido is male for both sexes speaks to a problem I shall look at later (chapter 9) – the problem of the 'maleness' of so-called gender-neutrality, whether it be at work or in sexual activity: 'she is promiscuous like a man'.

Because psychoanalysis has followed culture into subordinating sexuality to reproduction, it has lost sight of its own revolutionary insight into the importance of sexuality; it has necessarily moved from the understanding gained from grasping the psychic symptom as a sexual manifestation to following the interplay of fantasies. The clinical transference which should represent the impasses produced by fantasies (Lacan 1982a) can become the be-all and end-all of therapeutic resolution and theoretical research. To be or not to be married; to have or not to have a baby, the mark of 'the cure'. To restore sexuality to its central place would entail resolving the symptom back into the unconscious representations of the sexual drive which composes it; a large part of this sexual drive, even in the married couples of the cornflakes packet family, is 'perverse'.

To reread Freud's *The Three Essays on Sexuality* (1905) is to be confronted with a paradoxical sensation. The essays' theses, in particular the presence of infantile sexuality, have long been completely accepted – yet one is faced with what is still today a brief but revolutionary volume. This is not only because what it argued in 1905 was path-breaking, but because it still is. The argument has not now, and never has, collapsed back into common sense or acceptable ideologies: despite apparently being accepted, it is as radical as it ever was.

Octave Mannoni called *The Three Essays* 'the book of the drive' (Mannoni 1968). It is in this book that we can find the lost sexuality of psychoanalysis: a book which starts with the human being as necessarily perverse and which puts in question any idea of natural and normal sexual desires of 'sexual difference' and reproduction. The radical implications of the concept of 'gender' within psychoanalysis should be heir to *The Three Essays*, for 'gender' does not imply the necessity of genitality or of a fixed sexual object or of reproduction. Although gender is deployed in the construction of difference, it is not structured around it. The difference between the sexes to which gender necessarily refers lies outside its framework, and thus no explanation of hierarchy is called for – the term applies indifferently to women and to men. Analogously to race, gender produces its own differences; difference is not intrinsic to the concept as it is to 'sexual difference'. 'Gender' is the polymorphously perverse child, grown up. Its morality comes from elsewhere than the subjection of sexuality to reproduction. It comes from the relationship between sexuality and violence in the struggle for psychic survival, which at a certain stage is interpreted as dominance.

I suggest then that the morality of gender has to do not with accepting sexual difference but with the resolution of violence, being able to accept instead of murdering the other who is so like one. This self-same other is both the same as the self in human needs while simultaneously other than oneself – likeness in unlikeness, unlikeness in likeness. In reproductive, 'sexual difference' relationships, the other object illusorily offers what the subject has not got; that is not the case with gender. 'Gender' does not revolve around what is constituted as 'missing' – such as the absent phallus – nor implicate its replacement, such as its compensation in the baby (the equation 'baby equals phallus'). *The Three Essays* are on the perversions, infantile sexuality and puberty. There needs to be a fourth to complete the stress on non-reproductive sexuality, a fourth which might have been quite as shocking as the notion of infantile sexuality in its time: the sexuality of the post-menopausal woman. (This was noted early. Helene Deutsch (1947) recorded with pleasure a response of Princess Metternich when asked about sex in the elderly woman: 'You will have to ask someone else, I'm only sixty.' As with the 'discovery' of infantile sexuality, everybody except the experts has known about it all along.)

Since the 1960s reproduction and sexuality have become unlocked from each other – Freud once remarked that whoever found the means of achieving this would have accomplished something of untold benefit to mankind. In the Western world there are now very few countries that are replacing their populations through births; the higher the economic success of the woman, the greater the chance of 'childfree-ness'. Where children are wanted, this can be socially detached from heterosexuality, from reproductive age – even partially from life. This is not quite so biologically, although now reality is nearly in line with fantasy sex, and the anus will be able to house the embryo. It is not, I believe, that these social or technological changes play out immediately into psychic life. It is rather that there is something latent in psychic life that responds to them, indeed that must have been part of their precondition – because asexual reproduction is a prevalent fantasy, with many versions, in time it can be realized technologically. Judith Butler, the promoter of 'gender trouble', asks questions that are pointing not so much to something universally radical, as to a potentiality of a particular historical time in a very limited geographical place:

> Is the breakdown of gender binaries . . . so monstrous, so frightening, that it must be held to be definitionally impossible and heuristically precluded from any effort to think gender? (1999: viii)

> [This] text asks, how do non-normative sexual practices call into question the stability of gender as a category of analysis? How do certain sexual practices compel the question: what is a woman, what is a man? (1999: xii)

For 'non-normative' I believe we should substitute 'non-reproductive'. More fundamentally, I would argue that we can challenge 'gender binaries', as Butler suggests, precisely because gender, unlike sexual difference, is not constructed as a binary (see chapter 6).

A plurality of sexual relationships has been on the agenda since the very onset of second-wave feminism in the 1960s; that was the conclusion to my own first work in this field (Mitchell 1966). I now believe that the very notion of gender came into being as an expression of this proposed pluralistic programme. However, where we have hitherto looked for a relationship between social change and the psyche along the lines of a very slow alteration in the content of the ego, I now would argue for a much greater interaction between the two spheres.[2]

At the end of the nineteenth century the patriarch was the most visible social force – Freud's theories of the mind implicated the father. However, subterraneously the period saw the rise of the overwhelming importance of the child, and with it the mother. It was not only that this social change eventually impacted, some two decades later, on psychoanalytic theory with the so-called 'mothering of psychoanalysis' (Sayers 1991), it was that the child and its mother were always crucial aspects of psychic fantasy which became more dominant with changing social practices; these latent psychic factors assisted the social change. So too with the recent rise of a recognition of siblings. The point is obvious – however, it is difficult for any of us to perceive what has not yet emerged.

My argument is threefold, my third point being my greatest concern: (1) that the shift from the deployment of the concept of 'sexual difference' to that of 'gender' indicates a move from the dominance of reproductive object-relations, Oedipal and pre-Oedipal-maternal, to a gamut of 'polymorphously perverse' sexual arrangements; (2) that the previous dominance of reproduction was, in part, responsible for the demise of the determinative role of sexuality within psychoanalysis; and (3) that, although there is always interaction, the perpetuation of the polymorphously perverse, non-reproductive sexuality takes place through lateral, not vertical relationships, starting with siblings in the context always of peers and later of affines. In other words, as the infant-maternal was latent in the heyday of patriarchal psychoanalysis, so the sibling/the lateral has been latent throughout the reproductive (inevitably more matriarchal than patriarchal) period. The evidence and suppression/repression of this can, I think, be noted in work arising from the two world wars.

What would/will this lateral gender sexuality look like? How will it affect our theory? What follows are some suggestions for clinical research into this question; I will expand on aspects of them in later chapters. The advent of a sibling (or awareness of the older other who is so like the emergent infantile subject) produces ecstasy along narcissistic lines and despair occasioned by the sense of annihilation of being displaced/replaced or just 'not there'. The baby no less than the parent is entranced by the child's self-sufficient playfulness. But the other child, usually the sibling, delights for its own reasons too. What are the psychic mechanisms involved?

Instead of *Oedipus Rex* we will have *Antigone*: murderous brothers, a sister, Antigone, who knows the meaning of death, and one, Ismene, who doesn't. My suggestion of an 'Antigone complex' negotiates the life-and-death conflict of the 'self and other'. It implicates power, violence, love and hate. Then instead of the father's 'no' phallus for the mother of the castration complex (and what earlier I have argued is the mother's 'no' you cannot be pregnant), we have a sister, Antigone, insisting that one must acknowledge two brothers, not just one – even if they are different from each other and at war, they are equal in death. Instead of the hiatus of 'latency' between Oedipus and puberty (dyphasic 'sexuality'), lateral sexuality is subject to the social/educational enforcement of Antigone's law: different but equal. Lateral desire does not involve the symbolization that comes about through the absence of the phallus (or womb); it involves seriality. As part of a series, girls and boys are 'equilateral', in other words, they are not defined by what is missing. Girls and boys explore what is *there*, not what is not.

There seems to be no use of an intrinsic difference here in the way that marks the social construction of sexual difference for reproduction. Gender sexuality can be realized in transgendering, homosexuality and heterosexuality. 'Latency' has been noted to be less marked than in earlier historical periods; this may well be because the increasing role of the school in relation to the family privileges lateral and peer over vertical child–parent relations. The dominance of a lateral peer group facilitates non-reproductive sexual exploration of all kinds. But the violence that is the response to the danger of 'death' or the subject's annihilation marks the sexuality and may be what establishes the enforcement of male supremacy. Sisters and brothers mark the nuclear point of sameness and difference – is that your sister? 'Closer than that' for the transsexual or transgender, but further than that for the affine whom one might marry. At one end of laterality is a minimal differentiation, at the other much greater separation when brothers and sisters love, cherish and protect, kill, rape or simply lose touch. An 'Antigone complex' is only one aspect of laterality – Shakespeare's comedies can provide a playground in which we might search for the pleasures of sibling sameness and difference; the joy of the child in the child.

6

Who's been Sitting in My Chair?

In 'The myth of structural analysis: Lévi-Strauss and The Three Bears', E. A. Hammel pointed out that if a binary logic was universal (as Lévi-Strauss proposed) we would not need to think about it. Hammel argues that to think in binary terms is a reductive but not universal tendency of the mind. He notes:

> Analysis is always the examination of variation, not of uniformity. Thus if binary logic is indeed universal, then there is not much point in examining it, and if it is not, but is only fundamental to the philosophical and analytical techniques of the observer, it cannot be demonstrated to exist in another culture. (1972: 7)

This is a major challenge to any theory that proposes universality. It should be addressed to psychoanalysis no less than to Lévi-Strauss. In the case of psychoanalysis, though Hammel's critique is often valid, I believe that to an extent the fault lies with lacunae between the observation of the clinical material and its transformation into a theory. On an analogy with binary logic, it is absolutely true and crucial that the Oedipus complex is claimed as a universal; however, the various pathologies that are objects of study give us nothing but the variations of this. To the best of my knowledge, most clinicians do not address the universals (the Oedipus complex, envy, hysteria, etc.), but only the various specificities in their practice. As a feminist in earlier work I used the Oedipus and castration complexes as universals to see if we could explain what is now called the 'transversal' oppression of women (Mitchell 2000b); my own experience later as a training analysand did not fit this usage, though it did not invalidate it. I remember my shock when one day my training analyst (Enid Balint, see chapter 3) said: 'Oh bother! I suppose we'd better talk about dear old penis-envy.' We did – thus clearing the debris of the uninteresting universal. As Hammel says, there is not much point in examining a universal; however, there is some point in establishing whether or not the variations are each and every one discrete entities or are subterraneously related to each other. I do not consider that the Oedipus complex, hysteria, envy or the importance of siblings are in the mind of the observers. The questioning of binary logic is another matter.

Within psychoanalytic theory it is hoped that the triangulations of the Oedipus complex will sophisticate the binary propensities of fort/da (here/there),[1] absence/presence, paranoid/schizoid, mother/baby to which we are initially subject. An anthropologist, Hammel too notes the prevalence of three as intersecting the two, much as in psychoanalysis we use the Oedipus complex to indicate the move from a binary system to triangulation – a child's relationship to its two parents making three in all. However, Hammel further demonstrates that the story of Goldilocks and the Three Bears importantly exceeds this triangular structure. The story of the three bears in fact indicates the difficulty in our thinking and practice not so much of going beyond three as going beyond two or three into seriality – the problem of how to move the either/or of Goldilocks and Little Bear into a both/and of making room around the table for yet another chair. The Little Bear is a happy bear if he can contemplate two parents and they him, but what if someone takes his place? The intruder doesn't like the father's large chair – too hard – or the mother's middle-sized chair – too soft – but Little Bear's chair is just right – she wants his place. In taking baby Bear's chair Goldilocks – the older sister – breaks it. We could say that she breaks the binary logic that subtends the triangulation of the Oedipus complex.

However, was the binary ever the sibling mode of thinking? The binary relates to the reproductive parents; siblings come in sequential numbers: 'Mrs Klein asked who the second fish was. Richard replied it was Paul [his brother] . . . Then he quickly began to write lots of numbers, beginning with 1 . . . Richard, without hesitation, said they were all babies' (Klein [1961]: 293–4).

Even the best psychoanalytic theorists of the importance of recognition of another person's subjecthood, such as I believe Donald

Winnicott or Enid Balint (see chapter 3) to be, consider it as a problem along a binary axis of you and me (mother and baby) and back again. Recognition is in their work an awareness from the mother of who the baby is (or is becoming) and what the baby feels. These analysts pay respect to the importance of the Oedipal third but the marginal structural position of the father indicates that the Oedipus complex is not resolved in their theories. Lacan, who criticizes all Object Relations analysts for their effective omission of the castration complex, recognizes that just as there must be three to perceive two, so there must be four to perceive three. He introduces a fourth term, the dead father (the place of the law), in relation to whom all must find their place if psychosis is to be avoided. This relates to why death can only be represented (according to Freud–Lacan) in the unconscious by castration. What I want to argue is that we have overlooked the sequence that underpins this fourth term, she who will be scapegoat, the marginalized or the murdered in war.

A person needs a different kind of recognition as someone who is both utterly like a sibling and yet is acknowledged to be different too. The problem underlies group psychology, which definitionally goes beyond three; it is the problem of lateral identification and then either displacement or differentiation. It may be that in some cultures recognition of lateral sameness and difference has initially to come to the subject from elsewhere: that the parents must recognize the differences between their children. But the children too have to recognize each other. This recognition cannot ultimately be reflective, it cannot stay as the mirror relationship that is the danger with twins. Each child or social group must accord the other the recognition of its autonomy. Simone de Beauvoir can be deployed for this argument because she found this mutuality of recognition always missing in the relationship of men and women. De Beauvoir argued that men do not accord women subjecthood and neither do women claim it. The two groups do not relate to each other on the basis of a mutual recognition of the other's consciousness. When this recognition is missing then either idealizing love or demolishing hate or a love without boundaries (incest) or a hate without boundaries (murder) become rampant and social relations predicated on equality cannot be established. De Beauvoir's thesis on men and women in *The Second Sex* (1947) now sounds to me remarkably like unresolved sibling relations (de Beauvoir 1972).

As outlined in chapters 1 and 2, it was working with the problem of hysteria that led me to a lineal model that incorporates the fourth and beyond. In this chapter, I shall emphasize the normality of the sibling reaction – the need both for the trauma of non-uniqueness and for its resolution in which one takes one's place in a social series. Sociality involves series as well as nexuses.[2] Everyone has felt non-existent when a fourth seems to replace him and there can be no recognition for him from anywhere. The experience recurs throughout life. However, its initial exemplary instance is the advent of the new sibling or, as for the Little Bear, the sudden recognition of the meaning of the older one who, as it were, intrudes dramatically and traumatically on his consciousness. The one who feels displaced refuses to recognize the new or new-found sibling – the other. In other words, the normal sibling predicament underlies the hysterical reaction in which the hysteric needs to be unique. It is not that the hysteric is moving between fertile man or reproductive woman or, in Lacan's terms, asking 'am I a man or am I a woman?' – this unsymbolized binary is the expression of the hysterical symptom much as blindness might be. Lacan is taking the hysterical message for the meaning. The meaning is do I or don't I exist – to be or not to be, that is the question, as Hamlet, the 'hysteric', realized.

The hysteric cannot emotionally afford to recognize the intruder, who must therefore be assimilated by the seductions of sameness or excluded by the expulsion of difference. In this situation violent death or incest implode on the scene, destroying the social possibility of recognition of likeness and difference. Goldilocks, that other child, the fourth, fifth or sixth . . . in the family, needs to be read into our Oedipal and pre-Oedipal schema. Goldilocks is the sibling whom the Little Bear, *fils unique*, does not want in his family. Goldilocks is an excellent metaphor for the sibling predicament for, by condensing in her person both older sister and intrusive newcomer, she shows us that psychically they are the same, they represent an identical problematic even if the phenomenal forms are different.

Some early versions of the story of Goldilocks and the Three Bears make the intruder, Goldilocks, a vagabond – someone homeless and with no family of their own: just as any child wishes the intrusive sibling to be so that they can be expelled, but also as the older child who has been sent away from home can feel himself to be. Thus, when the bears return from their walk in the woods, Goldilocks escapes discovery by jumping through the window 'and whether she broke her neck in the fall; or ran into the wood and was lost there; or found her way out of the wood, and was taken up by the constable and sent to the House of Correction for the vagrant she was, I cannot tell if the Three Bears ever saw anything more of her' (Jacobs [1890]: 98). This is any child's view of what should happen to someone who tries to disrupt or steal his place as his parents' only child, but also it is the actual fate of the anti-social child and older psychopath who is likely to end up in prison – the house of correction.

Freud, and following him Anna Freud, regarded sibling relations as an extension of the Oedipal situation. To the contrary, Lacan placed them firmly within the pre-symbolic, imaginary realm as an aspect of the mother's pre-Oedipal domain. In the clinical accounts by Object Relations psychoanalysts (either Kleinian or Independent), brothers and sisters proliferate but remain at a descriptive level. It is not that they have not been noted observationally; it is that psycho-analytic theory in all its versions omits them from a structuring role in the production of unconscious processes. Again their *prevalence* in such processes has been noted. For instance, Freud in *The Interpreta-tion of Dreams* (1900–1) remarked in passing that he had *never* encountered a woman patient who had *not* dreamt of murdering her sib – but he makes nothing of this. Volkan and Ast (1997) devote a study to the enumeration of siblings in the unconscious. Away from psychoanalysis, in a recent collection of anecdotes and accounts entitled *Sisters* (Farmer 1999), one woman tells how every night when she was eight or nine years old she had nightmares that her older sister was murdering her, only to discover in adulthood that, at the very same time, this older sister was dreaming that she *was* murdering her younger sister.

However, what is being observed in most of these instances are manifest contents. The so-called latent contents, the story that lies beneath the surface picture of the dream, can only be reached by the 'free association' of the dreamer. The person represented in the dream is usually a stand-in for someone who must *not* be thought of in this context. The sister or sibling therefore could be a stand-in for some-one else. But equally, someone else could represent a sibling. What is crucial is that for siblings to affect or bring about unconscious mental structures they must be in themselves objects of desires and prohibitions, totems and taboos. As social presences, only their being the objects of a forbidden desire shifts them from the conscious to the unconscious level.

What is it that sets up such unconscious processes? Classically it is the repression, denial and foreclosure on Oedipal desires which makes these wishes and the prohibitions of them unconscious. The object of these forbidden desires follows the presentation of these desires into unconsciousness and becomes 'forgotten' as such. The mechanisms for instituting amnesia meet an originary 'id', which is some unknown constitutional and psychically hereditary fill-in of a mental lesion. This lesion has been engraved in the future subject by the potentially traumatic helplessness of the human condition. My argument is that siblings offer a set of other desires than the vertical, Oedipal ones which operate with a binary perspective and that these must likewise be subject to various defences and hence productive of unconscious processes. The repression of incestuous sibling desires in our culture may be far weaker than the repression of desires for the mother but it is extremely forceful among the Trobrianders (chapter 9). Above all, it is, I believe, the wish to murder the sibling that must be repressed and hence made to this degree unconscious. However, there is too either a prohibition on lateral incest or in rare cases, such as the Ptolemies, a firm control of its forms.

Whatever the psychoanalytic orientation, the dominant *practice* of all the therapies interprets and reconstructs largely within the vertical paradigm of parent and child. To look at this other structure demands we look to the hidden issues behind the many observations of sibling significance. The focus of these observations is nearly always on sibling rivalry and violence. Such rivalries are crucial. But sibling or childhood-peer sexual desire is clearly present, as are the widespread prohibitions on sibling incest. If these prohibitions and controls exist – and they do – are they represented somehow in unconscious processes; represented not just as manifest contents but as latent structures?

In the absence of siblings as paradigm or theory, in the disappearance of hysteria (and, in particular, of male hysteria) as it inaugurates the new science of psychoanalysis, and in the nearly undiscussed psychology of psychopathy, I believe we find a nodal point of what is missing. What is missing is non-binary thought process, conscious and unconscious.

Psychoanalysis is perceived by outsiders or breakaway therapists such as Carl Jung as an individual psychology. Object Relations theory

—— 135 ——

was in part a response to this accusation: it was Freud who was interested in one-person psychology, Object Relations looks at two – mother and child. Current 'intersubjective' psychologies aim to go beyond one and two towards three, four and more. They thus address Hammel's concern and use of Goldilocks and the Three Bears as a model for this enterprise. But I believe that this enterprise misreads history. With a misread history, it has a misread problematic that it is trying to resolve; the misread problematic enhances the likelihood of a false solution. These false solutions are additive – adding first one, two, then others. What we need instead is the emplacement of another structure: a structure of seriality as a transformation of a counting game.

As I have emphasized throughout, it was clinical work with hysterics that led me to the missing siblings. However, it was not the presence of hysteria in the consulting room but its presence outside in dramas of the street, the battlefield or bedroom that led me to question the unique interpretation of an Oedipal problematic. The more I consider the issue, the more it seems that what is squeezed *out* of the consulting room should receive our attention. What is pushed out of the consulting room is the social expression and origin of mental illness, and in its turn this omission allows for the misapprehension that psychoanalysis is an individual psychology. Psychoanalysis is not and never has been an individual psychology. However, I suggest that the omission of the lateral has allowed for this mistake to persist. Psychoanalysis is addressing the internalization in the individual of social relationships. However, it is the internalization of the parents who cherish and protect or could neglect and destroy and the responses to these that become part of the subject's psychic world. What is largely ignored here is that there are also children, even other babies and infants, out there in the field of giants. Siblings and peers can care for or destroy but also they can *mirror* – the baby can begin to form some image of itself through others who are like it. The social world is in part a hierarchy, but in part also a world that reflects and is like the baby. A social sense depends on the internalization of this wider world and at the same time a sense of the self *as* social being depends on an image of the self seen from the perspective of this social world. Here I want to note the connections between hysteria, trauma and psychopathy and then consider a case of male hysteria which demands a sibling reading.

In order to consider further the internalization of a social world, I shall follow a methodology that looks at its failure. The most obvious instance of failure is psychopathy, which I shall consider further in chapter 9. The psychopath, I suggest, has not achieved an internalized concept of self or other; thus he has no self-esteem or respect of others. Something has failed to happen, the social world is ingested but is without meaning. Yet the psychopath is not a discrete category – as in cases of the neuroses, we are looking here at a continuum: we can all behave psychopathically or lapse into psychopathy at moments. It is not only people who are incarcerated, as was Goldilocks, in 'houses of correction' who steal, lie, cheat and kill – in certain conditions we all do. If institutions such as prison restrain psychopaths, institutions such as big businesses also produce them; there is a thin dividing line between legitimate and illegitimate psychopathic behaviour. The soldier who loots and rapes and massacres civilians is also the soldier who is fighting for his country's democracy. We are looking at the evil in all of us.

Hysteria and psychopathy are distinct states but there are areas of overlap. These overlaps relate, I believe, to trauma. I said earlier that a crucial distinction between hysteria and traumatic neurosis lay in the positioning of the trauma. In traumatic neurosis, the trauma is in the present, in hysteria it is in the past. The hysteric uses every obstacle that stands in the way of his getting what he wants as a new edition of this past trauma. Trauma features in psychopathy – as indeed it almost certainly does in all mental states. Where the hysteric is regressing to his past trauma, melodramaticizing his uniquenesses to ensure the attention he needs if he is to feel he exists at all, and where the sufferer from traumatic neurosis has had his existence blasted by a present-day occurrence which has produced the overwhelming fear that he will be bombed like his mate, the psychopath has not moved on from a past that is experienced as a perpetual present. He does not regress, because there is no place to regress from; time is a level playing-field with no before and after, there is no discrimination, no transgression because there are no rules. The psychopath continues to live in the predicament of early childhood to which the hysteric returns and which the sufferer from traumatic neuroses re-experiences in a near annihilating present-day event.

All three, psychopathy, hysteria and traumatic neurosis, present some important and similar behavioural characteristics: a tendency to intense irritability at the presence of other people, although it is also hard to be alone; habitual lying and cheating; an inability to love except in flashes; a lack of boundaries which would, if they were there, limit and contain violence and sexuality. The sufferer from traumatic neurosis is, according to all who know him, 'a changed person'; the hysteric oscillates between fascinating charm and uncontrollable nastiness; the psychopath is characteristically sullen, sarcastic and kicks his misery around like a football.

Of all the characteristics which the three conditions have in common despite all the differences in their presentation, irritability seems to me the one that calls most loudly for a lateral interpretation. I plan to look first at a published case of hysteria and later at one of psychopathy to illustrate the importance of siblings and peers in the aetiology of the two conditions. The case of hysteria is one that was first diagnosed as an instance of traumatic neurosis. The differential diagnosis between hysteria and the psychic effects of trauma was a crucial issue in the First World War. The following case, which I previously looked at from a different perspective, was, I believe, originally part of a polemic showing how behind hysteria but not behind traumatic neurosis is the malnegotiation of Oedipal desires and prohibitions. This argument helped to entrench the vertical perspective in the face of lateral evidence. (As with Sarah, I referred to this case history, this time for a rare account of male hysteria, in *Mad Men and Medusas* (Mitchell 2000a); the significance of siblings now seems to me to extend, even in this case, beyond but including hysteria.) In comparing it this time not with traumatic neurosis (Eisler's purpose – Eisler 1921) but with psychopathy, my intention is to show not how they differ, but how they overlap and how both have a sociopathy in sibling relations at their base.

The hysteric has been dethroned by a sibling from his position of omnipotence and uniqueness, and he tries to get back there at all costs. Of the psychopath, Winnicott pertinently wrote on a number of occasions that before his psychopathy, he was an anti-social child and before that a deprived infant. We could say that, far from being dethroned, the psychopath was never king of the castle; deprivation, lack of care or protection never allowed him to be 'His Majesty the Baby'. There is no omnipotence, no sufficient sense of being to regain. But in both cases – hysteria and psychopathy – the presence of others easily causes extreme irritation, as though the other person is always rubbing the subject up the wrong way. Though parents can clearly fit the bill, siblings seem to me to be the first culprits.

To look at these issues I have questions from my own clinical practice in mind, but for hysteria I have chosen to use 'A man's unconscious phantasy of pregnancy in the guise of traumatic hysteria'. This case history by the Hungarian analyst Michael Eisler, from an analysis conducted in 1921, was reviewed and reinterpreted by Jacques Lacan in 1956 (Lacan 1993). The material is rich in sibling relationships – the patient had thirteen brothers and sisters: however, Lacan's theory, having subordinated siblings to the mother's 'imaginary' pre-symbolic realm, makes no mention of them whatsoever. Unlike Lacan, Eisler does give us the material of siblings but has to content himself with subordinating any understanding of this material to his explanation in Oedipal and castration complex terms. He subjugates issues of pregnancy to a single localization in anal eroticism. Eisler's patient appears to be suffering from a traumatic accident, but he is in fact not a 'traumatic neurotic' but a 'hysteric', and his problem is not the fact that he fell from the tram he conducts, but that he wishes to give birth.

During the First World War large numbers of invalided soldiers displayed hysterical symptoms. There were no organic problems behind their various paralyses, their body contortions, their mutism or their fits. It became a debate among psychiatrists and psychoanalysts as to whether or not there was an Oedipal aetiology, which would make it hysteria, or whether it was only a trauma, which in today's idiom would make the symptoms post-traumatic stress disorder (PTSD), or in yesterday's terms, 'traumatic neurosis'. Eisler writes his case history to demonstrate that although his patient seems to be suffering from today's PTSD, he is, in fact, an Oedipal hysteric with 'passive' or feminine Oedipal sexual fantasies of receiving a child from his father. In this account of male hysteria, as in a number of others, pseudo-trauma appears as manifest hysteria, which is understood as latent homosexuality. The hysteric, however, ends up labelled feminine in part because of what I see as a misrecognition of the meaning of the pregnancy fantasies. It is as though the commentators cannot acknowledge the boy's dreams of pregnancy and parturition and thus cannot free themselves from the notion that even psychically it is only women who give birth.

The case history then is an account of the symptoms and relevant history of a male tram conductor with an unconscious fantasy of pregnancy. I give the following dream in full as I shall use it as a reference point.

> An unknown friend invited him to come to his farm. There he showed him first the stabling, where one could see animals for breeding arranged in splendid order, and labelled according to name and pedigree. In a small niche, separated off, he saw a great number of hens' eggs covered with straw. He took up a strikingly large bean-shaped sample, and examined it with the greatest astonishment, since there were isolated letters on it, which were becoming clearer and clearer. On his friend's return, he hastily replaced the egg. They then went out into the yard, where animals reminiscent of rats were being reared in a pen-like enclosure. They gave out an intolerable odour. The whole farm was on a ridge; below lay a deserted churchyard with a meadow in its middle. Under a tree he saw a grave fallen in, and a chapel near it. He went in to this with his friend, and to the right and left of the gangway were placed children's coffins, and on their lids could be seen modelled and painted, figures representing the dead. He stepped through a glass door to the inner chamber, where stood the adults' coffins. As he turned round by chance, and looked back through the glass door, he saw that the dead children were dancing; directly they saw him however, they lay down again in their places. He was startled, and could not believe his eyes, and therefore tried again. Every time he found the children dancing and lying down again as soon as he looked at them. In the meantime the friend had disappeared, and he was seized with intense dread since he could only emerge into the open through that gangway. (Eisler 1921: 285)

The tram-man's story follows: the tram conductor fell from his tram, lost consciousness, sustained minor injuries to head, forearm and leg, all on the left side. After full and repeated X-ray investigation, he was discharged perfectly well. But a few weeks later he had acute pains under his left rib. These occurred fortnightly and lasted for fourteen to sixteen hours; they were sometimes accompanied by a stitch, also on the left side, whenever he was excited. After the second year the pains became incapacitating, with the patient losing consciousness on three occasions. The tram-man suffered too from untreatable constipation. Twenty-four hours before his pains began, he would suffer great restlessness, excitement and intense irritability. (Freud's later description of Dostoevsky's hysteria (1928) shows that the novelist had similar symptoms before the onset of his hysterical epileptic fits.)

After neurological investigations revealed nothing, the tram-man was finally diagnosed with hysteria.

In fact it turned out that the apparent trauma – the accident when he fell from his tram – was only a substitute or disguise for hysterical pregnancy fantasies activated by the X-ray treatment he had received after his fall to ascertain if there were any breakages. He was adamant in demanding more and more X-rays. The X-rays proved to be the switch point, shifting him from acting out his problems to manifesting his hysteria. There was no organic cause and the tram-man was referred to Eisler for psychoanalysis instead of medical or surgical intervention. The X-rays had provoked a recollection of when, as a ten-year-old boy, by staring through a window he had witnessed a pregnant woman whose labour terminated in a forceps delivery of a dead, dismembered foetus. The tram-man's symptoms, fantasies and dreams indicate that he imagines he is pregnant.

I want to stress here what both Eisler and Lacan ignore – that he is pregnant, by association, with a *dead* baby, just as that other famous 'psychoanalytic' hysteric, Dora, was fascinated by a mother – the Madonna – whose child would be crucified. If there is imitation of the mother, the mother is pregnant with the child's sibling. It is not just babies, but dead babies that are important both in sibling fantasies and in hysteria where sibling rivalry comes into play. The child wants its sibling dead – the psychological child still present in the adult repeats those dreaded wishes. In the dream all the tram-man's siblings are dead – though, as in a child's play, they can get up again and dance. Death is still a game; the tram-man does not yet understand its significance. Steiner's patient who struggled to become a truly creative artist (chapter 1) had to allow the dead siblings he wished for in the guise of earlier great masters to die properly and take up their place in the past, so that he could identify with a great tradition. Eisler's tram-man's brothers and sisters 'play' dead. Their death has thus not been understood; though they can be fantasized, they cannot be represented. I suggest that because they cannot be represented as dead they cannot contribute to the tram-man's express wish to be a creative writer.

The tram-man is the eldest of fourteen children of whom eight survive. When he is three, his mother throws a knife at him to stop him taking a piece of bread left by his father on the table. (Along with the patient's thumb having been trodden on, this for Lacan is the all-important determining moment of future castration dread.) At the time of the knife-throwing, which cuts the boy's hat, his mother is engaged in breast-feeding his youngest, nine-month-old brother. As the tram-man is three and the baby, we are told, is the young*est*, not younger, brother, there must be another one of around two years between them. In the dream there may be the tram-man's unconscious feelings towards a brother who was born and nursed when he was around a year old and who really died but was unmourned by the one-year-old, so that his death haunts the tram-man.[3] The Oedipal rivalry of wanting to stand in the father's place is well illustrated by the boy snatching his father's bread; his mother's castrating response of throwing the knife at him is obviously crucial. Both Eisler and Lacan make much of these incidents. However, I would argue that these must be interwoven with the tram-man's intense ambivalence or negativity towards his suckling sibling and probably another – dead – brother.

In fact, it is the birth of his first sister, born when he is six years old, that is the ostensible start of problems for the tram-man. We should note once more that like Sarah at the age of incest, the tram-man is six. It is this sister and his youngest sister, the thirteenth sibling, born just before his tram accident when he is thirty-three – and acknowledged by Eisler as crucial to the outbreak of his neurosis – who provoke the very superior attitude which he maintains towards women. He is not dismissive of his mother. He is irritable and denigrating to his wife on the model of his sisters. This sibling superiority is the name of the game of sibling rivalry and envy – if I am superior and enviable I will not myself suffer the pangs of envy of others. That it is often, as with the tram-man, expressed as the superiority of maleness is a crucial aspect which I will consider later.

The tram-man longs for children but has none. He is married to a woman who brought an illegitimate daughter to the marriage. Although he knew his wife for a long time before the marriage, he claims to have known nothing of his wife's pre-marital affair or of her child's existence. He is fascinated by hens and their eggs, by seeds or fruit stones that germinate in the human faeces left around the farmyard, and by bread dough, which he loves to knead and which one can imagine must therefore rise like a pregnant stomach through his own action.

Eisler and Lacan see various actions as indications of the tram-man's latent homosexuality. This I think is wrong; it is an inaccurate analysis of what the case history demonstrates of the tram-man's relationships. No more than with heterosexuality can we tell whether the relationship is dominantly one of identification (sameness) or object choice (difference). Homosexuality implies an object choice even if the basis is biological same-sexness. Homosexuality and hysteria are clearly distinct in practice – but an analysis often confuses them. In hysteria, as opposed to homosexuality, there is replication but no real possibility of object choice. Eisler understands this absence of object choice as an aspect of the narcissism of the tram-man's pregnancy: the tram-man wants to have a boy like himself. In fact, surely what we are dealing with here is not just fantasized pregnancy, but once again parthenogenetic fantasies of self-replication.[4] The apparent homosexuality so often referred to in cases of male hysteria is on the contrary a sexuality without an object choice; it comes from identification with the baby, the mother, or both at the same time – for instance, in the child's imitation of pregnancy and even parturition. The florid sexuality or apparent femininity is a manifestation of this look-alike identification. It is linked to separation anxiety and more forcefully, to what is experienced as a threat to the subject's unique existence.[5] The annihilation of the subject's self which the sibling brings about sets up the type of identification which aims at preventing the mother being lost – the child will be 'one' with the mother by being a repeat of her or of her and her baby who is another version of the child. The hysteric becomes like the mother (and/or like her baby) in order not to lose her.

This is not an identification modelled on a representation of her which has come about through acknowledged loss in which the image and memory stand for the missing object. It is an identification without a representation, a palimpsest, often referred to as a 'fusion'. The fusion of baby and mother in this hysterical identification can be reproduced in the later parent–child relationship when the child grows up and has its own baby. However, the insistence on being the same as the mother or as the mother-and-baby, the insistence that is to say on being one (or even being 'as one' and 'at one' in peace and not conflict), is a psychic refusal to enter the fray of counting: 'if I don't count why should I count others?' – a sibling's dilemma.

The tram-man remembers the excitement with which his parents anticipated and greeted his first sister's birth. As mentioned, it is probable that there had been three boys by the time he was three – between then and when he was six there may have been another boy, a miscarriage or a delay in conception, all of which conditions make it feasible that the parents of either four boys or three boys plus a gap of three years hoped for a girl. At six, the tram-man himself may have looked forward to the advent of a sister, but then felt very displaced by her both in terms of her position – his parents' child – which repeated his, and by her gender which would have meant people said she was like her mother, the mother whom he cannot bear to lose, with whom he is therefore identified and whose recognition of his own uniqueness and all-importance he demands.

I will return now to the tram-man's dream. It is the second part of the dream I wish ultimately to emphasize; the first part is rich in reference to parthenogenesis through hens' eggs and anal births – a fantasized mode of parturition which is gender indifferent and central to hysteria. The foul-smelling rats are surely siblings. We do not have the tram-man's associations to the dream so my use of it can only be to point to a neglected scenario. In the dream, the tram-man has invited an unknown friend to visit his family farm. 'There he showed him first the stabling, where one could see animals for breeding arranged in splendid order, and labelled according to name and pedigree' (Eisler 1921: 285). These siblings are imagined as rats, horses, effigies, dead children, letters carved on a beautiful egg – these objects are *displacements* of the siblings, not literal representations, and hence they bear the hallmark of unconscious processes. But we should note too that the tram-man is the eldest child – when he was born there were no siblings. Yet his dream makes use of replication in the world of the farm that would have surrounded the infant. If birds can count up to five, what numbers can pre-verbal infants register? I recall the proud parents of one of my god-daughters: they were pushing the child of about eight or nine months through the flat Lincolnshire fields when she pointed to the sky and said 'Two' as two planes flew overhead!

The dilemma of the tram-man seems well captured in the dream's images – the anxiety arises from the no-win situation: he is anxious because he has wished all the children/sibs in the latter part of the dream dead, and his evil eye (his envy) seems to realize this wish so that when he looks towards them they hastily get back in their coffins (or back inside the womb). Death has a double dominion with siblings – they arrive from non-existence and they threaten non-existence. Womb and tomb are equivalents – before birth and after death are treated identically in hysteria and therefore in part by all of us. But the tram-man is also anxious for the opposite reason: his wish for their death may have failed and they are, in fact, alive and dancing – he is nowhere near the acceptance and sorrow for his murderousness shown by Steiner's artist patient. His ambivalence means that he will have wished for his wish not to work and then wished this wish undone.

The tram-man in his dream has gone by a gang-plank through a glass door to where he will be able to see into his parents' coffins, or into their insides. We can remember too that he looked through a glass window at the neighbour woman's appalling childbirth. Although he would have been used to nature red in tooth and claw, to witness this may well have been traumatic. I recall when I read an account of the breaking up of a dead foetus with no anaesthetic for the mother in contemporary North Africa, I was horrified just by reading about it. One would want to press the dream here to see what is being 'forgotten' as the horror is transferred to the tramman's looking back and seeing that his siblings are already out and about: only his glance ensures their death or non-birth.

When he drove trams the tram-man was involved in a large number of accidents; he became a conductor perhaps because somewhere he realized these accidents were not entirely accidental. The interpretation of the tram-man's hysterical pregnancy offered by Lacan emphasizes that these road accidents echo the neighbour's dismembered foetus which he witnessed as a ten-year-old. I would put the stress differently: the dismembered foetus (witnessed in late latency or early puberty) has such significance because of his death wishes against his siblings, which are also compulsively enacted in his dangerous driving. Eisler does, in passing, note a link between these accidents and a drowned brother. In wishing the death of another child, who is the same as oneself, the subject's own body gestalt crumbles into fragments – it is one's own death too. The dead foetus had been dismembered in order for it to be extracted – it surely indicated the collapse of the tram-man into a state where his ego had not come together. Yet the dream is dreamt by a very coherent ego. It is as though somewhere this tram-man knows what he is doing and thinking and is not overwhelmed by neurotic symptoms – rather he is preferring the pains of childbirth to the relinquishment of this way of thinking. The certainty of his ego is probably bound up with its omnipotence. From the height of his farm he can see a deserted graveyard – he is doing OK in emptying the world; there is even a meadow in the graveyard's midst. He has one friend in this empty world to whom he sometimes shows things, sometimes not – is this friend-analyst really a parent or someone between a replica of himself and a peer?

Both Eisler and Lacan link the tram-man's fascination with the X-rays he was given after his fall from the tram to the forceps used in the dismemberment of the neighbour's foetus.[6] In fact I would argue that the glass doors of the dream and the neighbour's actual window bring together the fact that what X-rays and forceps have in common are ways of seeing or feeling into bodies to find out whether there are babies inside – and are these babies dead or alive, and if dead, who has killed them? But the dancing children seem like a Hungarian version of the game of 'grandmother's footsteps' – they become like the effigies on their coffins, the frozen players when 'grandmother' looks round. The game, at least as I always experienced it, is one in which one really frightens oneself. Is the wish fulfilment of the dream a joke at the expense of the analyst – that this is all a game?

If we now read back this latter part of the dream into the early part we get a clear account of a child's view of sibling replication: the children on either side of the gangway that represents the tram-man's precarious path through life are in rows of coffins, one after another. At the beginning of the dream the tram-man is introduced by his unknown friend (as Eisler indicates, this is the doctor-analyst) to some animals which are *labelled according to name and pedigree*. The doctor-analyst is there to name them and indicate their lineage. Eisler saw himself as analyst in a paternal role. However, the dream makes him a lateral 'friend'. It is possible that the dreamer is teasing the doctor, effectively saying, you have explained to me that each of my siblings has a different name and pedigree but the joke is on you – pedigree animals may have the same sperm donation but most have different mothers (as in polygynous societies) – so there is nothing for me to be worried about.

The possible joke goes on: the friendly doctor's efforts to explain the seriality of siblingship comes to nought – the analyst leaves the scene, taking with him his vain advice about how siblingship works and the importance of the father in giving pedigree. However, 'separated off' from these rows of thoroughbred horses, alike but individually named, there is a small niche crammed with 'a great number of hens' eggs'. The tram-man can discover another model: lots of eggs, not in neat rows like the horses but crammed together. If all the horses had in common was male sperm, all the eggs have in common is one hen – no cock is needed. His friend the dream doctor-analyst has temporarily vanished. On his return, the tram-man has to quickly put back the trophy he has discovered: this is 'a strikingly large bean-shaped' egg which he examined 'with the greatest astonishment, since there were isolated letters on it, which were becoming clearer and clearer'. This big egg is the tram-man. He is the biggest and best, his siblings are discrete letters engraved on his skin, which as they become clearer are there to glorify him. His strikingly large, wondrous egg-self has these isolated, bright letters on it – here one could introduce Klein's ideas about children's learning (Klein [1923]). Klein showed how inhibitions in reading, writing and arithmetic and other school subjects had a basis in the child's inhibited or repressed sexual curiosity – one child cannot add up different objects, which Klein sees as an inhibition about thinking about male/female sexual intercourse. These letters on the big egg – the tram-man's self – are not linked up into words. The letters are isolates, like siblings without an acknowledged relationship to each other.

After this wondrous narcissistic moment in which he is by far the best of the bunch and nobody relates to each other, only to him, the tram-man and his friend go out into the yard 'where animals reminiscent of rats were being reared in a pen-like enclosure'. While his friend is away, the tram-man can believe his idealization of his siblings as letters on his surface – his friend must show him the other side of this idealization: like smelly babies in play-pens, these sibling rats give off an intolerable odour. However, just as he sees no relationship between the individual letters, so too the tram-man does not know the relationship between the animals. It is as though he has heard the children's names – the labels – but has not yet grasped the meaning of the relationship between them. Replication too, rather than seriality, may be seen in a child learning to read his letters or to count. 'Words are like labels, or coins, or better, like swarming bees' (Sexton [1962]). In fact, words are not like this: such words as Sexton's are signs and not able to form sentences; words that are numerous but all alike generically, while being individually different, are something you count. This counting seems simple but is not. I remember my daughter, aged about four, being preoccupied with a large billboard advertisement: 'you are never more than five minutes from a Renault 5.' I thought she was worried about the distribution of garages or the number of specific cars on the road, but this was not the problem – the difficulty was how did you map time (5 minutes) onto place or object (a Renault 5)? In some cultures different objects demand different forms of counting.

In 'Some mechanisms of jealousy, paranoia and homosexuality' (1922), Freud concluded that a homosexual patient had taken an older brother as a model. He had reversed his sibling hate/rivalry into love/emulation. Eisler's patient evinces strikingly similar features to those of Freud's patient: he has paranoid fantasies, delusional jealousy of what he imagines is his wife's infidelity, and Eisler considers him to be, like Freud's patient, a latent homosexual. Faithful to a vertical Oedipal schema, Eisler notes: 'Surely these phantasies are to be regarded as new editions of similar ones in childhood, in which it was a question of the mother and father. As link may serve his jealous attitude with respect to his eldest sister' (1921: 272). Eisler makes nothing more of the sister, just as Freud makes nothing of the brother in his paper. Yet the sister's importance seems evident everywhere: he is intensely jealous of his sister, both consciously and, more importantly, unconsciously, and his wife is this sister's reincarnation, but so is the tram-man himself. The wife is not an object choice but a replication on the lines of identification. He is murderously jealous of his wife because, like a sibling, she occupies what he deems to be his place. That his wife fits so well the bill of his jealousy and narcissistic identification (having a child 'on her own' just as he wants to reproduce parthenogenetically) would also have been the source of the compulsive attraction he felt towards her – he was involved with her, he probably gave her up when she became pregnant by another man, but returned to marry her when the child was older, claiming to have been unaware of the child. He plans to defend his or her honour by killing the lover – this is the role of the brother who protects the family's name. In his fantasy she is what he is and does what he does: produces a baby from 'nowhere' or just from herself.

The absence of siblings in the theory has colluded with the invisibility of male hysteria, in particular, within the practice. We do not see when a man identifies with his sister along narcissistic lines. Yet he can still hate her and wish her dead and love her and want her incestuously – this is surely a familiar scenario in many a problematic marriage? One sign would be the easy irritability. Mental irritability is very like physiological irritability: an external agent stimulates the mind or body to excessive action. When someone with whom one was psychically fused, and of whom one was thus unaware as a separate person, suddenly is felt as not-quite-the-same as oneself, they act like an external agent: every little act grates if it is not identical with one's own.

The heterosexuality of hysteria has hidden too the fact that hysteria does not involve object-relationships but rather replications of the self. Eisler comments, 'He could never be reconciled to the idea that Nature had left the actual construction of the body, the important operation of carrying the baby, entirely to women. A further step in such phantasies is the belief in self-creation, which was demonstrably present in the patient' (1921: 273) Both boys and girls (for the hysteric there is no difference between them) can have babies – as 'Little Hans' put it, 'from themselves'. But at the same time, not being mad, that is not being completely deluded, the tram-man also knows that it is not the case – a woman is not the same as he is: hence she is seen as 'external' and not-quite-identical with him and to that degree she is the source of great irritation.

There is, however, something more interesting than this. Hammel asks whether the binary is a part of our thought. The tram-man not only does not want it to be, he also shows that it is not there 'in nature' and has to be forced into our thinking. Reproduction does not occur only from two sexes that are different/binary: it is easy to miss the stud sperm in the pedigree horse; one cannot see the difference between a fertilized and an unfertilized egg; cherry trees grow from stones fertilized by shit . . . The Oedipal story insists on heterosexuality and a binary, but what looks like heterosexuality may be psychically homosexuality or an imagined narcissistic cloning. If we analyse the variations of what makes up reproduction, the child born on the farm knows there are more ways of procreating and of having sex than one. It is not only that the child is 'polymorphously perverse', so is the world around it.

From siblings one learns, or fails to learn, that one is not the same child as the one who came before or as the next baby who follows, the baby who can still have the breast or the infant who can suck its thumb: that there are differences between siblings. We could say that this sets up the context in which the child makes symbolic equations (Segal 1986): two unlikes – baby and toddler – are alike in being siblings or children. But siblings suggest that it is also, and perhaps predominantly, the other way around – the achievement is to move from viewing all breeding pedigree horses as identical to seeing that each is different even if breeding makes use of the same sperm. There are commands and prohibitions involved: you must love your neighbour/brother as yourself and not kill him (Cain and Abel). Your love, however, must not be sexual.

The hysteric never accepts the law against parthenogenesis. He continues to 'give birth', to use his body as present, not to lose and then represent it. His body is thus unrepresented and unsymbolized (David-Menard 1989). When the arm becomes hysterically paralysed, the heart mocks a heart attack, the sighted eye goes blind, it is because these organs or body parts have not been symbolized – they can thus be used for all the myriad possibilities of conversion symptoms. The child that claims it has 'a headache in its tummy' is halfway to knowing its head can be represented by a word. A body part can only be represented when it is known it could not be there. Games of hide-and-seek are crucial in the acquisition of this knowledge. But the belief that one can give birth how and when one will is only a compensation for the child's fear that, if he is not omnipotent and omnicreative, he has nothing. The adult hysteric has not mourned the baby that as a child he cannot have – instead he enacts having it. The hysteric in all of us may make use of the binary of sexed reproduction falsely because we want to be both woman and man, but he does this in order to hide a deeper dilemma – how can he exist if there is anyone like him in the world?

The child wants to produce a baby from itself; in its fantasy, it produces its own replication and plays at this alongside its sibling or peer. Plants reproduce vegetatively: eggs, which look the same fertilized and unfertilized, fascinate and the chicks emerge not from parents but from an encasement like Marion's dinosaur (chapter 2); leaves fall in autumn and come again another day just as other children you kill in play stand up after falling down dead. Only reluctantly will the child agree to give this latter perception up, to allow that, for the time being and hence forever, loss can be absolute. However, there is much evidence that children can understand death quite early (Bowlby, chapter 7 below). The tram-man feels, and has internalized the experience, that no one has recognized that he is the same as but different from his oldest or youngest sister or future wife. But is he also playing a game? How we consider even the binary of sexed reproduction is historically and culturally different, not just in the fantasies of neurotics. Life and death are also very diversely conceived – if cherry stones you have eaten can grow into trees, immortality may not seem far away. On one level the tram-man is simply refusing his own culture's conventions. But these conventions count.

We need a place in psychoanalytical theory for the minimal difference that needs to be set up between sisters and brothers for replica-

'The minimal difference that needs to be set up between sisters and brothers'
Heneage Lloyd and his Sister by Thomas Gainsborough (*c*.1750), photograph
© Fitzwilliam Museum, University of Cambridge

tion to turn into seriality. (Although I have none better, the term seriality is perhaps unfortunate – the serial killer is surely seeing each murdered woman (or man) as a replication of the last.) Who is it that gets displaced or tries to displace someone else in a happy family? Goldilocks becomes either a good girl or an anti-social child. The hysteric regresses to this childhood stage; the anti-social child and psychopathic adult do not leave it. Confused or naughty (according to different versions), Goldilocks, the older sister or her vagrant alternatives, tries to take the younger sibling's place. Instead she breaks the baby's chair in her effort to find a place in a family that doesn't seem to recognize her needs. However, in some versions, pretty young Goldilocks takes mischievous catapult-shooting Little Bear by the hand: they don their satchels and go off to school together.

Attachment and Maternal Deprivation: How did John Bowlby Miss the Siblings?

I have long been curious about why the Second World War produced such an intensification of work that made the mother's care of her infant the alpha and omega of that child's subsequent mental health. The 'moral motherhood' (Davin 1978) of the latter decades of the nineteenth century and the second industrial revolution had made the mother responsible for her child's qualities of citizenship, its education and physique. The interwar years certainly moved the mother into a psychological role. The psychological decimations of the First World War, when the psychic casualties were far greater than the physical holocaust, go a long way to explaining why everything became secondary to psychological health in the wartime conditions of the mid-twentieth century. Wars are mass traumas for most of those engaged or caught up in them.

I started to study one part of the material from which this emphasis on the all-importance of the mother was derived, that of the mass evacuation of children away from their families in towns and cities to the countryside in Britain (Mitchell and Goody 1999). After finding the negative aspect of sibling relationships crucial in the production of hysteria, the positive importance of sisters and brothers started to jump out at me from the primary source material of the evacuations I was studying. Where in psychoanalytical studies of hysteria they seemed hidden behind the Oedipus complex or, more recently, the pre-Oedipal mother, in the evacuation studies siblings were altogether missing from the reports of investigations of the children's psychological welfare. Not so from the life and literature (for example, Cary 1947; Wolf 1945). The other day I heard on the radio a woman recount how, when she was taken as an evacuee to her billet, the lady who opened the front door exclaimed she had asked for only one, to which the billeting officer responded, 'But they are sisters and we couldn't separate them.' The image of Goldilocks and the Little Bear going off to school could be an icon for child-to-child-care of the evacuation. One wartime mother can stand for the general mood: seeing off her two small children for evacuation, she put a sign round each of their necks, 'Not to be separated'. I went back to the work of John Bowlby to rethink the omission of siblings.

An equation was made between the trauma of war and the trauma of maternal deprivation. Yet there was a paradox – saving the children from the worst of the bombing involved seeing them not as the product of nuclear families but as the responsibility of the nation and the community. The literature of Second World War evacuations is replete with references to 'our' children. Our, the nation's, children were siblings and peers – the success of evacuation depended on that. But its failures were put at the door of missing mothers. In this slippage the problem of what makes for good as opposed to bad sibling/peer relations was missed. Once more, the sibling situation had to be shoved into the vertical paradigm.

However, while work proceeds apace on the importance of attachment and its failures, the ground plan of why maternal separation causes anxiety is taken for granted because the importance of the mother is assumed to be a sufficient explanation. Bowlby did not expand his own notion that the baby lived in fear of predators and no one, I believe, has bothered since. I suggest the good sister or brother is a predator transformed. We need to look at the conditions of this transformation within its lateral terms.

I am going to start with two personal anecdotes and a very minor realization that came to me as I was rereading Bowlby's major works. Although these three instances may seem random and isolated, I hope to link them to Bowlby's central theme of 'attachment and maternal deprivation' – or, as I have come to see their point of unity, 'separation anxiety'. 'Separation anxiety' is, I believe, a major concept in constant need of re-emphasis and sophistication. Anecdotes are not 'experiments' or controlled observations, they are not about verification or falsification – they illustrate states of questioning, of wondering.

The first instance: a little while ago, I was stuck for the night in Bombay airport. My Aeroflot flight was greatly delayed, I had broken my leg and (somewhat surprising in the Indian context) no one seemed keen to push me around in the wheelchair I had eventually procured. I was thus stuck to the spot for many hours, and though I read a novel sporadically, mostly I just watched. I was absolutely amazed to witness the extraordinary screams of babies-in-arms. Numerous family members would be bunched together, seeing off a relative. The baby or babies would be held by what I took to be an aunt, an older sister, a grandmother, great-aunt or, less frequently, a male member of the party. Of course also by the mother. But irrespective of whoever was holding the baby, when the mother left the group to fetch a Coke, go to the lavatory, talk with a friend, the hitherto contented baby stretched out its arms, arched its back, struggled to escape the cradling arms of whoever was holding it and throughout emitted the most piercing yell. This all ceased on the mother's return.

Over and over again I watched this phenomenon. Then, as dawn broke, my stepson, who has long lived in India and who has his own family there, found me and started to push me towards my flight. I asked him about the babies, saying that I didn't think one saw that degree of piercing screaming as a normal occurrence in the West. Although he said he had ceased to notice it, he confirmed my observation, saying the behaviour was absolutely typical. By way of explanation, he commented on how in India there were always so many people available to look after and hold children that they grow up accustomed to multiple care. But the baby, multiply cared for, still responded above all to the *mother's* absence. Indeed, the desperation and the instant recovery from it were much sharper, more intense than one encounters in situations where the mother is more or less the only carer. Why?

Before commenting on this, I will give my second, more elusive anecdote. While thinking about the work of John Bowlby, I realized that I felt as if his work had been with me all my life. In part I could account for this by the general prevalence of 'Bowlbyism' as I was growing up in 1940s and 1950s North London; in part by the fact that, though I never directly encountered him myself either personally or professionally, I have known well a number of his close colleagues, friends and relatives. In the small world of this North London intelligentsia, my daughter was a friend of his grand-daughter and I had been at school with his daughter-in-law . . . not that I could have known that then! This familiarity was not all. I realized that although I had this background, I have a very particular nervousness when I think about Bowlby's work. I feel I am sure to get Bowlby wrong. I traced this anxiety back to the fact that on the few occasions in the past when I have publicly said anything about his work, I have been pretty emphatically 'ticked off': once for, in my salad days, making a classic feminist objection to his demand for round the clock mother-care; then later, while training at the Institute of Psychoanalysis, for underestimating his liberating effect on institutional child-care; and finally, recently in Cambridge, by ethologist Robert Hinde, one of Bowlby's most important sources of inspiration and his intellectual collaborator, for thinking that Bowlby was talking of 'the unconscious' at all – moreover, that nobody should.

The link between my two anecdotes only came to me after my minor revelation. My feminist reaction to Bowlby, felt throughout the 1960s and first published in 1966 (Mitchell 1966), was typical of the response of women protesting the *Feminine Mystique* (Friedan 1963) who blamed Bowlby for the postwar relegation of women to the family and motherhood. Social psychologist Wendy Hollway describes the response thus: 'Women had demonstrated their capacity for doing men's work during the war and *it is now routinely claimed* that their return to motherhood and the home afterwards was due to Bowlby's expert discourse on maternal deprivation and its harmonious fit with the government's desire to re-establish its traditional labour force and its post-war pronatalist policies' (2000: 7, my italics). Mothers who failed the Bowlby test were then held responsible for social and psychological ills.

The feminist denunciation of Bowlby thus had an obvious logic, even if a simplistic one. However, it is only now that I have seen another and very different logic beneath the feminist repudiation: I believe at a deep level the repudiation of Bowlby's work was a confirmation from the opposite direction of what it was opposing – a confirmation, that is, of attachment theory. The generation to which I belong that initiated second-wave feminism were the children whom Bowlby studied. We may not have been literally the forty-four young thieves (who were anyway boys) whom he studied for maternal deprivation in the late 1930s, nor may each one of us have been the child of a wartime working mother, a resident of a day-nursery, an evacuee or a latchkey kid going after school on our own or with friends to eat at a British Restaurant – but that was our generation and for many of us our actual experience. I believe that in protesting against such formulations of Bowlby's as '[the mother's] going to be [the child's] anchor – whether she likes it or not – and separations from her are going to give rise to problems',[1] in denouncing Bowlby, we were remaining attached to our 'bad' war-working mothers whom we were demonstrating were quite good enough for us. If we wartime and postwar babies had multiple carers through state, community, extended family or neighbourhood provision, we still metaphorically, like the Bombay babies, screamed piercingly for our mothers and felt safe on their return. Despite its repudiation of Bowlby and the hostile images of female harridans, particularly in the UK, second-wave feminism claimed (and reclaimed) both the mother and the child. Contrary to received notions, second-wave feminism evinced a touching love of the nursing couple and of mothers, endorsing Virginia Woolf's oft-repeated injunction to 'think back through our mothers'.

I started to think of my own daughter. When she was born I was completing my training as a psychoanalyst; she was used to my up-to-two-hour absences. When she was ten months old we went to work in California; shortly after our arrival I was away for four hours, leaving her with her father. On my return it was hard to make out which was the more distressed! Apparently after about 2 hours and 20 minutes, the baby had started to become very restless and half an hour later was inconsolable. I remembered how at six weeks old she had suddenly awoken in a bustling Italian restaurant in her carrycot which we had placed on chairs opposite and close by, but where she couldn't see us. Until I took her out of the noisy, crowded room and cradled her quietly on our own, her crying was desperate. These are anecdotal and extreme versions of the Strange Situation tests which observe an infant's reactions to its mother going and coming in the strange laboratory situation. Laboratories cannot factor in strange strangenesses. With my daughter there was my absence and reappearance of course, but in both cases (as in instances with other babies I've noted) there was also the presence of unfamiliar places – not the absence of the familiar but the unpredictability and the excess of the new. As a mother at these moments, one feels not like an interacting person – that would be too much – but like a familiar place; it is one's body, not the soothing expression on one's face, that is needed. Reading studies of infants in the Anna Freud wartime nurseries, I notice how often (though without there being a comment on it) the babies 'scream' – they do not cry. The bombs were falling. This screaming is so reassuring compared to silent, suffering babies.

And so back to my screaming babies in Bombay airport – or rather, to my stepson's explanation of their behaviour, in terms of their being entirely used to multiple carers. As he had said this, intellectually I felt myself on the dizzying pinnacle of a paradox – why should babies *used* to other carers writhe and yell blue murder when their mothers leave, and babies in the West, who are not so used to this, make far less protest? At the same time as my intellectual grasp slithered around, my body understood – I had what Melanie Klein called 'a memory in feeling', I felt I knew exactly how those Bombay babies felt. Then, back again in India a couple of years later, I read in Bowlby an exact confirmation of my earlier observation: children of multiple carers experience extreme anxiety when their mother leaves. But this time there was nothing intellectually problematic about this: such children were merely more insecure by definition as they had not had enough sole mothering. Yet why had Bowlby's understanding not come to me when my stepson first explained my observation? Why does the explanation still slip away from me and then come back but only with an obviousness that darkens the mind? There is, I think, something crucially important in the observation, but also some crucial shortcoming in the explanation. I am reminded that I get ticked off for my very standardized remarks about Bowlby; this happens, I now think, because I express my opinions childishly. That is to say, I speak from a childhood which hasn't had quite enough of a look-in and which thus returns like a symptom, a childhood of what was *technically* – that is, in Bowlby's terms – maternal deprivation. I had a full-time working mother from my very earliest infancy, two godparents who cared for me when my mother was away at work, and quite possibly there was screaming separation anxiety – except that what my mother recalled was my pre-verbal fury with her (not my relief) when she *returned* after an atypical weekend field-trip. Bowlby has been felt as a presence all my life because, metaphorically, I am the child he wrote about. Except that I cannot quite recognize myself in any of his descriptions.

On the question of multiple carers, Bowlby has been corrected by his own followers. Ainsworth's famous study of Ganda children showed that multiply cared-for and maternally cared-for children show similar levels of separation anxiety. Of this, Jeremy Holmes says:

> the evidence shows that Bowlby was just plain wrong about multiple care-givers. Going back to Mary Ainsworth's original Ganda infants, in whom multiple care-givers is the norm and for whom the Strange Situation was devised, the distribution of insecure to secure infants is more-or-less the same, whether the sample comes from middle-class Baltimore, Hampstead, or rural Uganda – the ratio is about one third to two thirds. It is only among the urban socio-economically stressed mothers of our impoverished inner cities that the insecure attachment rates go up dramatically, and here the pattern is predominantly disorganised – a descriptor which was only just being elaborated at the time of Bowlby's death. (Holmes 2000)

If this is so, then the problem must be one of a particular type of poverty and of devaluation, rather than the number of care-givers. And that explains why 'attachment theory' has an uncomfortable complacency to it – the well-to-do and the peasant in a simple society make good mothers. However, that does not explain the degree of terror and relief in relation to the absent mother. Good social provision could take a number of forms, but the mother remains crucial in some fundamental way. One could imagine that with multiple carers, the biological/bodily bond with the mother is retained more forcefully and the infant screams louder on its severance and is more instantly at peace on its return. Did something similar happen to us wartime children?

To ask this question, I am going to look at the study of Cambridge evacuee children I have referred to. This was led by Susan Isaacs, one-time president of the British Psychoanalytic Society, head of the Malting House School and of Child Development at the London Institute of Education. Among others on Isaacs' team were Melanie Klein and John Bowlby. The team had been assembled to look at the effects on child development of moving them away from home. The study, which incorporates a survey of a questionnaire given to the children, is remarkable for Isaacs' critical and self-critical reflectiveness (Isaacs 1941). We need to contextualize the practice of removing children from their families. Before the war, every year some 40,000 children, mainly from 'broken homes' or 'problem families', had been boarded out in other families. Bowlby's (and others')

war and postwar work was to stop this practice – the biological home
was supposed rarely to be bad enough to justify a child's removal
from it. But during September 1939 47 per cent, or some 750,000 of
the country's schoolchildren were transported with their teachers from
the towns to the countryside. (Until the call-up, Richard's brother
Paul (chapter 5) was one of these.) An additional 420,000 mothers
with young children and 12,000 expectant mothers were also moved.[2]
Of this army of children on the march, some 3,000 from the bor-
oughs of Islington and Tottenham went to Cambridge and formed
the pool from which Isaacs' survey was drawn.

What interests me is that this evacuation was relatively successful.
Parents missed children, children were homesick, but one clearly noted
difficulty was the pain experienced by parents because their children
had adapted so well to their new families; this was particularly true
of the young children – adolescents found it harder. However,
despite this, using this research for his later work for the United
Nations, *Maternal Care and Mental Health*, Bowlby emphasized that
the children 'suffered deprivation and were not yet emotionally self-
supporting' and noted how 'teachers reported that homesickness
was prevalent and power of concentration on schoolwork declined'
(Bowlby 1951: 28). This is true. But teachers also noted – and Bowlby
does not remark on this – not only improved health and personal
appearance, but better relationships with teachers and peers, a widen-
ing of interests and a tremendous increase in self-reliance (Isaacs
1941). Can we, perhaps somewhat poetically, imagine these children
sobbing into their pillows at night but happy, alert and friendly during the day? Answering the questionnaires, the children don't *say*
they most miss their mothers: what they mention is their cats, their
dogs, their toys and, above all, their siblings. Are they older versions
of my screaming Bombay babies whose dependence on their mothers
seems so natural as to be biological? I am reminded too of work by
the Balints which led them to compare and contrast neurotic and
psychotic patients in individual analytic treatment with patients in
group therapy: the first gained insight, the second achieved greater
maturity (Balint et al. 1993). The evacuees – like participants in group
therapy, but unlike patients with a special single relationship to a
single 'mother analyst' – became more mature in a positive way.
There may be a quasi-biological pain for the absent mother of early
infancy, but much goes on as well as this. These observations on

social versus psychic gains impact directly on the question of psychoanalysis itself. What is it seeking to achieve? The everyday assumption by outsiders that the treatment is self-indulgence should be countered because it is – or should be – a tough and painful procedure. However, this criticism's other side may have pertinence – the prevalence of psychopathy suggests that its virtual omission from psychoanalytic theory is matched by how widespread it is in the community. Does it escape the consulting room? (See also chapter 8.)

There is no doubt in my mind that Bowlby was socially concerned – concerned how children would live in a society; where Klein focuses on the child's self and then on its relationship within the family, Bowlby has in mind the wider world. Bowlby's place as a psychoanalyst seems somewhat ironic. Because he was unconcerned with the trials and tribulations of subjectivity, most psychoanalysts – anyway at the time I made my slightly disparaging remarks at the Institute of Psychoanalysis – kept his work at a distance. But he has also had his fair share of opprobrium from commentators such as Eysenck simply on the grounds that he *was* a psychoanalyst. It seems to me to be evident that Bowlby himself thought of his work as falling within the confines of psychoanalysis, and that this was important to him: 'Enough has been said, it is hoped, to show that recognition of attachment behaviour, sexual behaviour, and parental behaviour as distinct systems in no way imperils the fruits of psychoanalytic theory' (Bowlby 1969: 234). In particular, Bowlby refers his own theory to Freud's 1926 essay *Inhibition, Symptoms and Anxiety*, of which, rather quaintly, he writes: 'Not until his seventieth year did [Freud] clearly perceive separation and loss as a principal source of the processes to which he had devoted half a lifetime of study. But by then psychoanalytic theory was established' (Bowlby [1973]: 48).[3]

Inhibitions, Symptoms and Anxiety is, in fact, a remarkable volume, rich in its difficulty – a difficulty not of its theories, but of Freud's exposure of his own clinical and intellectual struggles.[4] In it, among other issues, Freud reconsiders the relationship of sexuality and anxiety. Instead of anxiety being the outcome of unsatisfactory sexual repression, as he had argued earlier, it comes, so to speak, 'first', acting as a signal of danger. For Freud, that of which anxiety gives warning is a danger both within and without – instincts present internal dangers and prohibitions against them indicate external dangers. For Klein this danger was almost entirely from within – her emphasis is on the effects of our innate envy and destructiveness. For Bowlby it was a danger from without – from what he designates 'predators'. I doubt if Freud, whether or not he grasped the import of separation and loss only in his later years, would have subscribed to Bowlby's development of this argument – which does not, of course, invalidate it, but simply situates it as something different. Freud's volume has no truck with the contention to which he had earlier given house-room: this was Otto Rank's notion that it is not sexuality, but the trauma of human birth that produces the anxiety that underlies all neuroses ([1924]). Freud did not believe it is birth, but nor, I think, did he consider it is separation in quite the way Bowlby later suggested.

The concept of 'separation anxiety' in Freud's work is an interesting one. Here I wish to draw attention to the fact that it comes up as a challenge to the notion of castration anxiety from the side of the girl; put crudely, how can a girl, who is 'already castrated' (that is, has no penis), feel castration anxiety? The girl must, Freud argues, rather feel the danger of loss of love, love primarily from the father to whom she has Oedipally turned. What is being introduced with 'separation anxiety' comes, then, from the side of femininity. But it is the reference point too for siblings. In so far as they get a look-in for Freud, siblings are seeking the fair distribution of love from their parents. I should make it clear that these links between Freud's notion of separation anxiety, femininity and siblings are mine – not Freud's. But it is important that for Freud there is no such thing as 'separation anxiety' without sexuality – they are not, as for Bowlby, different systems. Furthermore, loss of a person, of the crucial human object, Freud points out, causes not anxiety but pain. There is intense pain in the face of the eight- to ten-month-old baby suffering so-called 'stranger anxiety'; in the heart too of any mourner, it is pain that is felt. Anxiety forewarns of the dangers of separation; pain greets the loss. The pain within the baby's fearful response to the stranger's face may then indicate that the new face means the old face (of mother) has been lost – the anxiety is the fear that something is going to happen, not that it has happened. Commensurately one could say – though no one does – that the girl feels pain, not anxiety, that there is no penis. In so far as she is expressing 'castration *anxiety*', I believe it is because she is psychically bisexual and is preserving the illusion that she has a penis which she is in danger of losing. If she experiences pain it is because she is mourning its absence.

I cannot pursue this important question of pain and anxiety further here. I am not at this point interested in the differences between Freud's and Bowlby's concepts but rather in why this particular text of Freud's is Bowlby's psychoanalytic reference point. I am sure that 'separation anxiety' is the reason for his explicit conscious interest, but there is something latent too. *Inhibitions, Symptoms and Anxiety*, though written in 1926, seems to me to be deeply informed by questions left over from the advent of traumatic neuroses and psychoneuroses during the Great War. It is not like the earlier efficient reorganization, *The Ego and the Id* (1923), or even like the labile, intellectually fluid *Beyond the Pleasure Principle* (1920). *Inhibitions, Symptoms and Anxiety* is a troubled text in which Freud feels that there are few old certainties left; yet here, as elsewhere, he clearly maintains the distinction between traumatic neurosis and hysteria – between a state provoked by a specific event and one that treats a prohibition or a limitation of wish fulfilment as a traumatic experience. Yet Bowlby, some fifty years later, was to write:

> When mislocation [of the dead figure] is within the self, a condition of hypochondria or hysteria may on occasion be diagnosed. When the mislocation is within another person a diagnosis of hysterical or psychopathic behaviour may be given. *Such terms are of no great value.* What matters is that the condition be recognised as one of failed mourning, and as a result of a mislocation of the lost person's presence. (Bowlby [1980]: 161, my italics)

For Bowlby, traumatic neurosis and psychoneurosis are not meaningful kept separate. Coping with loss blurs any psychic distinctions. This argument here has crucial implications. At the opening of volume 1 of the trilogy *Attachment and Loss*, Bowlby (1969) asserts how his theory reverses psychoanalytic methodology. In classical psychoanalysis a patient's symptom is retraced to a possible event in which there may be a kernel of reality but the significance of which is its psychic elaboration. Bowlby's theory starts with the trauma and moves prospectively; it is thus predictive rather than retrospective. It is in this way that his work assumes social responsibility – we can take preventive action if we are looking forward. However, this begs the question – or leaves it wide open – of the hypochondriac, hysterical or psychopathic adult who can only change their future by changing their past. The transference takes on a new dimension here as else-where. In all cases, the pathogenic agent is the loss of a mother-figure. Although here Bowlby is writing of actual death, there seems to be in his theory an elision between death that causes pain and must be mourned and separation which properly speaking causes anxiety in anticipation of danger. Surely only if separation is experi-enced as an already established loss is there pain?

Structurally speaking, this event of separation-as-loss, then, resem-bles not only Otto Rank's notion of the trauma of birth as the cause of humankind's psychic woes ([1924]), but also, of course, Freud's own 'discovery' of the event of parental sexual seduction underlying the history of hysteria. Again, this does not mean it is wrong – quite the contrary. But it does give it a special status. Freud argued that at the beginning of life there is something traumatic – something breaks the protective boundaries and, as it were, implodes within. Bowlby's trauma of maternal loss comes later than neonatal life because attach-ment behaviour is slow to develop in prematurely born humans. Attachment starts to build up in the first month; separation anxiety is intense and what is feared is given by Bowlby the generic name of 'a predator'. Because of the possible predator, separation produces anxiety, not pain.

My mother died a few years ago in what she called 'extreme old age'. She left my daughter, her granddaughter, the diaries she had written most of her adult life. As part of my own mourning process, I read most of them. When I was born my mother was a botanist, researching and teaching in New Zealand. She would take me, a baby of a few months, into the bush with her when she went on forays with her students. One time she comments on how wonderful it is to be able to leave me sleeping outside the hut while everyone goes off in search of rare plants – she can leave me because in New Zealand there are no dangerous animals whatsoever. As I read, I found my baby self protesting: didn't she know that if I woke I would not know the spider was not poisonous, the Kiwi not a vulture and the lamb not a lion? For the neonate and beyond, the world may at times dance with harmonies, but I agree with Bowlby, it is also a very frightening place.

What Bowlby, I think, is talking about is the trauma in a traumatic neurosis. He then finds this actual trauma at the core of a psycho-neurosis. For the Freud of *Inhibitions, Symptoms and Anxiety*, although there may be a traumatic event in both psychoneuroses and traumatic neuroses, the two conditions are not alike. In the first, the trauma produces the response which if not helped, can become pathological, as Bowlby describes. But in the second something else – the sexual drive and desire – has intervened, been prohibited, repressed and the repression has failed. To use an old term, Bowlby is describing an 'actual' neurosis – and indeed, he actually finds, for instance, that Little Hans's mother really threatened to leave him and, as in many another heart-rending case which Bowlby recites, the little boy is not only frightened but has his fear misperceived and misinterpreted. There is no doubt parents say terrible things and usually can only perceive such things when they are said by other people. I remember being in Rome with a young baby and commenting to the friends we were staying with how pleasurable it was, as everyone seemed so kind to mothers and babies. My friend took me out into the courtyard and made me listen to the yelling at babies from the apartments around. She translated – it was a battlefield of violent threats and verbal abuse.

In volume 3 of the trilogy, Bowlby's reliance on ethology gives way to a use of sociological studies (Bowlby [1980]). At first I thought this switch of base gave me a pleasure which was additional to the book's important focus on failed mourning. Yet, to my surprise, I missed the ethology. I was worried by my reaction – I remembered how as a young feminist I had found abhorrent the 'me Tarzan, you Jane', the biological determinism of the Tygers and Foxes of the late 1950s and early 1960s. Was my pleasure now in Bowlby's use of similar ethology due to the fact that I have since come to know and respect the work and person of his collaborator, Robert Hinde, or was it an instance of calm of mind, all passion spent, of getting older and liking to feel we are all on some prehistoric continuum – a kind of compensation for the lost consolations of religion? And then I realized: it was precisely for that which his contemporaries criticized him that Bowlby was so interesting. The ethology is about a universal, common situation. There is nothing individual or subjective about the universal expression of separation anxiety – it is exactly a generic response to incipient trauma common to primates, and maybe to less complex forms of life, for instance to Hinde's birds for which Bowlby has been derided. Not birth, not sexual seduction, but the loss or threatened loss of the figure who protects against predators would seem a suitable candidate for a generalized original trauma. However, from this promising start, Bowlby seems to me to drop one half of his perception: someone must care for and protect, but from whom or what must the baby be protected? There is a tautology at work, the argument turns around on itself, the danger of the predator becomes instead the danger of the loss of the carer.

Were the babies screaming in Bombay airport, with their multiple and clearly loving care-givers, thus simply experiencing inadequate attachment to one constant figure, as Bowlby would interpret the behaviour? Yes and no. Maybe it was a mass instance of the disorganized attachment of impoverished urban living. Maybe it was due to the too sudden oscillation of attention, an absence, stimulation and abandonment which somehow the mother's absence signified. Yet maybe it had to do with the degree and type of danger – the predator, the strange environment, the *excess*. In *The God of Small Things* (chapter 3 above), Arundhati Roy poignantly describes and presents how Indians live in the proximity of trauma every moment of their lives. Large-scale trauma dwarfs personal tragedy:

> He [an American husband] didn't know that in some places, like the country Rahel came from, various kinds of despair competed for primacy. And that *personal* despair could never be desperate enough. That something happened when personal turmoil dropped by at the wayside shrine of the vast, violent, circling, draining, ridiculous, insane, unfeasible, public turmoil of a nation . . . Nothing much mattered. And the less it mattered, the less it mattered. It was never important enough. Because Worse Things had happened. In the country that she came from, poised forever between the terror of war and the horror of peace, Worse Things kept happening. (Roy 1997: 19)

The recent earthquake in Gujarat and subsequent religious riots make this vivid. A journalist, Michaela Wrong, recently lambasted those who were comparing the British floods, rail disasters and so on to conditions in the Third World; she quoted a friend in a phrase that has become all too common: 'To live in Kinshasa is like swimming among sharks.' The infants in the London wartime nurseries who did not cry but screamed were living in the Blitz.

The evacuee children from Islington and Tottenham were being moved out of what was effectively to become a war zone. In the presence of predators or equivalent dangers, multiple carers would seem a good investment – as the developing world develops, in sub-Saharan Africa at least, the rate of infantile deaths and malnourishment is rising: mothers die. AIDS has produced the 'child-headed' family. The attachment of the Bombay babies may be insecure not because, or not *only* because, it is not a solitary 'organized' attachment, but because there are simply more dangers out there than in an English garden; the strange situation always threatens the wretched of the earth or the distressed of the cities. Worse Things had happened. The child who screams may be making a healthy bid for its own importance before 'Nothing much mattered. And the less it mattered, the less it mattered. It was never important enough.' Danger threatens above all the migrant just as it also produces the migrant, who must get away from the excess of poverty or war but can get away only to an utterly new and therefore excessive place. It is the overwhelming qualities of the strange place that make the mother-as-safe-place essential. But this becomes confused and the argument bites its own tail, so that the excess of the strange place is made to equal the lost mother.

Bowlby's work was crucial for arguing what ought to be, but to some extent this was at the cost of what is. The Isaacs' study, which is not didactic or programmatic as is the work which Bowlby subsequently produced for the United Nations, nevertheless ultimately missed the opportunity of analysing what is there as opposed to what is not there. By and large the children adjusted to safe havens; those that did not, did not find them safe.

Who are these multiple carers, too quickly labelled mother substitutes? Writing up her experiences of the children in her wartime residential nurseries, Anna Freud noted how children who had had very disturbed experiences formed stronger lateral than vertical relationships. This was particularly marked in a group of Holocaust children who, deprived of all else, had formed a cohesive, supportive sibling family. To Anna Freud, as to her father, in a normal situation the Oedipal parental family relations come first and then spread out to the siblings. Anna Freud noted the reverse movement but decided it must be the hallmark of the problem situation.

That sibling groups represent something pathological was clearly a postwar anxiety that continued through the 1950s – it informs novels such as William Golding's *Lord of the Flies* (1954). Such pathologizing is, however, interesting. It is, I believe, the result of explaining faulty sibling relations in terms not of potentially good sibling relations, but in terms of failed mothering. If we transfer this explanation of the insufficient mother to the Bombay babies, it would be hypothetically to pathologize a population. When the mothers in the airport returned, the babies instantly calmed down in the arms of whomsoever they were with – they did not need to go to their mothers.

I suggest that although there are indeed true mother substitutes, such as an adoptive mother or a foster mother or a father who mothers, nevertheless the extension of the term to anyone who takes care of a baby indicates a misleading matricentrism. In fact, these other carers who are not mother substitutes do get an occasional look-in in Bowlby's work, although even in these instances their presence is used to make a different point once more about *mothering*: 'That an infant can become attached *to others of the same age, or only a little older*, makes it plain that attachment behaviour can develop or be directed towards a figure who has done nothing to meet the infant's physiological needs' (Bowlby 1969: 217, my italics).

These attachment figures to whom Bowlby refers are the same age or a little older. We need to realize there is another dimension in states of separation anxiety. Among the evacuee children, accompaniment even by a younger sibling diminished separation anxiety. Among Rhesus monkeys, Bowlby notes, sons and daughters stay close together. What for Bowlby, with his intense matricentrism, are 'sons and daughters', looked at from elsewhere are of course brothers and sisters or half-brothers and half-sisters. Baboons engage in social play with peers at around four months and by six months their play 'absorbs a large part of the young baboon's time and attention'. Yet they are not weaned until ten months; in other words, lateral relations are crucial at the height of 'mother-attachment'.

In polygynous societies, in contemporary reconstituted families in the West, in families such as Freud's which were structured by the prevalence of maternal deaths, aunts and uncles may be younger than their nieces and nephews. From the infant's point of view, distinction of category may be irrelevant; even from our point of view a description may not match an analytical category. These multiple carers may be both 'vertical' and 'lateral' kith and kin. Servants, even young nannies or au pairs, may well be considered lateral carers as well as vertical mother substitutes. Child-minders care for several children who frequently become close friends – who is to say that the vertical protection or love is more important than the lateral?

I find Bowlby muddled about sibling significance as Freud was after the First World War. I suggest wars force lateral relations on to a resistant theory and practice, leaving these theoreticians confused in this respect. Bowlby claims, for example, that sibling death in adult life rarely causes disordered mourning – this is not my own clinical experience, nor is it my impression from reading case histories, nor is it Freud's experience of the Wolf Man's response to the death of his sister. And Bowlby himself notes that fighter pilots court the same fate as a dead mate – what are these mates if not fraternal, what is this imitation of death if not disturbed mourning? Surely this is an instance of what Bowlby himself would have explained as the 'mislocation' of the dead person in the subject himself, as in hysteria, or hypochondria, or psychopathy. He also asserts that a sibling death in childhood affects the surviving children not in itself but only through the parents' changed behaviour. It is almost as though the urge to 'verticalize' has created an observational blind spot in this superb watcher of children. He notes, for instance, that when a child whom he names 'Lottie' is left at nursery school, she 'turns into' her sister, 'Dorrie' (Bowlby [1973]: 50). He writes of the child's circumstances:

> Mother's pregnancy and the expectation of a new baby can also be ruled out as anything but minor factors. In the first place . . . children whose mothers are not pregnant habitually show typical responses when they are separated. In the second . . . it was possible to make a direct comparison of the behaviour of thirteen children whose mothers were about to have a new baby with that of five children whose mothers were not pregnant. When a detailed comparison was made of the ways in which children in these two groups behaved during the first fortnight of their separation, no significant differences were found between them. (Bowlby 1969: 33)

And yet he also notes – and here I introduce the centrepiece of my thesis:

> In most young children the mere sight of mother holding another baby in her arms is enough to elicit strong attachment behaviour. The older child insists on remaining close to his mother, or climbing in her lap. Often he behaves as though he were a baby. It is possible that this

well-known behaviour is only a special case of a child reacting to mother's lack of responsiveness to him. *The fact, however, that an older child often reacts in this way even when the mother makes a point of being attentive and responsive suggests that more is involved.* (Bowlby 1969: 260–1, my italics)

I suggest there is indeed 'more involved'. Threatened by a strange lump in her mother's belly, Lottie, suspecting another sister, hopes it will be like one who has become familiar – Dorrie – or she hopes that she will be Dorrie and able to cope with the arrival of a new Lottie. May it not be that premature and unresolved separation from a maternal attachment figure produces a core situation for the development of what I have called an actual neurosis, and then that the advent of a sibling is exactly a new instance of this trauma? The sibling (or peer) who replicates one, in doing so threatens one's existence – who am I if there is another daughter, son, baby, teacher's pet . . . ? Hate for the rival comes before love for the playmate. Love comes as the unknown becomes familiar. I suggest that here, in the superimposition of this sibling trauma – the trauma of the sibling's presence – on the trauma of the unthought predator risked by maternal separation, the core not of an actual but of a psychoneurosis can be found. The first 'predator' is experienced through affects; the sibling demands thought. The incest and the murderousness, the positive love and the positive hate of lateral relationships set their own demands and need their own resolutions alongside the incest and murderousness, love and hate of Oedipal and castration complexes. From the dilemmas of laterality also comes the psychic transformation revealed in the symptom, the Freudian unconscious, the compulsion to repeat and the drivenness of the drive.

And here I join my beginning. For me, Bowlby – concerned, caring, endlessly creative, thoughtful and intelligent – is a great innovator. But Bowlby, maybe because he missed his own mother when he was a child,[5] made good the loss of mothers in his theory but lost what was good about siblings, which he enacted in his excellent relationships with peers but ignored in his understanding. There is no question in my mind that mothers matter; but they should not be used to answer other problems – the problem of the predator, the trauma of the excess. By 'not be used' I am not referring to the morality but to the logic at stake. That the trauma became the loss of she who should protect from the trauma has had many unfortunate consequences – one of which was the 1950s attempt to produce 'supermum' and the condemnation of mothers who did not fit the prescription. At stake is an absurdity – no Mother is a King Canute who can stop the waves of an earthquake, a war, or a cruel society. As with her giving birth to the child's sibling, she can only mitigate the effects if we look at them not her. This is what the evacuation plans so usefully tried to do.

I want to pay respects to, and recall affectionately, the sisters and brothers (actual and metaphorical), the friends and mates at nursery school and on the street with whom I fought and played, screamed and laughed, shared and half-enjoyed the infectious illnesses then so prevalent, while our mothers whom we adored as they adored us worked away from home and the bombs fell. The presence and memory of the richness of lateral relationships are an underestimated part of the fabric of psychic and social life.

—— 8 ——

In our Own Times: Sexuality, Psychoanalysis and Social Change

There have been considerable changes in family patterns since the 1960s, yet the work of psychoanalysts in this area uses theories and information either as old as the discipline (over one hundred years) or as old as the work emanating from the crises of the Second World War and ending, at the latest, in the 1960s. Today, as distinct from the periods of the dominant theories, there is in the Western world, by and large, a decline in the rate of marriage, an increase in the rate of divorce, a decrease in family size to less than two children, an increase in the number of children born outside marriage, and a large rise of single-mother families, of paternal absenteeism, of cohabitation, of serial monogamy and of different varieties of living arrangements, including homosexual couples with or without children. All these phenomena have been witnessed in other historical epochs or in other societies but they were not dominant practices in the Western world at the time – or times – of the creation of psychoanalytic theory. Nor have these features of family life previously come together in quite this conjunction. Alternatively, when one or more of these changes was prevalent, as in wartime Britain, they seem to have led to an ideology of a mythical nuclear family which was at odds with a theory that was focusing on the child, the mother and an absent father. Wartime clinical material provided the conditions for this theory of the essential mother–baby unit. Despite repeated proclamations about the importance of fathers, there was effectively no analysis of paternity or the child–father relation. Ironically the important texts read as blueprints for the future single mother; the 'nursing' not the marital couple was the focus of attention and has largely remained so.

I am interested in raising a number of what seem to me urgent questions about psychoanalytic theory and practice by exploring these in the light of social changes. A focus for me concerns the problems that revolve around our understanding of the heterosexuality which seems to me to have been endorsed rather than analysed in the context of changing social patterns. I am not concerned here with the plurality of sexual practices (chapter 5) but with the plurality of psychic manifestations which appear under the guise of the normative. Support for the normative, not only by definition, must exclude the non-normative but, as is commonly noted, this practice masks the presence of the non-normative within itself. Not seeing this is a consequence of any collapse of analysis into ideology (chapter 2). So long as we fail to correlate our theories of psychic life with social conditions – whether these seem 'universal' or specific – such theories will, without our intending it, become reflective of these very conditions. Indeed, I think this has already happened, in relation both to the concept of a castration complex and to notions of mother–infant relations. As a result of a slip into theories of first character, then personality (chapter 4), the castration complex is no longer seen as emanating from the place of the father. Instead it cast its shadow on the mother, so that what we had was the feared woman rather than the fearing child. The child did not give up its dual desires as a result of a threat from the civilized world; instead it became neurotic or psychotic because of its castrating mother. As a consequence the mother–infant idyll is only for the right mothers in the right places.

Let us trace a sequence: the problem of fatherhood, then of motherhood, and finally the status of siblings in this trajectory. All three questions take place within an interrogation of heterosexuality. Do siblings arise to psychic prominence in the absence of parenthood? But they also contribute to this absence. As early as 1963 the German psychoanalyst Alexander Mitscherlich wrote his book *Society without the Father* (1963); today, descriptions such as 'fatherless America' or 'dead-beat Dads' are commonplace. Absent fathers are a statutory category to such a degree that they have effected a change in English law – in future they will only have to pay 15 per cent for one child and 20 per cent for two of their net income in child support, a derisory figure. If unmarried, they have no say in their child's education or medical treatment. Both measures seem to institutionalize the vanishing father.

I would suggest that the waning significance of the castration complex in Object Relations theory, both for the Kleinians and British Independents (Middle Group), should be seen as an unacknowledged reflection of this social change. 'Society without the father' translates into a theory which asserts the importance of the Oedipus complex without paying any attention to the critical role of the castration complex. Although both Kleinian and Independent practitioners claim to subscribe to the notion of the castration complex, it is strikingly absent from both theoretical and clinical observations. To the best of my knowledge the late Adam Limentani is one of the few psychoanalysts to reflect on the absence of the castration complex, not in the theories but in the cases that confront psychoanalysts. Was Limentani witnessing the psychic effects of social change?

In his 1986 paper 'The limits of heterosexuality: the vagina-man' (reprinted in Limentani 1989), Limentani explores something that he had learnt from his many years of clinical work, that heterosexuality – as social practice and psychic experience – was perfectly possible for individuals who showed no signs of either having negotiated or having failed to negotiate the castration complex: the castration complex was simply missing. Both a successful and an unsuccessful resolution of it would have indicated its presence as an unconscious representation – however, according to Limentani, who worked extensively with sexual perversion, male heterosexuality was sometimes achieved without any awareness of a castration complex. Without fear of castration there could be no internalization of the prohibition of incest or the prohibiting father, and thus there could be no resolution into a protective, ethical superego with coincident sublimation, no transmission of civilization. Limentani's 'vagina men' had found a viable solution to their primitive 'nameless dread' (Wilfred Bion) by identifying with the woman they loved rather than electing her as their object choice. These men could be good, if brief, lovers because they could identify with what the woman wanted. The question would be: could they be fathers or accept their women as mothers of their children in a psychic rather than a biological sense?

Limentani was convinced (and convincing) that his 'vagina man' was not, as is usually argued, defending against homosexuality. Using the vertical model of all psychoanalysis, he claimed that instead of homosexuality the 'vagina man' is deploying a recourse to an original fused infant–mother relationship in which the father is psychically absent. But let us stop here to ask what is this heterosexuality?

It would seem to me that overt homosexuals may make exactly the same psychic choice – valuing 'sameness' and intense identification rather than object choice. However, to claim that homosexuals and heterosexuals may be engaged in the same psychic practice is not at all to argue that these heterosexuals are homosexuals in disguise. The social practice of heterosexuality merely obscures the psychic identification in a way that the practice of homosexuality does not. If this is so, then I would also argue that a woman can be a 'vagina woman' in a similar way to a man – the syndrome simply looks different because this 'normal-looking pathology' is so close to what she is 'meant' to be: a woman. In this case, the regression to identification from object choice is one in which the object choice of the mother has not been first relinquished and then internalized. The vagina woman has identified with a woman but has failed to internalize 'femininity' (Riviere 1929) or, perhaps more importantly, 'maternity' – that is, she has failed to give them meaning. The 'vagina man' or woman can be homosexual or heterosexual: he is a useful exponent of 'gender trouble' (Butler 1999). If this is so, reproduction will be problematic (chapter 5). The vagina man or woman may be a man or woman (we will look later at what that means) but he/she cannot psychically father or mother because he/she has made an infantile identification. Do we have here the preconditions for psychopathy as well as an expression in the vagina man/woman of hysteria? I now believe the hysteria that is excluded from the consulting room because of the limitations of the vertical model is found in the madness of the bedroom, street or workplace as an aspect of psychopathy.

If there is no castration complex in this heterosexuality, if there is no 'symbolic' father, has the father's existence been annihilated in the mind? If so, then we have an instance of a prevalent 'normal' heterosexuality whose psychic structures, however obscured beneath the masquerade, are psychotic. We also have a situation in which – although the heterosexuality may work well enough at the level of the temporary couple, the serial monogamy – 'fathering', both actual and symbolic, will be traumatic. This is because psychically any child of the 'vagina man' will be experienced not as the father's offspring but rather as the result of his wife-as-his-own-mother's betrayal in some imagined adulterous union. Is not this possibility the problem of the tram-man (chapter 6) who chose a wife who had betrayed him?

Limentani argues that a vagina man has identified with the mother. However, this again misses the sibling for, in this fused identity, the vagina man is both mother and child, as he was when his actual or imagined sibling was born. The displaced child, such as the 'Piggle' described by Winnicott, becomes not just the mother she has lost but the mother and the new baby both together. This childhood identification which is being regressed to means that in unconscious fantasy the vagina man shares his infantile generation with his own child. In this case, enormous sibling jealousy will be evoked between the father and child. The vagina man's loss has not been of his mother as an erotic object with her transformation into an affectionate one. She has stayed erotic but in his mind she has betrayed her baby (himself) by an adulterous affair: the mother is experienced as having a lover who is not himself. To this I would add that it is the nature of this identification that makes the vagina man, in adulthood, adulterous. When the vagina man's wife has an actual baby, to him it is evidence of this always dreaded adultery of his mother.[1] In Limentani's thesis, the man only identifies with the woman as an incarnation of the mother who protects one from a 'primal dread' – this omits its crucial sexuality.

In the childhood he still inhabits, the vagina man's mother has betrayed him to have an affair with his father – her husband; in identifying with his sexual mother, the vagina man, a hysteric and a Don Juan, has found his sexuality. He has identified with the erotic woman rather than acknowledging the inevitable loss of the mother of his infancy. Transposing Bowlby's insights, the vagina man/woman has mourned neither his infantile mother nor his infantile self. Interestingly, he rarely has an image or even a memory of his own childhood – by not giving it up, he has of course not been able to represent it.

As a psychic picture, Limentani's explanation of the causative effects of primal dread reminds me of the infant monkey clinging to the mother's fur in case the strange noise is a new sort of lion. But the mother who is clung to is the familiar mother one takes for granted. However, all the symptomatologies of the vagina man, such as his irritabilities, jealousies and the rest, indicate to me something else. The danger outside is double. It is not only that there is a lion out there, one of Bowlby's 'predators'; the mother herself becomes a strange shape, as unfamiliar as the noise in the forest, her unfamiliarity as dangerous. The mother is pregnant. The vagina man (or woman) identifies not with the changing mother but with an idealized woman, a mother who cannot change shape, become a stranger – cannot have another baby, grow old or be ill or withdrawn: the woman thus identified with is an illusion.

In a paradox that I believe underlies psychopathy it is the familiar that becomes frighteningly strange and the new that feels safely the same. The new, so long as it is constantly new, is not given time to change shape, to have a past, to be explored: a new woman, a new man, a new job, new child, ironically *preserves* the psychic status quo. Constant change is in fact only alteration; it prevents the real change of the life drive. It is, in fact, I would argue, a manifestation of the death drive – an urgent haste that ensures psychic stasis.

The defensive identification of the vagina man with an idealized changeless mother protects against the dread of the unfamiliar mother, when the changed shape of the mother indicates an other – a brother or sister. But then when the baby is born, the vagina man, like the Piggle, not knowing who he now is, becomes the new baby who is also the baby he was.

Limentani's portrait is benign. However, the combination of a number of factors might well give us an identikit prototype of the abuser of women and children. There is the absence of boundaries, necessitated by the 'vagina man's' mode of identification with both mother and baby combined with his deep sense of 'being empty of his self' (Balint) because he has not internalized 'others'. There is too his primary jealousy (Riviere) and the primitive untransmuted rage associated with it. I think we need to ask if the prevalence of the 'vagina man' in the context of our changing social practices could be correlated with the apparent rise in child abuse. I believe that Limentani is pointing to a possible widespread 'normal' trend: a prevalent type of heterosexuality.

However, this is only one aspect of the situation. As I have suggested, as well as the infantile fusion with the mother, the 'vagina man' is also perceiving the other person laterally, as a sibling-type extension of himself/herself who is thus indifferently female (a sister) or male (a brother). The same holds good for the 'vagina woman'. In this respect it is not only the failure of the family, but the failure

—— 177 ——

of the school that needs considering. The absence of the 'law of the mother' (chapter 2) with the absence of the 'law of the father' (the castration complex) has been compounded by an absence of making space for siblings/peers to transform their violence and incestuous desires into a respect for seriality. Structured peer-group relations should be the concern of the school and community.

The prevalence of the vagina man raises the possibility that the concept of gender is not simply indifferent to sexual difference (chapter 5) but that it is this very indifference that partly constitutes gender – gender as the relationship between two (or more) positions may allow the two points to change places. If the vagina man can be a woman and vice versa, then being either does not really matter. Limentani claims his 'vagina man' is a Don Juan, in my view a perfect exemplar of the person who is always on the move in order to ensure there is no real change.[2] A feature of post-1960s sexuality, with its freedom from fear of pregnancy, has been Don Juanism among women – again this is by no means unique (one only has to think of Restoration drama to see that) but its cultural acceptance is a crucial part of our social situation in the Western world. This is an ironic reflection on a psychoanalytic advocacy of heterosexuality.

Eric Brenman's 1985 article 'Hysteria' (1985) can help us see more of the coming into being of gender. The more I consider the portrait of a male hysteric that Brenman paints, the more I think that he is describing the same (or at least a remarkably similar) phenomenon to Limentani's 'vagina man'. Brenman also focuses on the Don Juan syndrome (1985: 423).[3] His account is explicitly of a male hysteric and is far more negative a portrait than Limentani's 'vagina man' as he illustrates how Don Juanism shows 'the negation of psychic reality'. This negativism adds an important dimension to our picture – one that helps link it (though Brenman does not suggest this) to psychopathy and possible child abuse. Brenman's Mr X is childless but is psychologically abusive of his wife.

Mr X presented himself to Dr Brenman with crippling anxiety and panic states and then a sudden miraculous recovery from these. His self-presentation was completely contradictory – for instance he claimed he was both ruthless and caring. He tried to control his analyst and the analytic process in a highly manipulative way, constantly putting Brenman into a double-bind (G. Bateson) situation. His sexuality was not for sexual satisfaction but for triumph over the other person, 'a pseudosexuality at the service of his narcissistic conquest' (Brenman 1985: 423). (How well this describes some sibling incest!) Brenman writes of the hysteria illustrated by Mr X:

> It is my belief that the hysteric is able to make an apparent relationship with live external objects. Such an external object, a person, is used to hold the hysteric together and to prevent more serious breakdown into depression or disintegration – schizophrenia.
>
> The basic theme of this paper is that the use of the external object relationship, which appears as a relationship to a whole object, is essentially narcissistic, and that an ostensibly whole object is used as a part object to prevent breakdown. (1985: 422–3)

This seems to me to be the negative of the 'vagina man's' positive – both are the self-as-another; Limentani's patient's identification prevents the breakthrough of 'primal dread', Brenman's patient's false use of a 'whole object' prevents disintegration, depression, breakdown – schizophrenia. Brenman, however, is also concerned with what this means for the human 'object' thus used. Don Juan's identification with the other will make for a degree of sensitivity towards its needs. The woman whom he has 'become' through such literal identification will initially feel her needs responded to before she feels usurped. But we also witness the mechanisms of seduction: as with incest, there are no boundaries here. At the other end, the extent of projection that becoming this other person entails will make for a 'takeover' that is a complete denial and abuse of the other's otherness. Where Limentani's vagina man is heterosexually sensitive, Brenman's Mr X, also heterosexual, destroys the other's psychic reality. This Brenman sees as a hallmark of hysteria. The mechanisms the patient uses in the identification with the apparent object are two ends of a psychic continuum ranging from fusion to extreme projective identification.

Any person or any event intruding into this coupling, including any action by the other that asserts the other's difference, will let all hell loose. Brenman's Mr X demands of his wife that she accept all his sexual liaisons as he would hers – except that she has none. When, however, his main mistress has lovers besides himself, he does his utmost viciously to destroy her, emotionally and professionally. His wife incurs his rage because, not being promiscuous, she does not accept promiscuity the way he does; his mistress incurs his rage because she does what he does, having a further affair with another man; one woman by acting differently, the other by acting similarly, force on him the fact that they are different from him.

There is no psychic parenting in the vagina man's or the hysteric's world – there is abundant heterosexuality – although, as in childhood, it could just as well be homosexuality. The Don Juan syndrome is above all one driven by jealousy and the use of sexuality for the ends of embedding this jealousy in the other's desperate response: the Don Juan, defined by infidelity, makes his lover/mistress jealous and thus relieves himself of the jealousy he otherwise feels. Just as being enviable protects against the pain of envying, so being the object of jealousy protects against the madness of feeling jealous. Envy hurts, jealousy makes mad; though often concomitant states, they are not the same. The Don Juan hysteric is enacting and trying to get rid of the madness of jealousy. Envy is about what someone has; jealousy about where someone else stands – it is about position rather than possession. Kleinian psychoanalytic theory has focused on the subject's primary envy – what it sees as the envy in the first instance of the mother's breast for containing all the baby wants. Brenman is theoretically committed to this approach but his material, I believe, escapes these confines. To some extent the focus on envy has always obscured the jealousies of the Oedipal triangle but in its turn the Oedipal jealousies have obscured the overwhelming jealousies of lateral relations.

Don Juanism is sexuality without reproduction; it is also sexuality in the service of evacuating jealousy – both arise within sibling relationships. Despite the fact that the Ur-Don Juan murders the father-figure, the Commandatore, the whole thrust of the story's action and passion is between 'equals'/peers not between generations. Thus, although Don Juan murders Donna Anna's father, the patriarchal Commandatore, he expects the Commandatore's ghost to behave like an equal, a peer, and accept his invitation to a feast.

There are a number of social factors in the Western world that promote this emphasis on lateral, equal, peer relations, which in turn are the background to a prevalence of psychic and enacted Don Juanism. These factors are the decline of the vertical family – grandparents are losing status as figures of respect and seniority, particularly with occupational mobility; the extension of schooling, with

'The madness of jealousy'
Hermes, Herse and Aglauros by Paolo Veronese (*c*.1576–84), photograph
© Fitzwilliam Museum, University of Cambridge

its peer group culture; the erosion through stepfamilies of generational exactitude (a new husband or wife can be the same age as his or her stepchildren); exchangeability of male and female positions and representations; the trend for sexuality in many of its central manifestations to be non-reproductive – it has always been partially non-reproductive, but this aspect hitherto has been legally and ideologically marginalized in such practices as prostitution, whereas it is now central.

Siblings' genders are not psychically as marked as is vertically derived sexual difference – or is it that it is not so much sexuality as violence that differentiates the male-female gender? The mother who screams blue murder at her pre-verbal infant may have had a young sibling to whom she was a 'little mother', perfect, ideal but partly play-acting. This 'little mother' of a younger sibling is deeply split, for she also wants to murder the newcomer. What we are witnessing is the impossibility of this degree of ambivalence. I was at supper with some friends recently and their ten-year-old daughter was regaling us with her school day, while showing great affection for her baby brother. She was charming – assured, funny, a delight to watch and listen to. But someone's attention was caught by the baby starting to crawl – we all turned to look and admire. The young girl quietly and decorously left the room. As she did so, I saw a change that she had not meant anyone to witness: a grimace between sullen misery and viciousness shadowed her face as she pulled the door harshly over her brother's fingers. This is not unusual; on the whole, as parents, we either do not notice, or forget.

Limentani considers a Don Juan character to be an exemplary instance of the 'vagina man', seeing Don Juan as heterosexual through identification with a woman rather than through object choice. Brenman's hysteric, Mr X, is a Don Juan whom he sees as promiscuous through his identifications with multiple others. (Klein had understood her evacuee patient Richard as in fantasy a Don Juan.) Brenman considers that the heterosexuality of Don Juan the hysteric prevents us seeing that he is, in fact, intensely narcissistic. Brenman's patient is also anxious to a point where he fears for his own sanity – is this anxiety fuelled by the unconscious jealousy he is trying to get rid of? He both exploits the catastrophic situation and denies it. He is unfaithful to his wife and outraged that she might restrict his freedom; he allows her to be 'free', knowing she will not be unfaithful.

When his lover is unfaithful, he wants to destroy her personally and professionally as he claims that she has betrayed all he gave her. For those of us who were young in the 1960s, this is so familiar a scenario as to seem normal. But behind it is the fact that the Don Juan character, male or female, is seeking to be adored, not to love. As Brenman so aptly puts it, 'I'll make you love me if I have to break every bone in your body' (1985: 427).

Two observations about Mr X and the vagina man need further exploration if we too are to move forward in thinking about sibling relationships as offering an autonomous paradigm underlying normative aspects of contemporary life. What is meant by identification[4] and what are the implications of wanting to be adored rather than to offer love?

Identifications, introjections, internalizations, what I have called 'ingestions', are different processes but there is no clear consensus on which one to use when. I have restricted the concept of internalization (or internal object) to a re-presentation of something that has been realized as not being part of oneself (thus acknowledged 'lost') – once 'other', one can take it in as an image within, it can be retained in the mind's eye. Internalization is essentially to do with the process of mourning; it is crucial for the development of the ability to mentalize as it facilitates a move from bodily enactment to thinking. Bowlby writes of the hysteric, the hypochondriac, the psychopath, that they have mislocated a dead person either in someone else or in themselves. The hysteric, the hypochondriac and the psychopath have not managed to see the other as different from themselves; to be mourned the dead person must be recognized as other – one's life goes on, but theirs does not. If they are mourned, they can be taken in as an 'internal object', be remembered and made use of. A person who has internalized psychologically separate 'lost' other people as others and/ or mourned dead ones is not 'empty of themselves' because these objects, which may be scenes as well as people, populate the mind. But they do more than this: in order to have been thus taken in they must have been perceived in their otherness and if other than the subject, then the subject can perceive that they themselves are likewise perceived by the other. Winnicott and Balint stress the developmental importance of the mother's recognition of the baby which enables the baby to be seen as itself. While agreeing with this formulation I want to emphasize the importance of the process I have just outlined. I have found its occurrence to be one of the most crucial transformative moments in clinical work. I can explain its importance best with an illustration.

In order to think about siblings and psychopathy, which is a psychiatric rather than psychoanalytic diagnosis, I read a psychologist's psychoanalytically informed account of his 'hypnoanalysis' of a psychopathic prisoner, Harold, the original 'Rebel without a Cause' (Lindner 1945). One of the things that puzzled me as I read was the movement of my own mood; I could not find a perspective, locate myself anywhere from where I could decide what I thought. As Harold told his story to his therapist (and I read it), I first felt that he was a victim of acute depression and a taken-for-granted level of violence in his home environment that should be unacceptable: the beatings he received, the cruel taunts, the mocking of his physical inadequacies. Winnicott's formulation for psychopathy helped me temporarily situate myself: the psychopath is the anti-social child, is the deprived baby. I felt sorry for Harold, the possible murderer. But then my mood altered – it was not so much that my perspective changed or that I saw something new, as that there was another level to my feelings: I felt sorry for all the objects he was smashing up, the people he was stealing from, treating like dirt. I realized I did not know where I was. Did I believe any of it?

Harold seemed to be making trouble for everyone – including the therapist. Much of his story was probably factually true, but it had no meaning for Harold other than as a means to an end. There was no dividing line between fantasy and reality and this worked in such a way that it made me recall an early comment of Melanie Klein on her play technique with children. In her treatments, Klein participated in a child's game, acting the parts the child assigned her with one proviso: that when the person she had to impersonate was too unbearably horrific, too gross a torturer or whatever, she would preface her enactment with the words 'I'll pretend to be . . .', thus, I imagine, protecting herself and her patient from the 'reality' of the fantasy. For the child of a certain age and for Harold, the fantasy is real and the real is fantasy; there is no dividing line, no 'let's pretend'. This is true too, for example, of the patient described in Bion's 'The imaginary twin' (chapter 9); indeed, it is episodically true for many people. It is the quality of the real–imagined fusion that must be of significance in psychopathy. This has something to do with the sheer pointlessness; most of the time there seems to be no gain from the fiction, just an indifference to the truth.

There are clearly many things to say about this, but I have introduced Harold to illustrate the importance of the process of internalization. The process of internalization is of the other person or object or place being seen to be other and then 'taken in', thought about, remembered, 'seen' with the inner eye. As this is achieved, this object, if it is perceived to be a human object, will be seen as someone who can see the subject. (With trees and places, animals, etc., one feels 'part of a landscape', 'loved by the dog' . . .) Harold in his psychopathy could not see the other, nor therefore perceive himself to be seen. As I said, it is a major turning-point when the subject *sees itself from the other's perspective*. This is an achievement of the subject and is different from and beyond the mother's (or anyone's) recognition; it is a major dimension of the process of 'internalization'. For a patient whose mother had died in his childhood, the breakthrough came when he suddenly saw how awful it was for his mother to leave him – rather than it being unbearable for him to have his mother die. It is the latter stance that is the immobile position of the victim.

Usually it is more complicated than this. Klein, in the case of Erna to which I have referred, helps her patient disentangle the real, kind mother from the torturing witch imago (which I call an introject). Rather than asserting this division of real (kind) and fantastical (witch), I would stress that the subject, Harold or Erna, needs to see that it was sad *for the parent* that he or she was the sort of person who was unable to perceive what was lovable in their child. This realization is almost the opposite of the experience that Sarah had – that she was misrecognized by a mother who thought she was happy when she was distressed. The latter has been well documented and variously described – it produces 'disorganized attachment' in the baby. What I am emphasizing is that it entails (or may be preceded by) the child's inability to experience itself from the point of view of the other, or to perceive the other *objectively*. But there is a further question to be taken up later: why do we believe the evil fantasies to the extent that we have to protect ourselves with a 'let's pretend', or indeed why do we enact the fantasies, becoming torturers, murderers, etc.?

It may be that things are taken in but not, in my sense of the word, 'internalized'. It is these I call 'introjects'. Sarah (chapter 3) was not only 'empty of herself' but her head was full of wild wolves; the convicted Harold is always 'buzzing' with ideas. But, as with Don Juan's women, none of these thoughts or animals connect up. The famous 'cleverness' of the psychopathic aspect of any personality seems to me to involve just this introjection of bits of information – often encyclopaedic – which cannot be thought through or developed; like Don Juan's use of a list of 903 women, this information is additive rather than linked. Introjects, then, are the objects in the world when they are taken in as disparate isolates – rather as the artist Francis Bacon presents through his depiction of unrelated people and things. Introjects are thus not 'internal objects', nor are they identifications.

Identification – as, over time, I have come to need to use this often ambiguous term – does not involve a taking in of the object in order that it can become a part of the subject. The subject is partly composed of those he internalizes; he is flooded with all he introjects; but though he may take in an identification to the degree to which he may examine it, it does not become part of him – he becomes it. The movement then is a going out to the other. 'I can identify with that argument, but not agree with it' means simply that you are able to understand the other's position *from their position*. It is crucial to be able to stand in someone else's shoes. But, of course, one can get lost there, in the place of the other. Identification is the technique of the trained observer: a going out to become the other, followed by a taking in that is just sufficient for looking and trying to understand, then a return of the 'identification' to the object and a disidentification of the observer. The observation cannot work as an observation if the observer retains or gets stuck with the identification. This is one of the reasons why a therapist as observer cannot take on any 'cause' of the patient – or ask the patient to identify with the analyst's 'cause'.

People, however, get stuck with or in identifications all the time. Before Freud, it was argued that a hysterical patient such as an anorexic girl was identifying with another girl who was startlingly skinny. Freud specified that the identification was with the other girl's desire – the first girl has a boyfriend and the anorexic wants one too, so comes to look like the lucky one. For both vagina man and Mr X, according to Limentani and Brenman, the main ways of being in the world are identifications with the woman whose love they demand. Brenman specifies that such an identification with 'a whole person' is used to prevent what would otherwise be the disintegration and fragmentation of Mr X. But there is a problem here, easiest seen with Mr X: it is a problem *for* Mr X and for us to think about through the identifications of observation. It is not only that the love his wife or mistress gives him is not enough; it is that whatever the two women do in loving him is wrong. He will break bones to get love because the love is never right. Brenman understands Mr X's problem as arising from an identification with his mother while he himself is the ideal baby – he can't decide which to be, mother or baby.

> Some time later when he was improving, he re-arranged his business affairs to give more pay and a greater share to his junior partners. He realised that he was assailed by a struggle with contradictory views. On the one hand he felt that everything should be given to the business, the profits should be re-invested and he and the partners should sacrifice their salaries. He realised he was the business – both the baby who had everything and the mother who supplied the food. At the same time he hated the business that made such demands on him, and thought that he should get everything out of the business and not look after it at all and it should supply him with everything.
>
> He realised that in the conflict he was both the ideal breast who should be everything and the ideal baby who should have everything. He was caught in the conflict of wanting to satisfy both completely, with no capacity to give and take. He linked this with what he considered to be the character of his mother . . . These features show a violent greedy dependency . . . (Brenman 1985: 426)

There is room in the above account for transference interpretations (and countertransference problems) along the lines of junior partners and siblingship. Mr X was emotionally abusive to his wife – could she not have been a sister, as well as a mother? His self-righteous infidelity was, among other things, a way of ensuring that it was she, not he, who was jealous – a lateral rather than vertical scenario. When the new baby is born, it is that baby that is in the place of the subject, with whom the subject identifies. He can be helped to see that he is not the same as the new baby – or he can get stuck in the identification with the new baby he is observing.

Without the identification with the sibling-as-baby we cannot get to why for the psychopath or hysteric nothing is ever OK. Brenman's understanding does not quite capture the so-familiar 'nothing is ever right' quality of Mr X's relationships. Yet any small (or not so small) child, confronted with new (or not so new) siblings, fits the case: Mr X tries to share with the younger brothers and sisters (the 'junior partners') but cannot bear to; he is the oldest and should get everything. A lot of people are very good at getting love but find it hard to love or know what that would mean; the love they receive (and they do) is never right so they go on trying to get the right love from someone else – or they do not bother. Everything having gone wrong with the advent of a sibling, it can seem impossible and not worth the effort of trying to put it right – better just to smash things up, as Harold, who had a younger sister with whom he had sex, proceeded to do.

What then is this identification in the place where it looks as though there is object-love – heterosexuality for Mr X and the vagina man, homosexuality for Harold in prison:

> [Perry] still tells me . . . that he loves me . . . A lot of fellows are asking me how he is, how I like it . . . Not that I don't dislike it: I don't want to do it in the first place because I might like it. You know, if I did anything like that I – I couldn't look at the person. Maybe I would do it if I don't have to look at the person. I wouldn't ever do it so long as I would have to see the person . . . I'm having a lot of fun with Perry . . . He's starting to curse: I really kid him about picking that up from me. (Lindner 1945: 139)

As with all Harold's accounts, it becomes impossible to know who did what and which is which. One of his persistent and most problematic symptoms (for which he has had operations) is that he cannot open his eyes properly; it is not only that he cannot see clearly – neither can we. This uncertainty extends to his gender and is probably an aspect of his sexual relationship with his sister. In his childhood incest with his sister he fondles his penis to show her, 'and himself', as he says, that he is better than she is. His father has mocked him that it is his sister who should have the penis.

It seems to me that the specific objects of the identification are secondary to the process of identification itself. I consider there are two dimensions to the process which will be differently balanced in different contexts and people. The first identification is a response to trauma; it is chameleon-like and protective – defending, as Limentani and Brenman assert, against a 'primal dread' or the subject's disintegration. This identification is certainly made with what is called 'a whole object', a complete person, but that does not mean the person is recognized as herself or himself, rather she or he is a familiar place. There is no desire in this identificatory response to trauma. But there is desire as the second aspect of the process – the desire to be loved in the right way, which means to be the only one who matters, which is why this identification never works. It has to be given up because the toddler can never be His Majesty the Baby again. But more than that, it also never works because the subject is not himself – in order to get the love he demands he has become his sibling-as-baby.

According to Brenman, the hysteric operates a switch between catastrophe (experienced in the symptom) and denial (expressed in the apparently healthy personality). Again one can imagine a social scenario beneath this description: the child denies that the sibling who has replaced him is anything other than absolutely adorable or admirable, yet he stops eating, even walking or talking, contracts physical illnesses, has night terrors and so on. Brenman writes of Mr X: 'The pretence of being loving and friendly is *not* designed to achieve a loving relationship, but to be the falsely adored object of love and to triumph over so-called loving objects who are then despised and annihilated' (1985: 425). This, I suggest, may be the end result of the false love for the sibling rather than for the mother. The love demanded from the mother entails triumphing not over her but over the sibling who has stolen this love.

Brenman elucidates the familiar observation of the labile, promiscuous, shallow identifications that hysterics make not with real but with ideal objects; these are to me the mother before she has changed shape, had *another* baby. He comments that these are always multiple identifications – presumably Don Juan's many idealized women. In commenting on one of Mr X's dreams he notes how hard it is to tell whether the psychoanalyst (himself) is the German navy who traps the Russian navy (the patient, Mr X) or vice versa. These processes are understood by Brenman along vertical, mother–child or father–child axes. But these confusingly interchangeable Russian and German navies seem to me more appropriately conceived as battles between fraternal rivals.

When one reads case histories or clinical accounts within psychoanalysis, or indeed theoretical propositions about the construction of the mind, one cannot but be struck by their complexity. Brenman's article is an exemplary instance of this. Likewise, when one reads ethnographic portraits, the social world and its relationships are intricate and nuanced, often difficult in their complexity for a lay-reader to grasp *in toto*. Yet, from a psychoanalytic perspective, the link between these complex worlds of the mind and the surrounding society is oddly simple. The Oedipus complex and the pre-Oedipal mother–infant relationship are presented as the only nexuses that link the internal world of unconscious thought processes and affects with the external social world. The triangular Oedipal pattern and the binary structures of Lévi-Strauss and others (in psychoanalysis, the pre-Oedipal) can go in multiple directions and be discovered in a variety of places; there are many dyads and many triangles, but as a residual structure this is still simple. The Oedipus complex is presented not so much as a reductive concept as a residual one, a core complex that draws everything to it or from which everything opens out.

The Oedipus complex is key because of its incestuous wishes and the prohibitions on these wishes. An ethnography, on the other hand, reveals the multiplicities of desires and prohibitions. Even a glance at current English marriage regulations gives us a hint of this multifariousness; the rules and regulations as to whom one may or may not marry are quite extraordinarily complicated, suggesting not an infinity of possibilities, but that the underlying pattern is likely to be more than only two or three.

The Oedipus complex is a metaphor for a nexus of relationships; with the acknowledgement of the castration complex both sexual and generational difference can be represented. Lateral relations such as Remus and Romulus, Cain and Abel, the twins who feature in various creation myths, form not a nexus but a series. Acknowledging that there is room for the next in line allows for the representation of seriality and with it a recognition of the taboo on sexuality – hetero- or homosexuality – and violence between siblings and their heirs.

The object of Mr X's, Harold's or the vagina man's so-called 'love' is strictly speaking, *as* object, a matter of indifference; the point is the identification with it. The 'object' can therefore be of either sex. The ideological reflective stance of psychoanalytic theory and practice leads, I believe, to psychoanalysis tending to find an outer edge for what it pathologizes[5] and missing the pathology of the centre. In this case its endorsement of heterosexuality at a practical level can hide the dangers inherent in some aspects of heterosexual practices. At a theoretical level it hides the siblings, and this in turn means

'Acknowledging that there is room for the next in line'
The Cholmondeley Ladies, British School (*c.*1600–10), © Tate, London 2003

something crucial is missing from the analysis. The hysteric or psychopath is psychically bisexual not heterosexual in his identifications – so is the sibling: in seeing himself mirrored in the younger or older sibling, the object the child sees as himself can, at least initially, be of either gender. This early mirroring is very clearly seen on the death of a sibling. For example, if a brother dies or is killed in war, his sister will retard an awareness of his loss by identifying with him (as will a brother with a sister). When Keats famously wrote about how as a poet he became the bird on the path, he was not concerned with species or gender boundaries. He was exploring a state in which, through identification, he was the *same* as the objects around him. It is safe for the subject to become the same as the object if the subject also knows he is different. To be the object might not be so good an experience – the bird may be understood by the poet but if the poem did not come to an end, Keats would have been like Mr X taking over his wife's (the bird's) life.

When the subject becomes the object, he is reversing an earlier danger in which it was the object that appeared to be the same as the subject. This meant that the subject feared being wiped out. I believe that this subject-object/object-subject identification along a lateral axis is present throughout life; it is from this, both as a source of understanding and as a protection against its dangers, that differences are constructed. For the baby and child there are of course already differences constructed by others out there in the world around it, so it will make use of these to construct its own differences, or reconstruct on an individual level the world's differences. Gender (like race) is one of the salient differences 'out there'. From the gender indifference of the sibling mirroring or sameness, gender is constructed as a defensive 'othering', a difference in which is inherent the violence of the displaced sibling's need to survive.

—— 9 ——

Conclusion: Siblings and the Engendering of Gender

In other places and other times

In the Trobriand Islands, according to Malinowski, the brother, sister and sister's son form the primary triangular relationship, with the sister's brother standing for authority but not, of course, being in a sexual relationship to the child's mother. Malinowski (1927, 1929) argues that this challenges the universality of the Oedipus complex. Ernest Jones, then president of the British Psychoanalytical Society fought back on behalf of the most important shibboleth of psychoanalysis.

The debate entirely missed the possibility of independent lateral structures. Among the Trobrianders, brother–sister incest is the supreme taboo and their mature relationship is characterized by extreme avoidance so that an intermediary has to pass objects between them. Related to the prohibitions, such incest is an important feature of Trobriand mythology: incest leads to death; Trobrianders become very anxious and denying when asked if they dream of sibling sexuality.[1]

Contrary to the Trobriand practice, in Ptolemaic Egypt the royal family were enjoined to have sibling marriages and progeny. The practice was probably quite widespread in the general population. Lateral endogamy ensures the maintenance of the royal blood and organizes the disposal of property within the family or clan (Goody 1990).

Looked at from a psychosocial perspective, the apparently opposite lateral taboos and positive injunctions to mating may serve the same purpose – they make the world a safer place (Parsons 1969). The Trobriand brother who is proscribed offers support and takes responsibility for his sister; fraternal or cousin marriages offer the same security. Intergenerational mating would not function in the same way because the mother or father dies. The prevalence of father–daughter incest in some communities takes care of the father in his old age but does not serve what may be a new or disrupted community in the same way that lateral injunctions or prohibitions can do.

Turning, if not this time to poets or novelists, but to films, the importance of the brotherhood is fascinatingly shown in Visconti's film *Rocco and his Brothers* (1960) (chapter 1). We will see how among the West African Tallensii, actors and observers alike ascribed the vast increase in madness (thirteenfold over a thirty-year period) to the increase in emigration for work in southern Ghana. *Rocco* portrays a more total migration.

Rocco and his Brothers 'anthropomorphizes' – the concept is Visconti's – a point of transition from a society built on known codes of sociality to one in which the key rules of a society or of culture itself are individualized. Caught between the old and the new, the main characters and the story are melodramatic – dramatizing their migrant predicament on a social level as a hysteric does on a personal level. But the melodrama has tragic implications precisely because the actors stand beside an abyss that fails to link an impossible past and an unwelcoming future.

The arrival of the Pafundi family by train at Milan's central station is pregnant with the family's tragedy, a particular tragedy that stands for the general historical tragedy of cataclysmic change. The train has come to a stop in the Mecca of progress, but for the Pafundis there is nothing there. Not only have they left their past, their past has abandoned them. Vincenzo, the eldest son on to whom should have devolved all the responsibility for the fatherless, deracinated family, is not at the station to meet them. Indeed, when they find him the clash of past and future makes it clear that there is only an unacceptable present for most of the Pafundi arrivals. The present is marginalized in the basement they will inhabit until they are evicted: Milan does not like to see its down-and-outs, so if they manage to be evicted they will be rehoused. Work is the very casual labour from which only the exploitative relegation to the bestial brutality of boxing is an escape – for a 'future' as a boxer, Simone has his teeth and jaw examined like any animal would have had done on the land back home in the South.

The absence of Vincenzo at the station indicates the end of the old fraternity. His fiancée Ginetta's family, also originally from the South, think the Pafundis have come, not to be taken care of by the oldest brother, but like any modern family to celebrate this son's engagement. The move then is from the centripetal fraternity to a couple who will go their own way, leaving to form an isolated nuclear family.

Quite simply a way of life is ending and the new one, for the central characters, is powerless to be born. In terms of both their pasts and their futures, these heroes and heroines are nobodies. Without a secure *place* in the group of Southern brothers or an *identity* in the nuclear families of Northern urban industrialization, each character is a mass of unrooted feelings. Imagistically, what we have is a cohort of brothers paying marked respect to a dominant mother, but visual evidence that this brotherhood is disintegrating in terms of values and structures. The fraternal lineage confronts the rising nuclear family, but is lost without meaning in the space between the two.

In a study of Naples, Ann Parsons (1969) demonstrates that the migrant group of brothers has transformed itself into the street gang with its all-male bar-life; this cohort is as strong or stronger than the urban family. Parsons notes the street's importance, but she has no model with which to examine it as also a kinship structure. Visconti's film at its best shows the gap between the clash of cultures; at its more limited end it reads the brotherhood through the emotions of the individualistic culture towards which it is heading. With neither psychoanalytic cultural anthropologist Ann Parsons nor with filmmaker Visconti can we get at a psychology of siblinghood, though the latter gives us a vivid portrait of it. This lack of understanding of the social psychology has implications in many contexts. For instance, already in the First World War it was realized that collective factors were far more crucial than individual responses to traumatic conditions (Shepherd 2002).

The street gang may not be a negative but an alternative to the ideologically hegemonic nuclear family. Although sister–brother avoidance is enjoined from the outset by the Trobrianders, formal prohibitions, responsibilities and respect come into being at puberty when fertility shifts the possibility of sibling incest from sexuality to reproduction – can we not assume it recognizes the infantile and latency attraction to each other of siblings? As with its only apparent opposite, Ptolemaic marriage, these practices and regulations would seem to indicate how the power of sibling feelings for each other can be put to good social use if regulated. The need for regulation indicates their force. In failing to perceive and analyse laterality, in not taking seriously either the incest or the violence, we are leaving to chance whether or not the good or bad potentialities of this power dominate. There is no doubt that other cultures are aware, or more aware, of it. We take our vertical model everywhere with us; but the material, as with Malinowski's Trobriand observations, quite staggeringly exceeds it.

Comparing schizophrenia among Italian migrants in a Boston clinic with its occurrence in a Neapolitan hospital, and controlling for the same diagnosis, Ann Parsons found that from any viewpoint one particular expectation of her model was *not* confirmed: 'no patient first became psychotic after the death of the mother, and only one after the death of the father' (1969: 110). Psychosis is thought to be linked to parental death – when Parsons finds it is not, she seeks no further.

Parsons is an unusually careful and perceptive observer, yet it seems to me that in her one individual case history of 'Giuseppina' she misses the significance of the death of a *brother* – older by ten months – at the time of the psychotic breakdown in early adulthood. There are to my mind two significant deaths in Giuseppina's history that are likely to have been relevant for the psychosis. First, her brother dies from TB, which is so dreaded a disease in the Neapolitan community in the 1960s that there are rituals to help deal with the fear. Second, a woman whom Giuseppina considers her friend (that is, a lateral relationship) dies from an abortion of an illegitimate baby. Totally breaking strict social mores, Giuseppina herself has had premarital sex with her husband. In her psychotic breakdown she interprets every gesture of her newborn baby as an act of aggression against her, and presumably this is a projection of her own aggression to her infant. That the woman friend who had the abortion is, in fact, a friend of the mother's rather than Giuseppina's as she claims only confirms the picture I would draw: on becoming a mother Giuseppina becomes confused in her mind with her own mother and all mothers, as she probably did when she was a child facing the prospect of a sibling. The new sibling she would have wished dead becomes confused with her just-older brother who has died. His death, her friend's, her mother's friend's death make her fear her own death. She has confused them all as she is probably confused about her baby and the friend's dead baby. The vertical models of both psychoanalysis and the cultural anthropology Parsons is using do not allow the lateral implications to be seen – but the material is there.

In 1963 anthropologist Meyer Fortes returned with his psychiatrist wife, Doris Mayer, to the Tallensi of Northern Ghana with whom he had worked from 1934 to 1937. In 'Psychoses and social change' they describe Tallensi family life in a way that indicates the pervasive influence of the psychoanalytic model (Fortes and Mayer 1965). The child's social world is illustrated through a series of boxes. The child's progress originates with the mother in the mother's room, is seen next in the father's quarters with his siblings and half-siblings from the father's other wives, and finally after about age five, among the wider clan of uncles, aunts, cousins, etc. This social configuration matches the internal schema of psychoanalytic pre-Oedipal (mother), Oedipal (father) and post-Oedipal (wider society) neatly. But this model aside, Fortes and Mayer's work instead illustrates something different: the structuring, autonomous area of sibling relations. Tallensi parents still in the 1960s abstained from sexual relations with each other from the clear conception of a baby until the time when the toddler could move and feed on its own. For the mother, birth-spacing was thus commonly from three to three and a half years. For the baby, on the contrary, it is quite likely that the nearest sibling would chronologically be a 'twin' as it would be a half-sibling with its own separate mother. However, it was expected that the mother's new pregnancy and a baby of the same mother (a matrisib) would cause the toddler to experience considerable disturbance and intense rivalry.

By the time the mother had a new baby, as Fortes and Mayer commented, there was already an extremely strong sibling and peer group in place so that it was not uncommon to see children of between two and three years going around with their arms affectionately around each other's necks. Along with the strong parental care and affection which they note repeatedly, Fortes and Mayer, as it were between the lines, are clearly curious as to whether this lateral bonding contributes to the robust psychic health of the Tallensi. When working in the nursery of a very liberal kibbutz near the Sea of

Galilee, Israel, in 1962 I noticed the same intimacy in small peer groups of children of around two years old. I had read about the dangers of their communal upbringing, but what one saw was its strengths: lateral bonding was widely acknowledged and considered significant. More recently, visiting with others the beautiful sixteenth-century churches in south-eastern Albania, our attention suddenly switched from the external frescoes to an idyll: two small children, somewhere between three and four years old, a boy and a girl, were carrying together a basket as they skipped and danced down a dirt track. They were laughing, singing odd snatches, chattering together; for stretches they had their arms around each other's necks, hugged then separated to dance on. When they saw us looking at them entranced, they shyly disentangled themselves from each other and scampered off. We had watched an icon of love.

There is an upside and a downside to the sibling story. My account has been biased towards the latter because I consider our failure to mark the significance of siblings and hence produce a lateral para-digm echoes our failure to look at the effects of intra- and intersibling abuse in violence, individual or collective, in wars or mental illness.

In 1965 Meyer Fortes noted that in 1934–7, the time of his first visit to the Tallensi, there had been one case of madness; thirty years later there were thirteen in the same social group (Fortes and Mayer 1965). The increase in migration for work seemed the explanation for this rise in 'madness'. The Tallensi were quite clear as to what constitutes 'madness' and differentiated it from eccentricity, mental deficiency and various strange behaviours. His wife, Doris Mayer, was looking for cross-cultural psychiatric differences, but instead she found that Tallensi 'madness' translated seamlessly into Western psy-chosis. One of the mad Tallensi had a post-partum depression, one was manic, one melancholic, the rest all suffered from schizophrenia. Today, forty years later, we would probably label some at least of these last borderline or narcissistic personality disorders, as seventy years previously they could well have been instances of hysterical psychoses. There was no paranoia and Mayer contrasted this with an observation by M. J. Field, who in 1960 reported a study of fifty-two schizophrenics among the Akan in Ghana: of these twenty-six men were paranoid; 50 per cent of the women were depressed. A pos-sible cause of the Akan disposition to paranoia and depression in adulthood is cited as the fact that in his or her childhood 'the adored small child has to suffer the trauma of growing up into an object of contempt' (Field 1960: 30). West African Asante and Ga behaviours are in strong contrast to the Tallensi. Where the Tallensi help the older child with its expected intense sibling rivalry, the other family systems push out the older child. This is described by an English doctor, Cecily Williams (1938), observing mostly Asante and Ga youngsters in the Children's Hospital, Accra, Gold Coast. Dr Williams studied a prevalent disease of childhood, kwashiorkor.

In sub-Saharan Africa in general, kwashiorkor, a protein deficiency sickness which can still be fatal, is known as 'the sickness the child gets when the next one is born'. Williams's first publication in *The Lancet* opens with these words: 'The name "kwashiorkor" indicates the disease the deposed baby gets when the next one is born' (1935: 1151). Caught early, good nutrition can save the child. However, in a fuller article on child health in the Gold Coast three years later, Williams describes the idyllic life of most small babies and the simultaneous rejection of the older child:

> A woman has a lot of time in which she likes to be with a baby. First she washes it slowly, lingeringly. Then she alters the disposal of the beads with great precision and leisure. She powders it . . . This meticulous love of the small baby is in striking contrast with the neglect and indifference with which the older children may be treated . . . Up to two the child leads a thoroughly spoiled life, but this existence is rudely broken. His mother either has another baby or goes away with a husband and leaves the child to his grandmother . . . I have seen great rage and bitterness in a child who finds the place on his mother's back is usurped by a new baby . . . after a period of *blind misery* the child gets used to this. People are good to him. (1938: 99, my italics)

Dr Williams explicitly labels the advent of a sibling as a trauma – even suggesting that the peevish, ill-considered articles by adults in the local Gold Coast newspapers can be laid at the door of this traumatic childhood experience – the jealousies of infancy are enacted in adult back-biting writing.

By 1962, writing more fully on kwashiorkor once again, Dr Williams uses cases reported by A. P. Farmer from East Africa: 'In 28 cases of kwashiorkor studied, there were 48 underlying causes. Four of these causes were poverty-related malnutrition, 17 others had underlying medical diseases', but 'social and psychological causes were responsible for 19 [and] another 8 were associated with "abrupt weaning"' (1962: 342). In vulnerable economies, food can indeed become insufficient when a new baby arrives and needs the only reliable source – breast milk. The same applies to twins. In simple cultures, what Western explanations consider infantile greed may well be infantile hunger. The toddler has a lot to lose when the sibling arrives. Some sub-Saharan people such as the Tallensi manage the older child's dethronement in a benign fashion, others do not try to mitigate the trauma – but that it is a trauma seems always to be recognized by all the various participants. In the interwar years a few Western observers perceived it but did not extend their observations into any comment on the significance of siblings. Normal sibling illness as a result of jealousy is thus widely recognized in other cultures. In fact, our failure to grant it a crucial place is, I believe, ethnocentric.

Psychoanalysis and siblings

I shall focus on three aspects of understanding siblings: psychoanalytic observation, the transference/countertransference, and the possible mechanisms and dynamics which might characterize the psychology of laterality. These are all aimed at situating the sibling from a psychodynamic viewpoint. At the time that Cecily Williams, A. P. Farmer and Fortes and Mayer were making their observations, Donald Winnicott, a paediatrician in London who had just started to train as a psychoanalyst, wrote not so differently about 'the disease the older child gets when the baby is born'. Here, in conditions of sufficiency, there is no question of actual malnutrition; however, the Western child often refuses to eat.

> You are taking the weights of a large number of children and it is easy to work out what is the average weight for any given age. In the same way, the average can be found for every other measurement of development and the test of normality is to compare the measurements of a child with the average. Such comparisons make it very interesting information, but there is a complication that can arise and spoil the whole calculation. A complication not usually mentioned in the paediatric literature. Although from a purely physical standpoint, any

deviation from health may be taken to be abnormal, it does not follow that physical lowering of health due to emotional strain and stress is necessarily abnormal. This rather startling point of view requires elucidation. Now take a rather crude example: it is very common for a child from 2–3 years old to be very upset at the birth of a baby brother or sister. As a mother's pregnancy proceeds or when the new baby arrives, the child that has hitherto been robust and has known no cause for distress may become unhappy and temporarily thin and pale and develop other symptoms such as enuresis, ill-temper, sickness, constipation and nasal congestion. If a physical illness should occur at this time, e.g. an attack of pneumonia, whooping cough, gastroenteritis, then it is possible that convalescence will be unduly prolonged. (Winnicott [1931]: pp. 3–4)

Instead of emphasizing the trauma, Winnicott points to the normality of distress. Winnicott's drawing attention to this, however, is important, because we can read into it other observations to see if we can move towards a psychoanalytic formulation of sibling significance. The sibling shock he observed would be a perfect candidate for his later notion that the catastrophe the adult patient always fears is about to take place has already happened in his childhood. In fact this famous idea of Winnicott's is, ironically, an observation that expresses immaculately the analyst's failure to see siblings – it is not only the patient who does not realize that his fear for the future is in fact an unremembered trauma in the past, the analyst too must have the prospect of siblings looming always in front of him because he has failed to notice their impact that has always been there.

While, like Klein, Winnicott seems to have forgotten his early paediatric observation of sibling importance, it seems to come through unrecognized in a number of his later formulations. For instance, it fits neatly into such later statements as the following account of the genesis of psychopathy:

[Psychopathy is an] adult condition which is an uncured delinquency. A delinquent is an uncured antisocial boy or girl. An antisocial boy or girl is a deprived child. A deprived child is one who had something good enough, and then no longer had this, *whatever it was*, and there was sufficient growth and organization of the individual *at the time of the deprivation* for the deprivation to be perceived as traumatic. (Winnicott [1959–64]: 134, first set of italics mine)

—— 201 ——

'Whatever it was' is surely the pre-sibling mother; the loss of the mother appears traumatic when she is stolen by the new baby.

> it was a loss of something that was good, and I am intending to imply that something happened, *after which nothing was the same again.* The antisocial tendency therefore represented a compulsion in the child to make external reality mend the *original trauma*, which of course *quickly became forgotten* and therefore became unmendable by simple reversal. In the psychopath this compulsion to go on forcing external reality to make good its failure continues . . . (Winnicott 1965a: 50)

After the sibling, nothing is the same again. Once more what is perceived in the patient or client applies to the analyst – the observed sibling trauma is quickly forgotten.

Winnicott in these statements is referring to the mother as the point of failure, but we can use the illustrations he gives to show how it is the advent of the sibling that makes nothing the same again, though of course, like the Ga and Asante child, the Western child can get over what is, in this context of psychopathy, specified by Winnicott as a trauma. Let us look at a portrait of an ill boy obsessed with string; Winnicott considers the separation from the boy's seriously depressed mother traumatic, but we can read in the younger sister: 'The mother cared for the boy until the sister was born when he was three years three months. This was the first separation of importance' ([1960]: 153). There follow a number of separations, as for instance when the mother is hospitalized. To Winnicott it is these excessive subsequent deprivations which make the original deprivation irreversible. Frightened of separations from his mother, the boy uses string to tie everything together, until one day 'the boy's preoccupation with string was gradually developing a new feature . . . He had recently tied a string round his sister's neck (the sister whose birth provided the first separation of this boy from his mother)' ([1960]: 154).

In Winnicott's overt account the use of string indicates the boy's benign effort to make links between separated objects. I would point to the fact that the linking is necessary because it is the original trauma of the sibling's birth which has been too severely re-enforced by broken ties. Thus the string is not entirely benign. The same string that would unite him with his mother is the string that would throttle his younger sister.

—— 202 ——

Or take the young girl of sixteen who came to see Winnicott and commented, 'I believe I came to see you when I was two, because I didn't like my brother being born.' Aged sixteen she starts to scream and scream and scream just as she had done at the age of twenty months when her mother was three months pregnant. (Are these screams the screams of the Bombay and wartime nursery babies, or Rahel's in *The God of Small Things* (Roy 1997) when something too awful has happened?)

Winnicott comments that it is at this point that the girl becomes ill. The uncontrollable screams of a sixteen-year-old echoing her infantile experience suggest that this original experience was beyond coping with. The boy obsessed with string had used it to tie things together, using it as though it would literally prevent his separation from his mother – this is Winnicott's focus. But surely when he ties the string around the sister's neck we have moved into a different realm of madness? Psychosis threatens when the trauma comes too early in life; psychopathy comes later, after the child has already been aware of something good about life. Psychosis manifests as a denial of reality; psychopathy as a wild compulsive demand for reality to change. Psychotics speak 'concretely' – words are the things themselves; psychopaths (like hysterics) use a period of development in childhood when words are not yet symbolic, they are used literally. This age coincides with the age when there is either an awareness of an actual or possible sibling who will or does dethrone the subject, as with the string-boy. Is the string-boy literalizing a taunt he heard – 'he's tied to his mother's apron-strings' – and then, slipping into madness, he thinks of 'stringing his sister up'?

André Green has argued that we need to reinstate madness as opposed to psychosis – it is here in being totally displaced by another that the source of the general response of madness lies. For the Tallensi, various Western psychotic categories are subsumed into one term which is translated as madness. The person also feels mad. In Shakespeare's *The Taming of the Shrew*, the play is performed for down-and-out Sly. When he wakes as a nobleman, he wants his old identity – the change to apparently being someone else makes him feel absolutely mad. This madness is missed from our sophisticated categories of psychosis – it is the madness of the small child displaced by the sibling.

This is madness's moment; the moment of taking things literally and of not knowing where or who one is; the child that is laughed at by grown-ups vanishes into nothingness; we are in the realm of total misunderstandings and mistaken identities. King Lear on the edge of lunacy asks 'Can someone tell me who I am?' 'Lear's shadow,' replies the Fool. Winnicott's Piggle was 'a shadow of her former self'. To be mad is to be outside what is understood as the social; the Tallensi who are good to the deposed child regard both the mad and the child who has not weathered the advent of a sibling as categorically asocial. The migrant has lost his place in the society he has left and has no identity in the one he has entered. The asocial or the anti-social person cannot perceive others *as* others who need respect as such, nor experience themselves as such others *to* others.

I will conclude the rare observations on siblings that I have excavated from Winnicott's work with two final instances that confirm our picture of the sibling-as-trauma that may or may not be resolved. The first is Joan, the child who illustrates Winnicott's paediatric comment in 1931; the second is from an analytical treatment described in 1978, the little girl who calls herself the Piggle.

> Joan aged 2 years 5 months was an only child when 13 months ago her brother was born. Joan had been in perfect health until this event. She then became very jealous, she lost her appetite and consequently got thin. When left for a week without being forced to eat, she ate practically nothing and lost weight. She has remained like this, is very irritable and her mother cannot leave her without producing in her an anxiety attack. She will not speak to anyone and in the night she wakes screaming – even four times a night. The actual dream material not being very clear . . . She pinches and even bites the baby and will not allow him things to play with. She will not allow anyone to speak about the baby, but frowns and ultimately intervenes. (Winnicott [1931]: 4)

Here it is the not eating that matches the child with kwashiorkor – the new baby has taken the old baby's food. Here too the screaming. Apart from these symptoms, what are the consequences of such a trauma? This is Winnicott the psychoanalyst in 1978:

> The mother said that there had been a great change toward ill health in the Piggle recently. She was not naughty and she was nice to the baby. It was difficult to put into words what the matter was. But *she was not herself. In fact she refused to be herself and said so: 'I'm the*

mummy. I'm the baby'. She was not to be addressed as herself. She had developed a high-voiced chatter which was not hers. (1978: 13, my italics)

As with the psychotic Giuseppina, here is the loss of identity and a need to be someone else. The Piggle takes on the identity of the mother she does not want to lose and the baby she still needs to be in order to remain herself. Here too is the ventriloquized voice that underlies later 'bull-shitting', compulsive, flooding chatter. There is a loss of the previous mother, but there is even more crucially, *the loss of the previous self*. When (and if) the child regains itself, it will have to be with a new perspective on itself and the world; in the concept of the Tallensi, it has become a social being – its self-awareness will be the ability to see itself from another's perspective, how it is, where it stands in relation to others.

I believe this new perspective is the beginning of self-esteem which involves the loss of the narcissistic self. The sibling experience organizes narcissism into self-esteem through accepted loss – through a mourning process for the grandiose self, the 'death' of His Majesty the Baby. This is the necessary acceptance that one is ordinary, which does not mean that one is not unique – just that all those other brothers and sisters are also ordinary and unique. Without this gradual and never fully established transformation of the self, the distress and disruption of the anti-social child or the maladies of madness are on the cards.

The shock of the sibling trauma will also be repeated and have to be reworked through in any future event that displaces and dislodges a person from who and where they thought they were. If the first or subsequent shocks are too great, then the trauma is introjected and forms a core of violence within the person. It is therefore not only jealousy but violence – the string round the sister's neck – which is an intrinsic possibility. Violence is thus always a potential of all sibling relationships and of sibling sexuality and incest.

The narcissistic love which extends to the sibling or peer when it is conceived as the same as the subject can be transformed at the same moment that the subject's grandiose narcissism is relinquished; the self-esteem and 'object love' for the sibling are on a par: self and other are loved – and hated –'objectively'. But the narcissistic love can likewise be retained so that the sibling/peer is only loved as the self and violence will erupt the moment it is conceived as marginally other – this is a real likelihood in incestuous relationships. The process will also very importantly affect wider social functioning. A psychopathic adult such as Harold has his finger on the trigger of violence and constant jealousy; the hysteric relives each setback as though it were the original catastrophe: both communicate the trauma's effects to others. At the core of both there is the possibility of paranoia: this has been done to me and I can make others commiserate with it. The psychopath tries to make the world put right the un-put-rightable outrage – to demand that the new baby be sent back; if this fails he shares and distributes the experience among others so that he projects and creates paranoia in the sibling (everybody thinks you are a nasty baby). This can become the classic social technique of making your opponent believe everybody hates him. Because the scene is set in a retained childhood, the fantasies have the quality of reality and the subject's conviction is participated in. The hysterical or psychopathic subject, like the disturbed child, appears quite well – it is the chaos around him that testifies to the problem.

The sibling occasions a degree of jealousy to which the response is a wish to kill. In the child this is quite conscious – it becomes unconscious when it is realized that it is forbidden. In time the child also realizes that not killing hopefully ensures not being killed. This awareness is arrived at through lateral play, and the play also creates and enacts rules which ensure that the murderousness either becomes unconscious or is directed into lawful channels, 'the right to kill'. The introjected violence of the trauma itself does not become unconscious: a trauma by definition cannot be represented, it can only be experienced as a hole within or violence to self or other until its effects are mitigated. Because the trauma cannot be represented, there is no representation of it to be internalized as an unconscious process – there is thus also no way of retrieving it from unconsciousness since it is not unconscious. The 'hole' or trauma is thus technically a hypothesis deduced from behaviour or symptoms. This means that a complex view of psycho-social interaction is necessary. For instance, the younger child can also introject the violence of the older sibling and then need to re-externalize it in others – one can easily select the wrong child for treatment.

Richard, the evacuee child whom Melanie Klein treated in 1941 (chapter 5), crossed out a biplane in his drawing – crossing out equalled shooting down. He told Mrs Klein he had drawn the plane as a representative of his brother Paul. Immediately he became anxious about his hostility and contradicted himself: he explained simultaneously that his older brother was a soldier and might easily really be killed, but that the plane he had drawn was Uncle Tony whom he didn't like. Melanie Klein explained that Uncle Tony was his bad Daddy. Maybe – but what has happened to Paul? The analysis has repeated rather than interpreted his desired and dreaded annihilation; if Richard's efforts at externalizing his fear of being killed by his older brother go unnoticed so that he wants him dead, they will persist and so too will his terror of death. And anyway, once again, why explain lateral experiences always as though they were vertical ones – there is enough sexuality and manifestations of the death drive in the former not to have to transpose them to the latter to make them fit the demands of unconscious representations of parents or their substitutes. Certainly Richard consciously knows he is jealous, but he does not know the depths of his paranoia, nor one of its probable, indeed salient, sources. If the trauma of possible annihilation can become conscious through an awareness of the ideas represented by the emotions it has evoked, it is on the way to being overcome, at least for the time being.

It is not that no psychoanalyst or psychoanalytical therapist ever interprets the transference or countertransference of the treatment setting as though each other were siblings. When I have asked colleagues about how siblings feature in their work, I receive a range of answers, but a certain uniformity – with some exceptions: one colleague told me that realizing the missed importance of her older brother made her return for a further full period of training analysis. Mostly the sibling comes in as the other patients or imagined or known children of the therapist and thus, because the transference is seen to be child–parent, this confirms the exclusive understanding of the vertical. Sometimes one does interpret laterally. With one of my patients neither of us could miss the extent to which I appeared as her older sister; not only was it almost conscious, but at times I felt I started to look like this sister – and as we lived in the same neighbourhood, I learnt that this was not just the patient's perception. With Mrs X (discussed in chapter 4), the patient whose younger brother and stepbrother were actors in her inner world, I find in retrospect that I missed important moments when I was one or other of them. This meant I did not realize the nature of my counter-transference – not so much as the sister to my own brother, that was easy, but how my younger brother must have experienced me. If this was so, and I did miss my brother's experience of me, I could not help Mrs X to see how she was seen by her siblings. However painful and difficult this may be (indeed because it is painful and difficult), it is a crucial stage in the post-traumatic stress of gaining self-awareness.

Not long ago, I was invited to comment on a presentation of a hysterical patient in such a way that it would demonstrate how my suggestion of introducing a lateral autonomous place for siblings would affect a case of hysteria. The patient was an only child. What the therapist selected to highlight was that at the beginning and at the end of the treatment she noted a countertransference reaction which she felt important but not fully resolved.

The therapist noted that near the termination of this successful analysis, she found her own thinking dominated by Shakespeare's *The Taming of the Shrew*. Although the overt association to this was of a battle with a shrewish patient, there was something left over that continued to trouble the therapist. At the time, although it was a 'lifetime' since I had read or seen the play (never a favourite), I remembered the following facts about it. Two sisters are at the very centre of the play. Katherina, the Shrew, detests her younger sister Bianca and is physically and verbally violent to her. Bianca is sweet, amenable and adored by their father. No one will marry the abusive Katherina, while they queue up for the hand of amiable Bianca. Yet there is a problem, for in the end the Shrew tamed is a nobler character than Bianca, whose charm is based on a degree of deception and manipulativeness. In the countertransference, where was the therapist, a woman faced by a female hysteric, positioned? Was she the tamer, Katherina's suitor and husband, Petruchio; or might she have been unconsciously worrying that the patient may still have been trium-phant, leaving the analytic arts as the cheap deception and manipula-tion that the patient throughout the analysis had proclaimed them to be? Was the therapist positioned as Bianca in a rescripted play in which the Shrew (only apparently transformed) in fact triumphs over sibling and, maybe, husband?

Was the therapist or the patient the forgotten Bianca? On rereading the play after the discussion, I learnt that Shakespeare had gone way beyond any of his sources in giving the sister relationship a central role. The forgotten Bianca seemed crucial. What I want to insert is the therapist *as* sibling. Because our own analysts on the whole did not explore this dimension with us, it is bound to be an unfamiliar part of our countertransference. Without thinking of siblings I suggest one cannot be aware of these dimensions. In particular, without a sibling paradigm one will be unlikely to think of siblings where there are none in the actual history – but only lots in the unconscious mind and in the social enactments. How are these actual or imagined siblings, peers or 'replacement' children such as Heathcliff, my brother, Mrs X's brother, us as our brother's sisters, Katherina and Bianca, dealing with each other? What is our problem?

To consider this, I am going to look at the sibling extreme in twinning. Twins everywhere are subjects of special regard – in sub-Saharan Africa, where they are more common than elsewhere in the world, they may be instances of evil and of good luck. Twinning can be what we might call a 'metaphorical' relationship in which two children of different ages and heritage are assigned each other as 'twin'.[2] As with kwashiorkor, the African context also gives us the real basis of jealousy and distress in that it is often hard to feed twins adequately. But the evil–good variance is interesting and echoed in psychoanalytic concepts: on the positive side, so-called 'doubling' is a protection against the threat of castration, which in its turn is the representation of death; on the other hand, the return of the subject as his own double is 'the uncanny'. Here it is not for their symbolism but because they offer an extreme instance of conditions of siblinghood that I turn to twins to see something of the psychodynamics of lateral relations. I have always found working clinically with a twin, or a parent of a twin, particularly interesting – probably a remnant of a fascination I recall from childhood.[3]

I remember a joke that repelled but intrigued me when young. A heavily pregnant woman never gave birth. After her death they cut open her swollen belly and inside were two identical wizened old men, each one saying, 'after you'. Wilfred Bion had a similar experience to this joke with a patient who had an 'imaginary twin'. After some work with the man, Bion tells him that he makes him, Bion, feel like a parent offering ineffectual admonitions to a refractory child. He records that after this comment, 'a difficult-to-express' change took place in the patient's sessions:

It was as if two quite separate co-existent scansions of his material were possible. One imparted an overpowering sense of boredom and depression; the other, dependent on the fact that he introduced regularly spaced pauses in the stream of his associations, an almost jocular effect as if he were saying 'Go on; it's your turn.' (Bion [1950]: 5)

Furthermore, even when actual people were referred to by the patient, Bion gradually realized these people could be versions of the patient himself. Bion, it is important to note, has interpreted his patient's behaviour by placing himself as the patient's remonstrating parent with the patient as his recalcitrant child. However, following this interpretation the patient has a dream which places Bion fairly and squarely as the imaginary twin. In the dream there are two people in a car, each preventing the other from getting out. Like the joke I recall, Bion translates the car as a womb, and the patient responds to this interpretation by getting into a cramped foetal position on the analytic couch. Bion explains that if he were to 'emerge' from the womb, the patient would be overwhelmed by hatred; however, were he to form a relationship with Bion as his imaginary twin, they would be consumed by mutual hatred. A further dream follows this lateral interpretation: a father is asking the patient to refer his daughter to a second eye-specialist. Certainly warranted by the material, Bion explains that the first 'I' specialist is the passive mother and the second 'I' specialist the more active father. Following this interpretation, Oedipal material starts to be produced. It is not that this is wrong, but that it seems to miss an enormous opportunity – the opportunity of siblings which Bion nearly got to when he realized he was the patient's imaginary twin. In the second dream, the child who needs her 'I' attended to in the dream is a girl, yet Bion makes nothing of the transgendering of his own interpretation. The male patient dreams his 'I' or ego as feminine.

Bion also makes nothing of the fact of which he informs us, that when his patient was one year old, his older sister died. A baby of this age would have been mirrored by his sibling – not only seeing himself in her, but beginning to see himself from her perspective. Is this dead sister not the root cause of the imaginary twin? When identical twins are young a twin's own reflection in the mirror is often identified as that of the other twin. Twins are so close together that it is hard for them to find the sibling perspective on the self. In a famous study of twins in a wartime residential nursery, Dorothy Burlingham (1952) describes the mirroring behaviour of two sets of twins. At nearly two and a half, Bill called Bert 'other one Bill', and in seeing his own reflection in a bathroom mirror he referred to this too as 'other one Bill'. When younger (seventeen months), his twin Bert had been ill and without any appetite, refusing all food. A nurse started to feed Bert in front of a mirror, pointing only to the reflection. Delighted, Bert started to eat like his healthy twin Bill; watching his reflection as though sick Bert were well Bill, he 'too' joyfully gobbled his food. When her twin, Bessie, was in the shelter set aside for the sick, Jessie, who was not allowed to see her, placed all her toys in front of a mirror and played with her reflection/twin as they had before they were separated.

Bion's patient does not imagine an older sister; instead he has 'a twin' because with his sister's death he would have lost the possibility of using her as a mirror or of being seen by her. At one year old he would have thought his sister was a reflection of himself – hence his emerging 'I' or ego that needs treating by a second optician is, I suggest, his older dead sister perceived as an unmourned imaginary twin. The one person whom Bion mentions in any detail as being experienced as a version of the patient himself is his homosexual brother-in-law, whom Bion believes may have been having an incestuous relationship with the patient's wife. This brother-in-law is surely another same-sex (boy here, girl in the dream) twin. Are the two 'I' specialists then not only the patient's parents, or the prospect of two therapists, but also the two 'I's of brother and sister, brother and homosexual brother-in-law, the twin mirror reflections, the imaginary twins, the patient and Bion as each other's mirror-twin?[4]

Commenting many years later on the analysis, Bion believed he was wrong to have been excited about the concept of psychological twinning (I disagree):

> I do not now regard the pattern of the 'imaginary twin' as of any central importance, though I have found it illuminating for some aspects of the psychoanalysis of an only child. It is then very often a particular fact of the more general pattern of splitting. The patient of whom I wrote was not an only child, but circumstances led him to feel so. (Bion 1967: 127)

For Bion twinning is just a particular variant of the general paranoid-schizoid phase, in which the baby splits the object and therefore itself into good and bad, and then fears that the bad into which everything negative of its own feelings has been projected will return to attack it. However, persecutory states which such splitting implies do not seem developed in Bion's patient; instead there is splitting into an imaginary twin. Bion later believes this is significant with only children. The only child who made the therapist accept her for treatment and reminded her of *The Taming of the Shrew* managed to get herself accepted as a favoured child over quasi-siblings with her neighbour's family and in her therapeutic treatment. Melanie Klein described at length an only-child patient Erna, who lived in a fantasized world of murder, torture, death and destruction of her mother and babies. However, we know nothing of why Erna was an only child – was it choice, or were there mis-carriages, abortions, deaths, as for most of the world's population there inevitably are? The aspect of the comparison of Erna with Bion's adult patient that strikes me as relevant is that Erna, aged six, lives almost entirely in a fantasy world. It would seem to me that both patients are using fantasy because a particular reality is too traumatic: the reality of a dead sibling will have to be dealt with by unresolved fantasies if it comes at a certain age and certain time and the child or infant is not helped to undertake a process of mourning. Erna is seriously pseudologic and lives her life in a dream-state.

It is remarkable that even when analysts such as Bowlby or Burlingham emphasize the importance of mourning, they do not be-lieve a sibling death has much significance. When Bion's remark about his being turned by his patient into a remonstrative parent produces the change to the patient's 'your turn now' communication, Bion then comes to realize that his patient's reports of his conversations with friends and family may be actual – or may be completely imagin-ary; fantasy, I suggest, protects against the reality of the dead sister. The patient's feminine 'I' is based on an identification with the dead sister, which, if Bion cannot see it, makes the patient want another 'I' specialist to help him.

Bion does not see the imaginary twin as a solution to the problem presented by the death of his sister: 'The twin was imaginary because my patient had prevented the birth of the twin – there was in fact no twin. His use of a twin as a means of alleviating anxiety was therefore illegitimate' ([1950]: 8). I think, to the contrary, producing a twin when your analyst, probably like everyone else, does not believe the death of your sister is significant is a very possible, indeed highly 'legitimate', psychic defence.

Melanie Klein is famous for her insistence that children's play is crucial for understanding unconscious processes and in fact play is crucial in its own right because it can serve the function of dreams: a well-playing child has the sensation with which dreaming leaves the adult – something important has been raised and resolved. It simply feels better to play and to dream.[5] But what is of relevance here is that dreams and play have in common the personification of aspects of the self: one plays and dreams others as the self and the self as others; in both cases the personification is both other and self – a doll is one's baby or one's little brother or school mate, all of whom will be both who one perceives these real or imagined people to be and the aspects of oneself one has used to understand them, one's identification with them. Eric Brenman's (1985) patient, Mr X, 'fragments' himself; so do all children in their play – so does Bion's patient with his imaginary twin. Bion's patient, like a child such as Erna, has got stuck in personified play, and like such a child, most of the time does not know that the doll is also a doll. One has to stop playing sometime and sometimes.

From the dream of two 'I's, Bion's patient awakes overwhelmed with rage and terror. In a film by Siodmark, *The Dark Mirror* (1946), Olivia de Havilland plays both Ruth and Terry, identical twin sisters. Ruth is pretty, kind and beloved, Terry jealous and a murderer. The psychologist in the film tells us of adult twins, one on the west, one on the east coast of the United States, having a tooth pulled at the same hour of the same day. One twin is a university professor, the other serving a jail sentence. Although as children, twins can take this route towards differentiation, there is in fact no evidence that twins turn out to be one good and one bad – it is, I believe, how we, the viewer, overcome the dilemma of someone being too nearly the same as another, we need to make crude differences. When the other who has been identified with dies, reality makes it harder to perceive that we were dealing with the problem through fantasy: the problem, whether actual or imagined, becomes death; the dark mirror in which one is not reflected signifies death.

Identical twins
Twins by Duffy Ayers, © the artist

If there are two 'I's, how can there be one – is there not even a joke in the terrifying dream: we do after all have two eyes? In Lacan's 'mirror phase' the baby is referred by its mother to the mirror in which its disorganized self is offered a coherent gestalt. Winnicott's mother mirrors the true baby to itself. Both ignore the active role of another child who looked *at*, looks like the self, but who looked *from*, sees that there are differences. When the toddler is expecting a baby to arrive it anticipates a repetition of itself; when it does arrive it literally *exceeds* all expectation – this excess is the trauma. But if the excess can be overcome, then the toddler seeing the baby as baby provides the conditions in which the baby will be able to see itself: for both children two 'I's will become 'you and me'. For twins, and where there is the death of a sibling, this is harder to achieve.

In negotiating this split into two 'I's, it is all too easy to make one good 'I' and one bad one – then later 'I' will become the good 'I' and you will be the bad one: war looms. Bion notes that his patient is violent in places where he should have been sexual. I would argue that for siblings the condition of sexuality is the violence of the nego-tiation of self and other, and vice versa. I love myself, I will love my sibling as myself, my sibling is not myself, I must love my sibling as another who is like me. I thus put at risk my unique, grandiose self: with luck I can see myself seen by my sibling. Rage and terror mark the overcoming of the trauma that necessitates the transition and transformation from narcissism to object-love, from self-importance to self-esteem, from the choice between murder versus being annihi-lated on the one hand, and, on the other hand, tolerance of self and other, self-esteem and respect for the other. When the subject becomes the object of the other's regard, both self and other are realizable. However, violence towards each other and incest with each other are born of the same problematic.

The engendering of gender

It is a little girl whom in his dream Bion's male patient sends to the eye/I specialist. He is also confused and probably shares his wife with his homosexual (surely bisexual?) brother-in-law. How does the 'I' and 'you' of siblinghood come to be gendered? When the excess of the newborn confronts the sibling, the differences will be a focus of all that is impossible about the situation. It was his older and young-est sisters (not his brothers) that triggered the tram-man's childhood and then adult hysteria. Jealousy relates to position – he stands where I want to stand. But it is implicated in the insatiability of desire: even the well-nourished baby wants all the milk, so jealousy oscil-lates with envy about what one has or has not got; he's got what I haven't got and I want it; or its other side, contempt – I don't want what he/she has got, or they have not got what I have got. What I believe we have to understand here is how the 'narcissism of minor differences' selects some small differences to become large ones – genitals, skin colour or whatever. In the case of gender most analyses suggest that it is its subsequent subjugation to the reproductivity of sexual difference that makes for the oppression of the woman as the future mother – idealized and denigrated. I want to argue a very different perspective. I suggest the sibling trauma instigates the construction of gender difference. Gender is engendered in the sibling (or sibling equivalent) relationship.

At first sight, social organization – and theories about it – would seem to bear out the widespread assumption of a relationship between child-bearing and women's status as the second sex. In order to challenge the primacy, at any rate, of this explanation, I first want to situate sexual differences, reproduction and madness in the Western world as a framework to my argument. Why madness? The first stage of my argument takes us away from siblings, to which I then return. The relationship between social change and psychic structures means that there are always latent mental structures that come to the surface both to inaugurate and to respond to social change: there is no one-to-one correlation between psyche and social, but there is an indubitable and necessary interdependence. From a psychoanalytic perspective, mental illnesses equal normal mental processes writ large: the so-called sane and the mad are not distinct psychic processes but are on a continuum. Psychopathologies are therefore useful exaggerations which can give us the key not just to the individual mind, but to the social world which produces it.

In the Western world it is common to note that men outnumber women in prison in roughly the same proportion as women outnumber men diagnosed with a mental disorder. The ratios tend to naturalize the gendering of crime and madness as though men are definitionally liable to offend against the civil order (crimes) and women by virtue of being women bring disorder and unreason (madness) to the human order itself. Men can be against society; women outside humanity. I suggest that the concept of mental illness and of criminality are already gendered. It is not a question of the disproportionate numbers of women who become mentally ill in a man's world, or even *because* it is a man's world, as is often (and probably rightly) contended (Porter 1987; Chesler 1997; Ussher 1997; and others); rather it is that 'women' and 'mental illness' are related terms. This general reflection has specific histories and it is to aspects of that specificity that I want ultimately to draw attention.

If women as women occupy a place outside the polity and hence share a terrain with madness, men as men will go against its structures from within it and within its terms – hence they will be criminals. However, at least in England at present, there is a striking escalation in the number of female criminals and simultaneously a concern that a very large proportion of criminals are quite seriously mentally ill. Are we watching some transgendering of madness and crime? Recent accounts of prisoners, male and female, in the United Kingdom consider that the majority are mentally ill, thus bringing the genders closer together.

Thus, as a general proposition cross-culturally since antiquity and in much mythology, women have been defined as marginal to the social order. Madness – the extreme of mental illness – occupies a similar position: it can partake of genius, divinity and/or the torpors of hell and the devil; it is the irrational, that which if it erupts must be excluded, even if, as in Foucault's premodern idyll, it is – like women – still catered for within the community; it is nevertheless outside the social law and order. For most of all human history, neither the mad nor women are full citizens. Yet madness and women are not identical; rather they occupy various and differing parts of that same extrinsic space. We should remember, too, that for the Tallensi a child before the advent of its matri-sibling is also asocial, though cared for of course as a human being within the community. I shall suggest that there is significance in an equation of women, the mad, the pre-sibling infant.

In 1989 Carole Pateman argued that the term 'patriarchy' should include fraternal as well as paternal forms of male dominance. I disagree with this conflation but find her controversial account of the 'fraternity' as patriarchal oppression both interesting and useful. Carole Pateman argues convincingly that the construction of modern political theory depends on the subordination of women; but this subordination is to the fraternity, not to the paternal patriarchy. The rise of the modern state in the seventeenth century with its subsequent emphasis on 'contract' ensured that brothers would be equal with each other and equally certain of their paternity. 'Perhaps the most striking feature of accounts of the contract story is the lack of attention paid to fraternity, when liberty and equality are so much discussed' . . . 'Only *men* are born free and equal. The contract theorists constructed sexual difference as a political difference, the difference between men's natural freedom and women's natural subjection' (Pateman 1989: 4–5). Women's duty is childbirth; men's to die for the state. The contract theorists who inaugurated the conditions we have still dominantly with us were in the seventeenth century opposed by 'patriarchalists'. In overthrowing arguments for the natural rights of kings and fathers and for the patriarchal family as the basis of the state, in insisting instead on individual rights, contract theory opened a space for the equality of all. But for the woman this was closed off in terms of her *natural* role, which was outside the social:

> The fraternal social contract creates a new, modern patriarchal order that is presented as divided into two spheres: civil society or the universal sphere of freedom, equality, individualism, reason, contract and impartial law – the realm of men or 'individuals' – and the private world of particularity, natural subjection, ties of blood, emotion, love and sexual passion – the world of women, in which men also rule. (Pateman 1989: 43)

Although the socio-political world is thus divided, this is obscured by the fact that all individuals have individual rights. In its turn, this fact of the 'abstract' individual with abstract rights means we do not see the fraternity behind it. The masculine fraternal subject masquerades as a bodiless, sexless private individual. One can extend this in a number of directions: the economy which depends not on the use-value of a person's labour, but on the surplus value they produce, is thus also rendered abstract and theoretically sexless. Does the concept of madness too start to fall under the sway of the neutral individual – a process only today being realized? Work and citizenship are abstract but marked masculine, and madness, which is marked feminine, becomes abstract. Within the abstract, gender positions can change.

In *King Lear* we see the old king and father of the patriarchal order become hysterical: 'I feel the mother rise in me.' The father was considered the one and only parent so Lear can feel hysterical; hysteria was a disease of women, 'the mother'; but as Lear is father and mother both, he can suffer the 'suffocation of the mother'. Hysteria's diagnosis shifted in the seventeenth century to become associated with the brain; even if 'the vapours' were linked to the womb, suffering from 'nerves' largely supplanted them. This meant men could be hysterical – not that they often were considered such, any more than women were considered politicians. If the new political theory brought into being the neutral political individual, the new socio-economic conditions, the neutral worker, attitudes to mental illness, I believe, were following suit. Psychiatry and pharmacology increasingly responded to and produced the gender-neutral sufferer. But if the neutral is still masculine in the polity and the economy, in madness it is still feminine. Nevertheless, a space, a possibility is opened up to demand what is offered – true neutrality in the polity. Are madness and hysteria thus comparably opened up to men and in turn de-gendered?

If women, as in Pateman's argument, were subjugated under the fraternity that denied them full equality and liberty because of their reproductive roles, how far is the increasing overcoming of the division due to changes in the actuality and in the conception of procreation? The higher the socio-economic level, the less likely is a woman to have children; in countries like Sweden, boys are educated with girls for an equal and gender-undifferentiated role in childcare. Maybe the changing relationship to reproduction signals the beginning of the end of sexual difference along clearly oppositional lines. This will mean 'gender' will be triumphant and the model will not be parents but siblings – but will there be a shifting of the goalposts of difference and an end to gender deference? I think not. Although ensuring a knowledge of paternity is a major factor in causing the freedom of wife-mothers to be restricted, it is not, I believe, all there is.

When the child is overwhelmed by the trauma of one who, in the mind, was supposed to be the same as itself inevitably turning out to be different, it finds or is given ways to mark this difference – age is one, gender another. Hopefully, familiarity soon enables the shock to be resolved; however, the violence inherent in the initial experience remains a possibility. The trauma guarantees that violence is always latent, and even if it is overcome between actual siblings, it is available for their replacements and substitutes in the wider world. The cradle of gender difference is both narcissistic love and violence at the traumatic moment of displacement in the world. Gender difference comes into being when physical strength and malevolence are used to mark the sister as lesser. Pateman did not take far enough the first part of her own observation that men must die for their country while women give birth. The soldier arises from the brother who has fought off the intruder, the man from the boy who has denigrated his little sister.

Here and now

The term 'patriarchy' has been widely deployed since the late nineteenth century, but more emphatically since the rise of second-wave feminism. We can consider one aspect of the concept of patriarchy as an analogy with the notion of 'the binary' which I considered in chapter 6. Hammel's (1972) critique of Lévi-Strauss's discovery of the binary as a universal rested on a double statement: either the binary is found everywhere, in which case there is nothing much to be said about it, or it is a particular mode of thinking, in which case it is important to interrogate the relationship between the modes of thought of the observer and the observed – does everyone, or only some people, or only some people some of the time, or everyone some of the time, think using an internal binary model?

The analogy with patriarchy is a weak, but relevant comparison. Okin (1989), Therborn (2002) and many others have claimed that 'patriarchy' is a universal. If it is, then it cannot be used as a variable, so what are we to make of it? As a universal it is not particularly interesting from an analytical standpoint. If, however, we consider that 'gender' is a category of analysis, then we must have terms to deploy within it. I suggest that just as the binary is not the only mode of thinking, so patriarchy, itself various, is not the only mode of male dominance. Within male dominance – itself the 'universal' – there will be various types of patriarchal and non-patriarchal but still male-dominant rule.

Second-wave feminism also adopted, developed and popularized the term oppression, deriving it mainly from the struggles against colonialism and racism; oppression was a general mode of which 'exploitation' was a particular subcategory relating to the taking of the surplus value produced by another's labour power. Postmodernism has critiqued the notion of oppression. However, as the flip-side of domination, it seems to me to still have some uses. Women's oppression and male domination are, I suggest, the two aspects of a universal that a gender analysis must posit as its terms of reference. It does not mean, indeed quite the contrary, that as universally present they are everywhere alike or manifest in each individual instance at all times. Analytically, they too are uninteresting as such; it is their variable and changing relationship which needs to be the object of enquiry.[6]

However, in suggesting we distinguish 'gender' and 'sexual difference' along the lines of non-reproductive and reproductive distinctions, I am proposing a subcategory of the general terms female oppression/male dominance. In relation to reproduction male and female are psychically polarized (sexual difference); they are thought in binary terms which are naturalized as two parents. In non-reproductive relationships the term gender is not binary. Gender is not a binary construction. In other words, sexual difference is a mark of polarity, and gender is the continuum which at one extreme may indicate the disappearance or incipient disappearance of the terms.

Sexual difference in classical psychoanalytical theory, and re-emphasized by Lacan, is established with the traumatic subjugation of boy and girl to the castration complex ('the law of the father'). I have added that there is also a subjugation to the painful realization that children cannot make or give birth to babies (my suggestion of the 'law of the mother'). Whether this latter is a trauma or not, it certainly imposes a limitation on omnipotence. The child has to get over the fact that as a child it is infertile and not allowed to go on imagining otherwise. 'Sexual difference' is the culturally various representation of two 'opposite' sexes for reproduction. Everyone will be subject to this differentiation – or have to find a way of avoiding or denying it. It is the trauma that instigates it that is being resisted: no one wants the knowledge that they are 'incomplete'; it is, however, a condition of the psyche of humanity. The double aspect of the Oedipus complex, like mother like father – but as their child not in the identical position of either – means that everyone's sexual drive is subject to the fantasies of procreation, everyone is psychically 'reproductive', whatever their choices, denials or repressions.

These traumata or monumental restrictions are intimations of the inevitability of death, and weathering the storms they cause is essential to becoming a social being.

However, the crucial blow to the unique subject is the presence of the alike other, first represented by the sibling or sibling-to-be who has at least the same mother and maternal line. The child wishes to control all aspects of this dangerous situation. I recently heard a four-year-old retort, on being told the sister she was eagerly awaiting might be a brother, 'I don't have to have a brother if I don't want one.' Everyone has a potential sibling – the parents who conceive one in the past or future can conceive others: an only child is no more unique in her or his generic humanity than is the son of a chief who counted over one hundred brothers and sisters through his polygynous father (Goody 2002), or the child of Queen Victoria, mother of nine.

After thirty years of active campaigning and discussion, Brazil in January 2003 instituted gender-equal legislation; women have the same rights as citizens as men; the male as 'head of the household' has been abolished. In France, the movement for the implementation of complete parity is having some success at taking forward the literal implication of notional equality – female/male representation must be on a fifty-fifty per cent basis, each individual citizen must have the same rights. At the same time, Brazil has instituted a hundred women-run police stations to enforce a woman's right to equal respect: there must be no rape, no beating, no incest. The legislation points to the practices that need remedying – sex and violence. What is changing?

The sexual basis of gender difference is alive and well in the world-wide gang cultures of the urban poor. However, there are some signs of the breakdown of gender divisions. Los Angeles has been deporting its criminal gang members and with them the Angelinos have exported an aspect of America's gender-equal ideology. Fifteen to twenty years ago, Salvadoreans fled their wars as illegal immigrants to California. While the parents cleaned or built the Angelinos' houses, their children, boys and to a degree girls, formed street gangs: robbing, raping, killing – mostly each other. Convicted offenders are deported to El Salvador, the country they left as toddlers. There girls as well as boys form violent gangs. As elsewhere, two 'solutions' are offered: prison or religion. Both prison and religious communities structurally repeat the social nature of the gang, but they place the gang under an external authority.

When I was growing up we formed unstable gangs, with one of the favourite groupings for warfare being 'girls after boys', or 'boys after girls' – at the time it seemed, and still does, a categorical division that was easier than remembering who was on whose side that day. Our violence took place on the street and in the school, but it was the school that set the rules: sticks no longer than your arm; no conkers in the honker-bonkers (tightly knotted football socks which were whirled like maces, but which must not be aimed at heads). The rules, however, could not equal the imagination – being cast in a specially dug pit with tall vertical mud walls, trussed and hung from a branch of a tree, dared to stay long in the fire and smoke with which we filled the air-raid shelters of the trespassed 'big house' . . . The fearful fun stopped, almost magically, at puberty. Through the adjustment to representations of the body image of secondary sexual characteristics, menstruation, body hair, voice timbre, breasts, sperm, sexual difference, a repeat of those Oedipal questions at age four or five, reasserted itself to reformulate 'gender' as binary sexual polarity. Adolescent sexual difference rearticulates gender difference as a repetition of Oedipal fantasies of sexual difference, but to do so it also builds on a bed of sibling gender difference; this difference, in childhood, adolescence and adulthood, is informed with all the implications of the lateral relationship.

The sibling situation introduces the threat of sameness – the clearer the difference established, the safer the dominant person; a major difference is the female other. Using the body to represent large/small, white/black, male/female, violence becomes the social means to establish the subject against this different other. Ann Parsons noted that as rural families moved to the slums of Naples, patriarchy declined. Women earned, mothers provided the money for children's food and their men's cigarettes: 'Like a soul in Purgatory, he waits for me with his mouth open just like the children when they cry for bread' (informant, Parsons 1969: 97). Trapped in her father Talcott's famous intergenerational paradigm, Ann Parsons, whose observations exceed her framework, notes that families became more matrifocal and, with no patriarchal model, males took their masculine definition from male gangs. This is a familiar theme of the 'crisis of masculinity', which asserts the other side of the binary of dominance/oppression to produce the invariable backlash against feminism.

The model of siblings shows us this: there is always a latent crisis in gender relations, with its predictable resolution of big/white/ male superiority. Such superiority is culturally codified as individual or collective omnipotence which depends on either annihilating or confining the other to powerlessness. It is a sad irony that despite the Angelino/Salvadorean girl gangs with their frighteningly violent egalitarian pre-pubertal mores, the more conventional girls of the ganglands, in trying to rescue their men, are nostalgic for a past family. This past family lives in an imagined nuclear community on a rural farm. Yet Brazil is typical: Brazil's farms were slave sugar plantations and it is in the countryside that male violence against women has been institutionalized as a male right. Where older men marry young women, patriarchally they may beat their wives with the father's benign discipline and keep the uncontrolled violence of lateral self-differentiation for those women who are not supposed to be the mothers of their children. And perhaps sometimes the smaller, the weaker, the constituted other, like Bianca, find ways of getting back, by deploying substitutes for violence.

In an article on 'the death of a twin', psychoanalyst George Engel (1975) described how on the anniversaries of the unexpected death of his twin brother, he re-experienced the extreme confusion of selves that the two of them had known subjectively and from others' perceptions which they both dreaded and exploited as children. Not only in dreams, but awake, he answered to his brother's name, saw his brother in the mirror, and more or less a year to the day after his death, had as a self-diagnosed hysterical conversion symptom the 'same' heart attack (from which – unlike his brother – he naturally recovered).

Twins also demonstrate the mutability of psychic positions, the play of sameness and difference. From birth, even in an identical 'clone' type twin, there are differences; life experiences will facilitate differentiation. However, pulling in the opposite direction is the tug of identificatory processes – as a twin becomes more different, both also become more alike. The roles, dependent/independent, stronger/ weaker and so on, will become to a degree settled, but at each of a child's life crises they are also renegotiated. Thus there is nothing fixed for all time and every situation. As the place from which 'gender' emanates, these lateral relations indicate that gender difference is likewise a flexible marker. Sometimes the genders will be far apart, at other times close together; like twins, the characteristic of each can swap places. This indicates the possibility of transformations of what seem, but are not, the binary rigidities that are claimed for gender. Twins are not so much the exception that the literature considers them to be – they are the extreme instances that highlight the problems, the glories and nightmares of the 'sibling' norm. With twins, with siblings, friends in a gang, in a religious community, in a marriage, in the repetition of yourself, you get more than you bargained for – for better or worse.

There is a general tendency for economic success to indicate one or no children at a general and individual level. We might soon be asking: where have all the siblings gone? Yet psychologically speaking, siblings are crucial also to the only child who expects their arrival and fears what may have happened to them. An actual sibling is considered important in allowing the access to hatred in a way that can be resolved so that sociality results. Siblings provide a way of learning to love and hate the same person. Siblings matter in their own right, and at the same time are central to any kin group. To an extent they may be replaced by friends and enemies from among the peer group – everyone has to take on board that they are not unique and omnipotent. The loss of the grandiose self and the acceptance of others who are like one will remain crucial. The subject must also survive in a world of other people; self-esteem and respect for others are two sides of the same coin.

Meanwhile in a world where siblings still flourish, we can see their importance not only in themselves, but for all lateral relationships. The psychic means through which siblinghood is negotiated are crucial. The splitting of the ego and object, identification and projection, and the simultaneous reversal of love and hate, all followed, it is hoped, by the transformation of narcissism into object-love and murderousness into an objective hatred for what is wrong or evil in the self and the other: these are the building blocks of a lateral not vertical paradigm. Siblings also point to the importance of laterality for understanding the interpenetration of violence, power and non-reproductive sexuality; for the engendering of gender as a difference forged out of the matrix of sameness.

Notes

1 Siblings and Psychoanalysis

1 Recently France became the exception to this trend. Concerned for almost two centuries about its exceptionally low birth-rate, France has always been at the forefront of pronatalist policies; it was recently rewarded with a 2.2 rate of reproduction compared, say, with Italy's 1.7.

2 The Oedipus complex is named after the mythical Greek hero Oedipus, whose life, death and the subsequent history of his family are vividly portrayed in Sophocles' trilogy *Oedipus Rex* (or *Oedipus the King*), *Oedipus at Colonus* and *Antigone*. In order to avoid a prophecy that their son would kill his father, Oedipus' parents had him exposed on a mountainside. A shepherd, however, saved him and he was brought up as a son in the royal family of Corinth. Because he does not know he is adopted, fate leads him to unwittingly kill his natural father, Laius, and marry his natural mother, Jocasta, with whom he has four children. The Oedipus complex is the constellation of unconscious ideas focusing on the wish to possess the mother and kill the father (the girl's wish for father and hatred of mother is her Oedipus complex, not as is often claimed, an Electra complex).

3 The work culminated in Mitchell 2000a.

4 I refer to psychopathy (and other such conditions) in the psychoanalytic rather than the psychiatric sense – that is, as a dynamic set of symptoms related to unconscious processes rather than as a personality disorder (renamed antisocial personality disorder in DSM-IV-TR).

5 The problem arose in part because by the time of Tudor England people could read the Bible and learn that God allowed certain relations that they had previously believed were prohibited.

6 Ernest Jones used the term 'aphanasis' for his clinical observation of this phenomenon, which, of course, he did not relate to siblings.

2 Did Oedipus have a Sister?

1 *Sophocles: The Three Theban Plays*, trans, R. Fagles (London: Allen Lane, 1982): *Oedipus the King*, pp. 66–7 (my italics).

2 Julia Kristeva (1982) explains this hatred as rising sui generis from the birth situation itself. She uses the concept of 'abjection' to describe the mother's response to parturition. The hatred has no psychic history. The same problem of psychic reactions arising for the first time ever with the advent of motherhood – i.e. that there is no *childhood/infantile* history of mothering – is inherent also in the work of Mary Kelly in *Post-partum Document* (1983). Kristeva's account, like Winnicott's explanation, begs a question – from where in the mother's infancy does the hatred arise? I suggest that the hated baby is a reduplication of the sibling that the mother hated in her childhood. As a casual observation, it is notable (or not!) how many mothers accidentally refer to their own babies by a sibling's name.

3 André Green (1995) considers failure to mourn the prevalent characteristic of most contemporary psychoneuroses. While agreeing with the observation, I have a different explanation from Green: this failure to mourn is the expression of the hysterical sediment in all the so-called 'borderline' cases.

4 Here I am making use of some of the observations of D. W. Winnicott and Anna Freud rather than those of Melanie Klein.

5 I am thinking of work done with mothers and premature babies in the slums of Lima, Peru, reported to me by E. Piazzon.

6 When critics like Elaine Showalter reassess these illnesses and their modern equivalents, such as Gulf War Syndrome, and argue that after all they are hysteria, they then redefine hysteria as the manifestation of an impotent response to untenable conditions. This leaves out hysteria's crucial sexualizing and compulsive proclivities. More importantly, it doesn't explain why the symptoms of hysteria express unconscious processes. Why can't the protest be conscious?

7 Their parents could not have done, and continue to do, more to help the situation. Possibly the early handicaps of the older child and the very difficult uterine experience and birth of the younger made the two girls particularly vulnerable to the threat posed by each other.

8 Since writing the above, I have heard Michael Rutter deliver the Eighth John Bowlby Memorial Lecture (City of London School for Girls, March 2000) in which he described some outcomes of his studies of children from Romanian orphanages adopted in England. These traumatized children come from horrific institutional situations; they like to be with babies, as though the baby gives them their lost baby-selves. Emmi's

excessive caring for babies may be analogous: the orphans' desires indicate the importance of trauma in early infancy and of how it can be resolved. Emmi is looking after 'herself' as she would have liked her sister to do.

9 I was struck when rereading Helene Deutsch's work (1947) on motherhood that it shows how frequently eggs feature in sexual curiosity. Eggs are easy images of both anal birth and parthenogeneticity. Deutsch's notion of an 'as if' personality is, I believe, a refinement and specification of hysteria. Eggs also feature prominently in Eisler's (1921) study of a man's hysterical pregnancy (see chapter 6).

10 Two years later (2002), Emmi now reluctantly goes to school. However, once there she resolutely refuses to speak at all – either to the teacher or to other children. She nods or shakes her head. Unlike her older sister, Emmi learnt to speak extraordinarily early – at nine months. She is extremely fluent, with a wide vocabulary and an unusual answer for absolutely everything. Marion now often invites her to play; she nearly always refuses, playing instead with the dolls (never to be referred to as such), which are no longer babies, but her little brothers and sisters – each one carefully named.

11 I read Anton Blok's excellent book (2001) after this was written. Blok emphasizes that violence takes place when differences cannot be maintained – my point, with a different emphasis because it is made the other way round. Blok notes the number of conflicts which are labelled 'fratricide'.

12 World Service of the BBC, 'It's a girl', 29 Jan. 2002.

3 SISTER–BROTHER/BROTHER–SISTER INCEST

1 Shakespeare, *King Lear*: this was Lear's hope for an old age cared for by his daughter Cordelia.

2 I think there is another story to be told about sibling incest from the boy's point of view (see chapter 9). Like the girl, the boy also has to realize he is not fertile *as a child*.

3 The recent report of the National Society for the Prevention of Cruelty to Children (Cawson et al. 2000) which notes that sibling incest and abuse is prevalent also indicates that it is widely overlooked.

4 John Donne, Sermon, 24 Feb. 1625.

5 Sadly, Enid Balint died in 1996, so I was unable to discuss the case history further with her.

6 I am grateful to Dr Estela Weldon, author of *Mother, Madonna, Whore* (1988) and retired senior psychiatric consultant at the Portman Clinic,

London, for psychiatric confirmation of this psychoanalytic observation and expectation.

7 Karen Horney and Melanie Klein give girls a primary womb awareness; Robert Stoller, among others, insists on primary femininity for both sexes. What I am pointing to is something these accounts do not address – the self-representation of the body-ego, the womb as 'me'. Eric Erikson's essay on 'inner space' (1964), which studied children's play and proposed the gender difference in terms of inner-directed and outer-directed activity, is a good account of representations of the gendered body-ego.

8 Both Freud's 'Wolf Man' and Eisler's male hysteric imaginatively retain their bowels as wombs.

9 Estela Weldon's *Mother, Madonna, Whore* (1988) followed by Louise Kaplan's *Female Perversions* (1991) have established the presence of female perversity once and for all. One should note that Freud's 1919 ' "A child is being beaten" ' (chapter 4 below) is about understanding perversion in women.

4 LOOKING SIDEWAYS

1 In ' "A child is being beaten" ' Freud insists on the crucial importance of memories being retrieved during analysis.

2 I wonder if an awareness of this integration into a potential hysterical neurosis together with a realization that siblings were omitted from the explanation were behind an observation that Anna Freud made towards the end of her life when she claimed that psychoanalysis had not yet understood hysteria (see Mitchell 2000a). Anna Freud had been notoriously highly competitive with her five older siblings, one of whom, Freud's favourite daughter Sophie, died just before ' "A child is being beaten" ' was written.

3 See Deutsch (1947) for good accounts of this difficulty.

4 Frau Cecilie in Freud's *Studies on Hysteria* (1895) recounts a similar trauma to this latter in her childhood. It is undoubtedly very common.

5 This may relate to a frequent observation that full orgasm is harder for girls/women to achieve. I am very doubtful about this. However, if this is so, it may be that it is not women but hysterics – male and female – who have a difficulty with orgasm.

6 In a recent book, *Hysteria* (2000), Christopher Bollas sees the mother's failure (arising from her own psychosexual pathology) to accept and safely foster her child's sexuality as the causative determinant of the child's future hysteria. Here we can see a line that leads from Abraham (perhaps through Klein) to today. It once more spotlights the hysterogenic

mother. One might ask simply: how do analysts know? Have they experienced themselves as anally erotic mothers who have not resolved their castration complexes, cannot acknowledge their patients' sexuality, etc.?

7 It is quite frequent that psychoanalysts who write of the female castration complex produce accounts which coincide with popular renditions to mean that the female is a castrator. This would seem to be Abraham's intention. Properly speaking, this cannot be a 'complex', which involves a number of conflicting unconscious desires – it would only be a singular acting out of the penis envy in the destruction of the object envied.

5 THE DIFFERENCE BETWEEN GENDER AND SEXUAL DIFFERENCE

1 I have read several times all Klein's published, and some of her unpublished work, producing a selected edition (Klein 2000). In my psychoanalytic training I took courses on her work and was supervised by Kleinians. I mention this because in looking for siblings, I was struck by the extent and depth of my own earlier oversight of them in the material of her first work.

2 In a forthcoming study, Mauthner (2003) claims that sistering contributes to feminine psychology as much as mothering and daughtering. This confirms my argument that the neglect of sibling relations underlies our blindness to this social shift. On the greater interaction of the social and psyche, see my own volume (Mitchell 1984: ch. 3); from the outset the neonate takes in the social as well as its own bodily experiences.

6 WHO'S BEEN SITTING IN MY CHAIR?

1 'fort/da' refers to a game of throwing away and retrieving a cotton-reel. Freud observed his eighteen-month-old grandson engaged in this game and used it to illustrate the idea of a 'compulsion to repeat' ([1920]: 14–17). Lacan converted it to the advent of a crucial phonemic utterance of absence and presence, the 'fort/da'.

2 The phrase comes from R. D. Laing's, 'Series and nexus in the family' (1962). Laing is modifying Sartre's concept of series and I am using it in a somewhat different sense from either author.

3 If this child had died, as six siblings did, the apparent realization of the tram-man's murderous fantasies would have aided the pathologization

of the whole situation. See a reference to Freud's own comparable history of a dead brother in Mitchell 2000a.

4 Eisler notes that fantasies of self-creation are a characteristic of psychoses but rare in neuroses, yet acknowledges they are a strong feature of this neurotic patient's inner world. See Conran (1975) for the prevalence of these fantasies in schizophrenia. In Mitchell 2000a I argue that such fantasies are very prevalent in hysterics.

5 Might not this be an element in the couvade also – that the man fears he will lose his wife when she becomes a mother, so stays attached through an identification with her?

6 Realizing that this takes the psychoanalytic determining moment to be set well before the limits of the onset of the castration complex, Lacan (1993) indicates that there must have been an earlier instance behind this, but he still makes no use whatsoever of the siblings.

7 ATTACHMENT AND MATERNAL DEPRIVATION

A version of this chapter was first presented at The Bowlby Memorial Conference, London, March 2000. I am very grateful to Jeremy Holmes, the discussant, for agreeing to the incorporation of some of his comments.

1 Quoted in Riley 1983: 101.

2 By January, no urban bombing yet having occurred, 87% of the group of mothers and 93% of the schoolchildren returned home, only for many to go again later.

3 For Bowlby, who did such pioneering work in advocating that quite young children should be helped to mourn, the omission of Freud's 1914 essay 'Mourning and melancholia' or of the place of loss for Anna O in *Studies on Hysteria* (1895) is, to say the least, puzzling.

4 I believe it is also a work very marked by the questions that arose from the war, with its demand for group psychology. It is in this volume that Freud reapproaches the problem of hysteria and draws back from it again.

5 In the discussion that followed the first presentation of this paper, Juliet Hopkins, herself a psychoanalytic therapist and niece of John Bowlby, commented that it gave her a new perspective on her uncle. According to Juliet Hopkins, her uncle was 'maternally deprived' and with his siblings had been brought up more or less entirely by nannies 'in the attic'. Only one of these nannies did the children love and compete for – a very young girl, a kind of older sister. Juliet Hopkins went on to say that she felt she now understood why her uncle was so wonderful with colleagues and groups – lateral relations.

8 IN OUR OWN TIMES

1 Interestingly, there is a Hollywood version of the Don Juan story which accounts for the character's Don Juanism by his mother's adultery.

2 Don Juan, the fictitious symbol of sexual licence, killed the Commandatore, the father of one of the noblewomen he had seduced. On meeting the murdered man's stone effigy, Don Juan invites it to a banquet – the statue attends and drags Don Juan, still arrogantly challenging even death, down to Hell. The Don Juan figure, used from a different perspective – that of a case of lying – is the subject of half a chapter in *Mad Men and Medusas* (Mitchell 2000a).

3 I spoke about Don Juan as a male hysteric at an International Symposium on Mythology in Cusco, Peru in 1989, reported in *Mitos: Sociedad Peruana de Psicoanálisis Simposio Internacional*, p. 20. I used Limentani's 'vagina man' but having been trained as an Independent Object Relation's psychoanalyst, I was then shamefully unaware of Eric Brenman's article. This experience, however, only strengthens my sense that we were (diversely) seeing the same thing in our clinical practices.

4 I have discussed this in relation to hysteria; here I need to re-examine it for siblings.

5 For an excellent brief account of 'homosexuality' in psychoanalytic theory, see Bogdan Lesnick's contribution to a forthcoming *Encyclopaedia of Psychoanalysis*, ed. R. Skelton.

9 CONCLUSION

1 Hegel's perception of the sister–brother relationship as ideal because of its closeness without sexuality is another version of this.

2 Personal communication from Professor Murray Last, University College London, about practices in Northern Nigeria.

3 I have always been both fascinated and intellectually inhibited by the thought of twins; wanting to understand and not knowing how to think about them at the same time. I can trace this back to a clearly remembered incident in childhood – but it only indicates that my problem predates it. I must have been about seven years old, and was sitting with a group of school friends on some logs on the edge of the school playing field. Identical girl twins from the class above were part of the group – I had long been drawn to them (or rather to what they represented) and my question popped out, 'What is it like to be twins?' My humiliation was probably as much for the revelation of the urgency of my unconscious curiosity as for the obvious put-down of a younger child when

one of them – I've always imagined it was the 'older', but it also in my memory merges into both of them – replied, 'What a stupid question. How can we know what it's like when we've never been anything else?'

Maybe it was that answer that led me to psychoanalysis – not only the more obvious problem of how can one know another person but how, given one is no one else than oneself, can one know one's self? This now seems to me to be the question of siblings. When I was ten or eleven I was committed to becoming a doctor and used to pester everyone with my medical first aid box treatments. At that time, like a *sotto voce* theme, there was a barely audible interest in being 'a psychoanalyst'. I had a friend whose father was one, but he was a great embarrassment to all of us. The positive inspiration came when, aged eleven, on Saturdays I looked after the young twins and baby sister of a woman who was in psychoanalytic training. As I write this I think that the series of the World's Twin books, which were adored reading, must bear some responsibility for my love of different countries. But probably underlying that very vivid memory from schooldays is a 'universal' twinning that belongs to the splitting of the ego in the paranoid-schizoid phase of the small baby in all of us.

4   'The imaginary twin' is a very interesting paper, but it nevertheless seems as though in some ways Bion has lost the plot: the disguise of the patient as a teacher does not seem apt; comments such as that a defence is 'illegitimate' imply an untenable distinction between legitimate and illegitimate defences; the incestuous brother-in-law must be bisexual, not, as Bion says, homosexual. Is it that this patient – like the therapeutic group – left it difficult to produce only a primal parent and Oedipal paradigm? Bion surely would have understood J. K. Rowling's defence of setting Harry Potter in a boarding school: children are interesting away from parents. Sent from India to an English boarding school at the age of eight, Bion was a successful schoolboy and got the Victoria Cross in the First World War. Did having all his own crucial lateral experiences understood analytically as really vertical ones drive him first to the very earliest mother-and-baby 'before I was', then to abstract grids and then to *A Memoir of the Future* (1975)? A 'discourse' analysis of 'The imaginary twin' would, I think, indicate the terrible difficulties for an analyst of the moments when there are 'two I's' and they are one of them.

5   The mother of one of my first patients had died from an abortion when my patient was six months old – of course, she had no memory of her. However, one day she came transformed into liveliness – she had dreamt of her mother for the first time in her life: 'it was only a phone-call from her, it seems a long time [my patient was middle-aged] to wait for a phone-call, but it *was* nice to hear from her.' She added, 'she must have

known I was there.' This enabled the patient to think about her mother's feelings in leaving her baby daughter, and from this we could move to the beginning of self-perception. I am arguing that such a perspective is an issue in the trauma of sibling relationships. Of course it builds on and diverges into other areas such as the mother's recognition; see chapter 3.

6 Feminism (itself a consequence of the coming closer together of female/ male relationships) is characterized by its social foregrounding followed by its apparent disappearance. Each time it re-arises from its quieter modes, feminist work, my own included, inevitably tries to explain the universal cross-cultural, transhistorical, still persisting, gender inequity.

References and Select Bibliography

Dates in square brackets are those of first publication, given where it is helpful to place these works in their time. In these cases, the page numbers cited in the text belong to the later edition.

Abraham, K. [1913] Mental after-effects produced in a nine-year-old child by the observation of sexual intercourse between its parents. In Abraham 1942, pp. 164–8.

Abraham, K. (1922) Manifestations of the female castration complex. *International Journal of Psycho-Analysis* 3, pp. 1–29.

Abraham, K. (1942) *Selected Papers on Psychoanalysis*. London: Hogarth Press and Institute of Psycho-Analysis.

Agger, E. M. (1988) Psychoanalytic perspectives on sibling relationships. *Psychoanalytic Enquiry* 8, no. 1, pp. 3–30.

Alexander, F. (1923) The castration complex in the formation of character. *International Journal of Psycho-Analysis* 4, pp. 11–42.

Anzieu, D. (1986) *Freud's Self-Analysis*. London: Hogarth.

Ariès, P. (1962) *Centuries of Childhood: A Social History of Family Life*. New York: Vintage Books.

Bainham, A., Day Sclater, S. and Richards, M. (eds) (1999) *What is a Parent? A Socio-Legal Analysis*. Oxford: Hart.

Balint, E. [1963] On being empty of oneself. In Mitchell and Parsons 1993, pp. 37–55.

Balint, E., Courteny, M., Elder, A., Hull, S. and Julian, P. (1993) *The Doctor, the Patient and the Group*. London: Routledge.

Balint, M. (1952) *Primary Love and Psycho-Analytic Technique*. London: Tavistock.

Balint, M. (1968) *The Basic Fault: Therapeutic Aspects of Regression*. London: Tavistock.

References and Select Bibliography

Bank, S. and Kahn, M. D. (1982) *The Sibling Bond*. New York: Basic Books.

Barker, P. (1996) *Regeneration*. London: Viking.

Bion, W. R. [1948] Experiences in groups. In Bion 1961.

Bion, W. R. [1950] The imaginary twin. In Bion 1967.

Bion, W. R. (1961) *Experiences in Groups, and Other Papers*. London: Tavistock.

Bion, W. R. (1967) *Second Thoughts: Selected Papers on Psychoanalysis*, London: Heinemann Medical.

Blok, A. (2001) *Honour and Violence*. Cambridge: Polity.

Boer, F. and Dunn, J. (eds) (1992) *Children's Sibling Relationships: Developmental and Clinical Issues*. Hillsdale, N.J.: Lawrence Erlbaum.

Bollas, C. (2000) *Hysteria*. London: Routledge.

Bowlby, J. (1951) *Maternal Care and Mental Health*. Geneva: World Health Organization.

Bowlby, J. (1969) *Attachment and Loss*, vol. 1: *Attachment*. London: Hogarth and Institute of Psycho-Analysis.

Bowlby, J. [1973] *Attachment and Loss*, vol. 2: *Separation, Anxiety and Anger*. New edn, London: Pimlico, 1998.

Bowlby, J. [1980] *Attachment and Loss*, vol. 3: *Loss: Sadness and Depression*. New edn, London: Pimlico, 1998.

Breen, D. (1993) (ed.) *The Gender Conundrum: Contemporary Psychoanalytic Perspectives on Femininity and Masculinity*. London: Routledge.

Brenman, E. (1985) Hysteria. *International Journal of Psycho-Analysis* 66, pp. 423–32.

Brunori, L. (1996) *Gruppo di Fratelli / Fratelli di Gruppo*. Rome: Borla.

Brontë, E. [1847] *Wuthering Heights*. Reprint London 1949.

Brown, D. (1998) Fair shares and mutual concern: the role of sibling relationships. *Group Analysis* 31, pp. 315–26.

Burlingham, D. (1952) *Twins: A Study of Three Pairs of Identical Twins*. London: Imago.

Butler, J. (1999) *Gender Trouble: Feminism and the Subversion of Identity*, 10th anniversary edn. London: Routledge.

Byatt, A. S. (1992) *Angels and Insects*. London: Chatto and Windus.

Carveth, D. L. and Carveth, J. H. (2003) Fugitives from guilt: postmodern de-moralization and the new hysterias. At www.yorku.ca/dcarveth.

Cary, J. (1947) *Charley is my Darling*. London: Michael Joseph.

Cawson, P., Wattam, C., Brooker, S. and Kelly, G. (2000) *Child Maltreatment in the United Kingdom: A Study of the Prevalence of Child Abuse and Neglect*. London: National Society for the Prevention of Cruelty to Children (NSPCC).

Charles, M. (1999) Sibling mysteries: enactments of unconscious fears and fantasies. *Psychoanalytic Review* 86, no. 6, pp. 877–901.

Chen, X. and Rubin, K. H. (1994) Only children and sibling children in urban China: a re-examination. *International Journal of Behavioural Development* 17, no. 3, pp. 413–21.

Chesler, P. (1997) *Women and Madness*. New York: Four Walls Eight Windows.

Cixious, H. (1981) Castration or decapitation. *Signs* 7, no. 1, pp. 36–55.

Clement, C. (1987) *The Weary Sons of Freud*. London: Verso.

Coles, P. (1998) 'The children in the apple tree': some thoughts on sibling attachment. *Australian Journal of Psychotherapy*, nos 1–2, pp. 10–33.

Colonna, A. B. and Newman, L. M. (1983) The psychoanalytic literature on siblings. *Psychoanalytic Study of the Child* 83, pp. 285–309.

Conran, M. (1975) Schizophrenia as incestuous failing. Paper to the International Symposium on the Psychotherapy of Schizophrenia, Oslo, Aug.

Coren, V. (2002) Why I need to beat up my brother. *Evening Standard*, 29 Oct.

David-Menard, M. (1989) *Hysteria from Freud to Lacan: Body and Language in Psychoanalysis*. Ithaca: Cornell University Press.

Davidoff, L. (1995) *Worlds Between: Historical Perspectives on Gender and Class*. Cambridge: Polity.

Davidoff, L. (2000) Sisters and brothers – brothers and sisters: intimate relations and the question of 'incest'. Paper for workshop, European University Institute, Florence.

Davin, A. (1978) Imperialism and motherhood. *History Workshop Journal* 5, pp. 9–65.

de Beauvoir, S. (1972) *The Second Sex*. Harmondsworth: Penguin. Originally published in French, 1947.

Deutsch, H. (1947) *The Psychology of Women: A Psychoanalytic Interpretation*, vol. 2: *Motherhood*. London: Research Books.

Dunn, J. (1985) *Sisters and Brothers*. London: Fontana Paperbacks.

Dunn, J. and Kendrick, C. (1982) *Siblings: Love, Envy and Understanding*. London: McIntyre.

Eisler, M. J. (1921) A man's unconscious phantasy of pregnancy in the guise of traumatic hysteria. *International Journal of Psycho-Analysis* 2, pp. 255–86.

Engel, G. (1975) The death of a twin. *International Journal of Psycho-Analysis* 56, pp. 23–40.

Erikson, E. [1964] The inner and the outer space: reflections on womanhood. In Erikson 1975.

Erikson, E. (1975) *Life History and the Historical Moment*. New York: Norton.

Farmer, P. (ed.) (1999) *Sisters: An Anthology*. London: Allen Lane.

Fenichel, O. (1945) *The Psychoanalytic Theory of Neurosis*. New York: Norton.

Field, M. J. (1960) *Search for Security: An Ethno-Psychiatric Study of Rural Ghana*. London: Faber.

Fortes, M. and Mayer, D. Y. (1965) Psychoses and social change among the Tallensi of Northern Ghana. *Études et Essais* (Revue du Centre National de la Recherche Scientifique), pp. 5–40.

Freud, A. (1923) The relation of beating-phantasies to a day-dream. *International Journal of Psycho-Analysis* 4, pp. 89–102.

Freud, S. [1895] *Studies on Hysteria*. In Freud 1953–74, vol. 2.

Freud, S. [1900–1] *The Interpretation of Dreams*. In Freud 1953–74, vols 4 and 5.

Freud, S. [1905a] Fragments of an analysis of a case of hysteria. In Freud 1953–74, vol. 7.

Freud, S. [1905b] *The Three Essays on Sexuality*. In Freud 1953–74, vol. 7.

Freud, S. [1907] On the sexual enlightenment of children. In Freud 1953–74, vol. 9.

Freud, S. [1909] Analysis of a phobia in a five year old boy. In Freud 1953–74, vol. 10.

Freud, S. [1913] *Totem and Taboo*. In Freud 1953–74, vol. 12.

Freud, S. [1918] From the history of an infantile neurosis. In Freud 1953–74, vol. 17.

Freud, S. [1919] 'A child is being beaten': a contribution to the study of the origin of sexual perversions. In Freud 1953–74, vol. 17.

Freud, S. [1920] *Beyond the Pleasure Principle*. In Freud 1953–74, vol. 18.

Freud, S. [1921] *Group Psychology and the Analysis of the Ego*. In Freud 1953–74, vol. 18.

Freud, S. [1922] Some neurotic mechanisms in jealousy, paranoia and homosexuality. In Freud 1953–74, vol. 18.

Freud, S. [1923] *The Ego and the Id*. In Freud 1953–74, vol. 19.

Freud, S. [1925] An autobiographical study. In Freud 1953–74, vol. 20.

Freud, S. [1926] *Inhibitions, Symptoms and Anxiety*. In Freud 1953–74, vol. 20.

Freud, S. [1928] Dostoevsky and parricide. In Freud 1953–74, vol. 21.

Freud, S. [1933] Femininity. In Freud 1953–74, vol. 22.

Freud, S. (1953–74) *The Standard Edition of the Complete Psychological Works of Sigmund Freud*, ed. J. Strachey. 24 vols, London: Hogarth and Institute of Psycho-Analysis.

Friedan, B. (1963) *The Feminine Mystique*. London: Gollancz.

Gallop, J. (1982) *Feminism and Psychoanalysis: The Daughter's Seduction*. London: Macmillan.

Girard, R. (1978) Narcissism: the Freudian myth demythified by Proust. In A. Roland (ed.), *Psychoanalysis, Creativity and Literature*, New York: Columbia University Press, pp. 293–311.

Golding, W. (1954) *Lord of the Flies*. London: Faber.

Goody, J. (1990) *The Oriental, the Ancient and the Primitive: Systems of Marriage and the Family in the Pre-industrial Societies of Eurasia*. Cambridge: Cambridge University Press.

Goody, J. (2002) The African family: yesterday, today and tomorrow. Paper to seminar Gendered Family Dynamics and Health: African Family Studies in a Globalizing World, Legon, Ghana, Oct.

Green, A. (1995) Has sexuality anything to do with psychoanalysis. *International Journal of Psychoanalysis* 76, no. 5, pp. 871–83.

Hacking, I. (1995) *Rewriting the Soul: Multiple Personality and the Sciences of Memory*. Princeton: Princeton University Press.

Hammel, E. A. (1972) *The Myth of Structural Analysis: Lévi-Strauss and The Three Bears*. Addison-Wesley.

Herman, J. L. (1992) *Trauma and Recovery: From Domestic Abuse to Political Terror*. London: Pandora.

Hobson, P. (2002) *The Cradle of Thought*. London: Macmillan.

Hollway, W. (2000) Psychological and psychoanalytic discourses on partnering and parenting: the post-war period. Paper, University of Leeds, at www.leeds.ac.uk/cava.

Holmes, J. (1980) The sibling and psychotherapy: a review with clinical examples. *British Journal of Medical Psychology* 53, pp. 297–305.

Holmes, J. (2000) Reply to Juliet Mitchell. John Bowlby Memorial Conference, London, Mar.

Hopkins, K. (1980) Brother–sister marriage in Roman Egypt. *Comparative Studies in Society and History* 22, pp. 303–54.

Hopper, E. (2000) Sibling relationships in groups, organisations and society. Lecture and workshop for International Association of Group Psychotherapy (IAGP) Project, Professional Exchange for Further Education (PEFE), Istanbul, May.

Hufton, O. (1995) *The Prospect Before Her: A History of Women in Western Europe*, vol. 1: *1500–1800*. London: HarperCollins.

Hunter, D. (1983) Hysteria, psychoanalysis and feminism: the case of Anna O. *Feminist Studies* 9, no. 3, pp. 464–88.

Isaacs, S. (ed.) (1941) *The Cambridge Evacuation Survey: A Wartime Study in Social Welfare and Education*. London: Methuen.

Jacobs, J. [1890] The story of the three bears. In *English Fairy Tales*, London: Everyman Library, 1993.

Jacobus, M. (1995) *First Things: The Maternal Imaginary in Literature, Art and Psychoanalysis*. London: Routledge.

Jones, E. (1922) Notes on Dr Abraham's article on the female castration complex. *International Journal of Psycho-Analysis* 3, pp. 327–8.

Kaplan, L. (1991) *Female Perversions*. London: Pandora Press.

Kelly, M. (1983) *Post-partum Document*. London: Routledge and Kegan Paul.

King, H. (1993) Once upon a text: hysteria from Hippocrates. In S. L. Gilman, H. King, R. Porter, G. S. Rousseau and E. Showalter (eds), *Hysteria beyond Freud*, Berkeley: University of California Press.

Klein, M. [1923] The role of the school in the libidinal development of the child. In Klein 1975, vol. 1.

Klein, M. [1932] The sexual activities of children. In Klein 1975, vol. 2.

Klein, M. [1952] On observing the behaviour of young infants. In Klein 1975, vol. 3.

Klein, M. [1957] Envy and gratitude. In Klein 1975, vol. 3.

Klein, M. [1961] *Narrative of a Child Analysis*. In Klein 1975, vol. 4.

Klein, M. (1975) *The Writings of Melanie Klein*, vols 1–4. London: Hogarth Press and Institute of Psycho-Analysis.

Klein, M. (2000) *The Selected Melanie Klein*, ed. J. Mitchell. London: Penguin.

Kristeva, J. (1982) *Powers of Horror: An Essay on Abjection*. New York: Columbia University Press.

Lacan, J. (1982a) Intervention on transference. In Mitchell and Rose 1982, pp. 61–73.

Lacan, J. (1982b) The meaning of the phallus. In Mitchell and Rose 1982, pp. 74–85.

Lacan, J. (1993) *The Seminar of Jacques Lacan: Book III, The Psychoses (1955–1956)*, ed. J.-A. Miller. London: Norton.

Laing, R. D. (1962) Series and nexus in the family. *New Left Review* 15, pp. 7–14.

Laplanche, J. and Pontalis, J.-B. (1973) *The Language of Psycho-Analysis*. London: Hogarth Press and Institute of Psycho-Analysis.

Laufer, M. E. (1989) Adolescent sexuality: a body/mind continuum. *Psychoanalytic Study of the Child* 44, pp. 281–94.

Lechartier-Atlan, C. (1997) Un traumatisme si banal. Quelques réflexions sur la jalousie fraternelle. *Revue Française de Psychanalyse* 1, pp. 57–66.

Lévi-Strauss, C. (1963) *Structural Anthropology*. New York: Basic Books.

Lévi-Strauss, C. (1994) *The Raw and the Cooked: Introduction to a Science of Mythology*. London: Pimlico.

Libbrecht, K. (1995) *Hysterical Psychosis*. New Brunswick, N.J.: Transaction.

Limentani, A. (1989) To the limits of male heterosexuality: the vagina-man. In *Between Freud and Klein: The Psychoanalytic Quest for Knowledge and Truth*, London: Free Association Books.

Lindner, R. M. (1945) *Rebel without a Cause: The Hypno-analysis of a Criminal Psychopath*. London: Research Books.

Malinowski, B. (1927) *Sex and Repression in Savage Society*. London: Routledge and Kegan Paul.

References and Select Bibliography

Malinowski, B. (1929) *The Sexual life of Savages*. London: Routledge and Kegan Paul.

Mannoni, O. (1968) *Freud and the Unconscious*. New York: Pantheon.

Mauthner, M. (2003) *Sistering: Powers of Change in Female Relationships*. London: Palgrave Macmillan.

Mitchell, J. (1966) Women: the longest revolution. *New Left Review* 40, pp. 11–37.

Mitchell, J. (1984) *Women: The Longest Revolution: Essays on Feminism, Literature and Psychoanalysis*. London: Virago.

Mitchell, J. (2000a) *Mad Men and Medusas: Reclaiming Hysteria and the Effects of Sibling Relationships on the Human Condition*. London: Penguin.

Mitchell, J. (2000b) *Psychoanalysis and Feminism* (with a new introduction). London: Penguin Press. First published 1974.

Mitchell, J. (2003) Natasha and Helene in Tolstoy's *War and Peace*: gender conventions and creativity. In F. Moretti (ed.), *Il Romano*, vol. 3, Rome: Einaudi.

Mitchell, J. and Goody, J. (1999) Family or familiarity? In Bainham et al. 1999, pp. 107–17.

Mitchell, J. and Parsons, M. (eds) (1993) *Before I was I: Psychoanalysis and the Imagination* by Enid Balint. London: Free Association Books.

Mitchell, J. and Rose, J. (eds) (1982) *Feminine Sexuality and the École Freudienne*. London: Norton.

Mitscherlich, A. (1963) *Society without the Father*. London: Tavistock.

Oakley, A. (1972) *Sex, Gender and Society*. London: Temple Smith.

Oberndorf, C. P. (1928) Psychoanalysis of siblings. Paper to the 84th annual meeting of the American Psychiatric Association, Minneapolis, June.

Okin, S. (1989) *Justice, Gender and the Family*. New York: Basic Books.

Parsons, A. (1969) *Belief, Magic and Anomie: Essays in Psychosocial Anthropology*. New York: Free Press.

Pateman, C. (1989) *The Disorder of Women: Democracy, Feminism and Political Theory*. Cambridge: Polity.

Pontalis, J.-B. (1981) On death-work. In J.-B. Pontalis, *Frontiers in Psychoanalysis: Between the Dream and Psychic Pain*, London: Hogarth Press and Institute of Psychoanalysis, pp. 184–93.

Porter, R. (1987) *A Social History of Madness: Stories of the Insane*. London: Weidenfeld and Nicolson.

Rank, O. [1924] *The Trauma of Birth*. London: Routledge, 1999.

Riley, D. (1983) *War in the Nursery: Theories of the Child and Mother*. London: Virago.

Riviere, J. (1929) Womanliness as masquerade. *International Journal of Psychoanalysis*, pp. 303–13.

Riviere, J. [1932] On jealousy as a mechanism of defence. In Riviere 1991.

Riviere, J. (1991) *The Inner World of Joan Riviere: Collected Papers: 1920–1958*, ed. A. Hughes. London: Karnac.

Roheim, G. (1934) *The Riddle of the Sphinx*. London: Hogarth and Institute of Psycho-Analysis.

Roy, A. (1997) *The God of Small Things*. London: Flamingo.

Rubin, G. [1975] The traffic in women: notes on the political economy of sex. In Scott 1996b, pp. 105–51.

Rutter, M. (2000) Eighth John Bowlby Memorial Lecture. City of London School for Girls, Mar.

Saadawi, Nawal El (2002) *Walking through Fire: A Life of Nawal El Saadawi*. New York: Zed Books.

Sabbadini, A. (1988) The replacement child: an instance of being someone else. *Contemporary Psychoanalysis* 24, no. 4, pp. 528–47.

Sabean, D. W. (1993) Fanny and Felix Mendelssohn-Bartholdy and the question of incest. *Musical Quarterly* 77, no. 4, pp. 709–17.

Sayers, J. (1991) *Mothering Psychoanalysis*. London: Hamish Hamilton.

Scott, J. W. (1996a) Gender: a useful category of historical analysis. In Scott 1996b, pp. 152–80.

Scott, J. W. (ed.) (1996b) *Feminism and History*. Oxford: Oxford University Press.

Seccombe, W. (1993) *Weathering the Storm: Working-Class Families from the Industrial Revolution to the Fertility Decline*. London: Verso.

Segal, H. (1986) *The Work of Hanna Segal: A Kleinian Approach to Clinical Practice*. London: Free Association Books.

Sexton, A. [1962] All my pretty ones. In Sexton 1991.

Sexton, A. (1991) *The Selected Poems of Anne Sexton*, ed. D. W. Middlebrook and D. H. George. London: Virago.

Shechter, R. A. (1999) The meaning and interpretation of sibling-transference in the clinical situation. *Issues in Psychoanalytic Psychology* 21, nos 1–2, pp. 1–10.

Shepherd, B. (2002) *A War of Nerves: Soldiers and Psychiatrists 1914–1918*. London: Pimlico.

Showalter, E. (1987) *The Female Malady: Women, Madness, and English Culture, 1830–1980*. London: Virago.

Showalter, E. (1997) *Hystories: Hysterical Epidemics and Modern Culture*. London: Picador.

Steiner, R. (1999) Some notes on the 'heroic self' and the meaning and importance of its reparation for the creative process and the creative personality. *International Journal of Psychoanalysis* 80 (Aug.), part 4, pp. 685–718.

Stoller, R. (1968) *Sex and Gender*. London: Hogarth.

Sulloway, R. (1996) *Born to Rebel: Birth Order, Family Dynamics and Creative Lives*. London: Little, Brown.

References and Select Bibliography

Szreter, S. (1996) *Fertility, Class and Gender in Britain, 1860–1940*. Cambridge: Cambridge University Press.

Therborn, G. (2002) Between sex and power: the family in the world of the twentieth century. Paper presented at the Yale Colloquium on Comparative Social Research, 24 Oct.

Ussher, J. (ed.) (1997) *Body Talk: The Material and Discursive Regulation of Sexuality, Madness and Reproduction*. London: Routledge.

Volkan, V. D. and Ast, G. A. (1997) *Siblings in the Unconscious and Psychopathology*. Madison: International Universities Press.

Walby, S. (1986) *Patriarchy at Work: Patriarchal and Capitalist Relations in Employment*. Cambridge: Polity.

Weldon, E. V. (1988) *Mother, Madonna, Whore: The Idealization and Denigration of Motherhood*. London: Free Association Books.

Williams, C. D. (1935) Kwashiorkor. *Lancet*, 16 Nov., p. 1151.

Williams, C. D. (1938) Child health in the Gold Coast. *Lancet*, 8 Jan., pp. 97–102.

Williams, C. D. (1962) Malnutrition. *Lancet*, 18 Aug., pp. 342–4.

Winnicott, D. W. [1931] A note on normality and anxiety. In Winnicott 1975.

Winnicott, D. W. [1945] The only child. In Winnicott 1957.

Winnicott, D. W. (1957) *The Child and the Family: First Relationships* (broadcast talks). London: Tavistock.

Winnicott, D. W. (1958) *The Anti-social Tendency: Through Paediatrics to Psycho-Analysis*. London: Tavistock.

Winnicott, D. W. (1964) *The Child, the Family, and the Outside World*. London: Pelican.

Winnicott, D. W. [1959–64] Classification: is there a psycho-analytic contribution to psychiatric classification? In Winnicott 1965b, pp. 124–39.

Winnicott, D. W. [1960] String: a technique of communication. In Winnicott 1965b.

Winnicott, D. W. (1965a) *The Family and Individual Development*. London: Tavistock.

Winnicott, D. W. (1965b) *Maturational Processes and the Facilitating Environment*. London: Hogarth Press and Institute of Psycho-Analysis.

Winnicott, D. W. (1971) *Playing and Reality*. London: Tavistock.

Winnicott, D. W. (1975) *Through Paediatrics to Psycho-Analysis*. London: Hogarth.

Winnicott, D. W. (1978) *The Piggle: An Account of the Psychoanalytic Treatment of a Little Girl*. London: Hogarth Press and the Institute of Psycho-Analysis.

Wolf, K. M. (1945) Evacuation of children in wartime: a survey of the literature, with bibliography. *Psychoanalytic Study of the Child* 1, pp. 389–404.

Young-Bruehl, E. (1988) *Anna Freud: A Biography*. London: Macmillan.

Index